DAVID
GARRICK

A BIOGRAPHY

DAVID GARRICK

A BIOGRAPHY BY
ALAN KENDALL

St. Martin's Press · New York

Library of Congress Cataloging in Publication Data

Kendall, Alan, 1939–
    David Garrick: a biography.

    Bibliography: p.
    Includes index.
    1. Garrick, David, 1717–1779. 2. Actors—
Great Britain—Biography. 3. Dramatists, English—
18th century—Biography. I. Title.
PN2598.G3K46 1986 792′.028′0924 [B] 86–20297
ISBN 0–312–18372–0

First published in Great Britain by Harrap Ltd.

First U.S. Edition

10 9 8 7 6 5 4 3 2 1

CONTENTS

PREFACE

C ONSIDERING his fame and his importance in the history of the English theatre, David Garrick has attracted remarkably few biographers in the land of his birth, and in the last seventy years or so, only two books — Margaret Barton's *Garrick* of 1948 and Carola Oman's *David Garrick* of 1958 — have presented lives of this commanding figure.

In America, where admittedly much original material is now to be found, the situation is very different, and there has been a steady flow of most valuable contributions to our knowledge of Garrick and the theatre of his day. Indeed, it is to American scholarship that we owe the magnificent three-volume edition of David Garrick's letters, edited by D. M. Little and G. M. Kahrl, which appeared in 1963. Subsequently, G. W. Stone Jr and G. M. Kahrl published their critical biography in 1979, to celebrate the two hundredth anniversary of Garrick's death, but for all its 771 pages, the book betrays its dual authorship, there are some unfortunate blemishes, and it is not readily accessible to British readers; above all, the personality of Garrick himself is very hard to disentangle from the wealth of material within.

Of course, even in his lifetime Garrick suffered from his own reputation, and the wealth of anecdotes had already begun to obscure the real person. For this reason, the publication of the correspondence was particularly welcome, though even that work was unfortunately flawed — through no fault of the editors — by virtue of the fact that it did not include Garrick's letters to Georgiana, Countess Spencer — a correspondence that is particularly important for what it shows us of Garrick's character. For that correspondence one must turn to the edition edited by Earl Spencer and C. Dobson for the Roxburghe Club in 1960. Here again, however, is a work that is not readily accessible to the ordinary reader. It is hoped, therefore, that the present book will serve as an introduction to Garrick as a person, situate him in his world, and serve as a point of departure for those who may wish to explore further.

In the hope of getting closer to the real Garrick, it was decided to use modern spelling, punctuation and capitalization when transcribing original documents — apart from some rare exceptions in the early letters from the actor to his father. Garrick was a compulsive letter-writer, even in an age when a letter was the primary means of communication for most literate people. He seems to have answered virtually anything that was addressed to him, no matter how insignificant — though, as we shall see in the following pages, this was a fundamental part of his constant need to justify himself. Often this pointed to something bordering on insecurity, and on occasion even paranoia. At the same time, he was a very efficient and thorough person, and an able administrator, who numbered among his friends some of the most significant and modern minds of the day. One feels that the idea that his letters should in any way read quaintly to us would have incensed him. All the more reason, then, for presenting his correspondence as directly and in as uncomplicated a manner as possible.

This portrait has few of the expansive brush-strokes of the sort dear to the lovers of anecdote, who need all the nuances to be heightened and exaggerated. Indeed, one wonders how so unhistrionic a personality ever achieved what he did in his chosen profession. Of course at times he was well able to turn a fine phrase and extract the drama latent in certain situations, but the wonder is that he did so on relatively few occasions, in view of the opportunities presented and the fact that the use of words was his life-blood — and one must also bear in mind the fact that he lived in an age and a milieu where hyberbole was common.

Hopefully, then, a more realistic portrait of the man will emerge. It is a much less romantic portrait than the previous ones — the flamboyant aspects are found to be less flamboyant, and at the same time the darker aspects are found to be much less sinister. In short, we have a very plausible character, with his talent and his foibles, who set out to achieve an aim in life and was successful. At this point, however, one cannot escape the wider issue, which is that in achieving his success Garrick had a profound influence on the development of the British theatre and did a considerable amount in restoring Shakespeare to his rightful place in the national and even international consciousness.

Alan Kendall

ACKNOWLEDGMENTS

MANY people have given of their time and knowledge, and in particular I should like to thank Dr Geoffrey Ashton, sometime Librarian of the Garrick Club; Madame Véronique Bouillot of the Musée de l'Opéra, Paris; Peter Day, Keeper of Collections at Chatsworth; Iain Finlayson; Dr Levi Fox, Director of the Shakespeare Birthplace Trust; Geoffrey Langley, County of Avon Reference Librarian; David Postles, Archivist of Sheffield City Libraries; Sir Roy Strong, Director of the Victoria and Albert Museum; Peter Thornton, Curator, and Miss Scull, of Sir John Soane's Museum, and the staff of the Mansell Collection, who treated me with unfailing courtesy and kindness, never baulked at requests for yet more files to be brought, and made such a valuable contribution to the visual content of this book.

Among various institutions I should like to thank the staffs of the Ashmolean Museum, Oxford; the British Library; the British Museum — in particular, the Department of Prints and Drawings and the Department of Mediaeval and Later Antiquities; the Chesham branch of the Buckinghamshire County Library; the Codrington Library of All Souls College, Oxford; the Hamilton Kerr Institute of the University of Cambridge; the Harvard Theatre Collection; the Lord Chamberlain's Office; the Folger Shakespeare Library; the National Portrait Gallery; the Royal Albert Museum, Exeter; the Society of Antiquaries of London; the Tate Gallery; the Victoria and Albert Museum, and Yale University Library.

For permission to quote from copyright material, thanks are due to the Trustees of the Chatsworth Settlement; Olive, Countess Fitzwilliam's Wentworth Settlement Trustees and the Director of Libraries, Sheffield; the Shakespeare Birthplace Trust, Stratford-upon-Avon; Earl Spencer; the Trustees of the Victoria and Albert Museum, and Yale University Library and the McGraw-Hill Book Company, Inc. Attempts were made to contact all holders of copyright material, and failure to include acknowledgment here is no indication of intent to avoid such acknowledgment. Any omissions notified to the publishers will be included in future editions.

Finally, but by no means least, I should like to thank Simon Scott, who nursed the project over a number of years, Pamela Ruff who edited the book, and David Warner who designed it.

CHAPTER ONE

EARLY DAYS

(see previous page)
Richard Pine's portrait of David Garrick, now at Christ Church, Oxford. The actor is seen with a copy of *Macbeth*, a play that he did much to bring back to favour, and the text of which he restored to something much closer to the original. To the announcement that the play would be given 'as written by Shakespeare', James Quin retorted, 'Don't I play *Macbeth* as Shakespeare wrote it?' The answer was — until the advent of Garrick — firmly in the negative. (*Mansell Collection, London*)

The Angel Inn, Hereford, where David Garrick was born on 19 February 1717. Garrick's father, a lieutenant in Colonel James Tyrrell's Regiment of Dragoons, had been sent with a recruiting party to Hereford, and his wife Arabella went with him. The baptism of the newly born son — their third child — took place nine days later in the church of All Saints, Hereford. (Engraving by J. Storer, 1823) (*British Museum, London*)

THE Garrick family were originally Huguenots, who came from the somewhat inhospitable country whose sparse vegetation is still known as *garrigue*, around Castres in southern France, not far from Albi. The actor's grandfather, David Garric (originally de la Garrique), was in Bordeaux, however, at the time of the revocation of the Edict of Nantes in 1685, and it was from there that he fled to London. It was felt that his son Peter, the actor's father, was too young to undertake the journey, and he was to wait until he was eighteen months old, in 1687, when a nurse clandestinely brought him out of France.

David Garric became a naturalized British subject in 1695, and thereafter adopted the spelling 'Garrick'. When Peter came of age in 1706, his father bought him a commission in the Army on 12 April that year. As an ensign in a foot regiment, Peter Garrick was quartered in Lichfield, where he met his future wife, Arabella Clough. Her father was a vicar-choral of the cathedral, and her mother also belonged to a Lichfield family. Peter and Arabella were married on 13 November 1706, but it was not until 1710 that their first son, also called Peter, was born. There followed a daughter, Magdalene, in 1715, and David Garrick was their third child, born on 19 February 1717.

Although he always regarded himself as a native of Lichfield — and indeed he spent the first twenty years of his life there — David Garrick was actually born in Hereford, at the Angel Inn. His father had been sent there with a recruiting party — he was a lieutenant by then — and his wife had gone with him. So David was baptized in All Saints' Church, Hereford, on 28 February 1717. In a letter to his brother Peter of 24 September 1773, Garrick referred to Lichfield as his 'own native place (as I always call it, though dropped at Hereford)'. There were to be four more children: Jane, born in 1718; William, born in 1720; George, born in 1723, and Merrial, born in 1724. George was to become his brother David's right-hand man for the greater part of his career, and barely survived him. So assiduous was he for his brother's wants that, after even the briefest absence from the theatre, he would return in haste. As Charles Dibdin recorded in his autobiography: 'George was always in anxiety lest in his absence his brother should have wanted him; and the first question he asked on his return was, "Did David want me?" ' In the course of a conversation in the Green-Room at Drury Lane, when it was learned how quickly George had followed David to the grave (a matter of some forty-eight hours), those present found it extraordinary. ' "Extraordinary," said old Bannister, "not at all — David wanted him." ' [1] This story is also attributed to Richard Cumberland, however.

In order to support his large family, Peter Garrick was obliged to give up his lieutenancy on half pay and take an active captaincy with Major-General Kirke's regiment. Unfortunately, the regiment was stationed in Gibraltar, and for five years, from 1731 until 1736, Peter Garrick was separated from his wife and family. Despite their unhappy situation, there was a benefit for posterity in that the first surviving letter of David Garrick dates from this period: it is to his father in Gibraltar, written in January 1733. The oldest Garrick brother, Peter, was a midshipman in the West Indies under Sir Chaloner Ogle, so whilst he, too, was away, at a tender age David shouldered his responsibilities as acting head of the family.

Through David's letters we see what a difficult time it was for the family as a whole, but especially for Mrs Garrick. As David wrote on 21 January 1733: 'It is not to be expressed the joy that the family was in at the receipt of dear papa's letter, which we received the 7th of this month. My poor mamma was in very good spirits two or three days after she received your letter, but now begins to grow maloncolly [sic] again, and has little ugly fainting fits. She is in great hopes of the transports going for

Although he was born in Hereford, Garrick always regarded Lichfield as his home town. It was there that his father had met and married his mother, and where the actor spent his childhood. Lichfield is a city still dominated by the red cathedral with its three spires, known locally as 'The Ladies of the Vale'. Daniel Defoe, writing in his *Tour* (1724-6), described Lichfield as 'a place of good conversation and good company'. (*Mansell Collection*)

13

you every day, for we please ourselves with the hopes of your spending this summer with the family.'[2] In fact, it was not to be, for this sequence of letters continues until May 1735, and it was a further year after that before Captain Garrick finally returned to England.

Meanwhile, Mrs Garrick had to try and pull the family out of debt, and at the same time clothe and feed her offspring. As David wrote in the same letter: 'As soon as she came down to us [from London, after saying farewell to her husband], not to her great joy, she found us very shabby in cloaths [sic], and in all our accoutrements, that we was rather like so many beggars than gentleman soldiers, but with much ado at last she equipt [sic] us out a little better, and now with a great deal of mending and patching we are in statu quo.'

It is interesting that David Garrick was even at this age acquainted with the stage, for in mentioning the new wife of one of their friends, he referred to her as does a character in one of Farquhar's plays: 'a very pretty woman (only she squints a little, as Captain Brazen says in *The Recruiting Officer*)'. In fact, Garrick produced the play with himself in the lead as Kite, in the Bishop's Palace at Lichfield, when he was only eleven or twelve. The Palace was then the home of Gilbert Walmesley, registrar of the ecclesiastical court and an influential person in Garrick's early career.

In June 1733 it was still the same theme in the letter to David's father: Mrs Garrick not well, and planning how to get her husband home, and no news from brother Peter, still away at sea. From a letter of 12 September that year we learn that David had been to Lisbon to spend some time with an uncle, also David. As Thomas Davies put it: '[Garrick] was invited to Lisbon by an uncle, who was a considerable wine-merchant in that city; but his stay there was very short, for he returned to Lichfield the year following.'[3] It is not clear exactly when this visit took place. Percy Fitzgerald has 1726, though other sources put it as late as 1732, but whatever the year, it was that visit which had, in David's opinion to his father as expressed in the letter of 12 September 1733, 'backened me a great deal', by interrupting his schooling. In this letter he raised the question of his going to university when he was eighteen or nineteen.

In the spring of 1734 the family received two letters from Captain Garrick, though one of them hurt David considerably by virtue of the fact that his father had thought his son 'neglectful of writing'. It provoked from him a considerable protest which seems almost out of context, and yet was to remain with Garrick as an important part of his character for the rest of his life: 'When I do but consider of what you find fault with me in your letter, I fancy to myself the most odious ideas of a disobedient son, and rather than I will be upbraided with that worst of names, I will employ for the future my whole care and time to be found in every respect Your most obedient son . . .'[4] Almost to the end of his days Garrick would treat with seriousness virtually everything addressed to him, even the sort of letters that today people in a similar situation would simply drop into the nearest wastepaper basket. He always seemed obliged to justify himself, and unable to ignore the most insignificant, and sometimes purely imaginary, reproach. Where his father was concerned, it must have been especially frustrating, since it is obvious from the correspondence that has come down to us that he wrote other letters to Gibraltar which simply did not get there. As David wrote on 10 April 1735: 'The great pleasure we have at the receipt of any of dear papa's letters is so well known that I need not enlarge upon that point. If any sorrow should appear amidst such transports of joy, the miscarriage of my letter must occasion it. If the sea was as sure to carry as I am to write, you would have no reason to complain of my neglect, or a son's disobedience. The wind and waves seem to be more favourable to us than to you. None of your letters have escaped our hands; there are four of ours which you don't mention, we suppose are miscarried.'[5] David chose this occasion to let his father know that he was sorely in need of new clothes, but he did so in as light-handed a manner as he could: 'I must tell my dear papa that I am quite turned philosopher. You perhaps may think me vain, but to show you I am not, I would gladly get shut of my characteristic of a philosopher, viz. a ragged pair of breeches. Now the only way you have to cure your son of his philosophic qualification is to send some hansome [sic] thing for a waistcoat and pair of breeches to hide his nakedness; they tell me velvet is very cheap at Gibraltar. Amen, so be it.'

On the whole, the impression of the relationship between father and son — at least on paper, and allowing for the distance and time that they were apart — is a happy one. When referring to a portrait of his father, in a letter of 24 April 1735, David jokingly wrote: '. . .it is the figure of a gentleman, and I suppose military by his dress. I think Le Grout [?Jan de Groot of Leiden] told me his name was one Captain Peter Garrick. Perhaps as you are in the Army you may know him; he is pretty jolly and I believe not very tall. I don't know what would be the consequence if he

15

Samuel Johnson (1709-84), in a portrait once attributed to Reynolds. Johnson's father, Michael, kept a bookshop in Lichfield. Although both Johnson and Garrick were pupils of the local grammar school, the former had left before the latter arrived. Nevertheless, despite the disparity in their ages, they were destined to set out for London together in March 1737, intent on making their careers and, hopefully, their fortunes in the capital. (*National Portrait Gallery, London*)

was at Lichfield, for my poor mama sighs whenever she passes the picture. You would be in danger, I can tell you, of horns.'[6] A pious hand subsequently deleted the last two words, but the idea is a refreshingly healthy one, even from a son to his father. Incidentally, in view of Garrick's own somewhat diminutive height, it is interesting to note that his father was not tall, either.

Although — from a letter of May 1735 — the family believed that Captain Garrick's return was imminent, as mentioned earlier, they had to wait until almost a year was up before they saw him again. Percival Stockdale told a wry little story about Garrick's comment to his father on his return, allegedly told him by Garrick himself in 1773. The son said to his father that he supposed he had a good many brothers and sisters at Gibraltar — which was hardly tactful, especially in front of his mother. Had Garrick then been only about twelve years old, the gaffe might have been put down to childish ignorance. As it was, he was now eighteen years old, which puts a very different complexion on the story. According to Stockdale, tears came to Mrs Garrick's eyes and Captain Garrick reprimanded his son.[7]

Once Captain Garrick was home, however, he survived less than a year. The relationship between father and son — or indeed any of the children — had not really had a chance to develop at a crucial stage. There were, however, other adult persons around who exercised a beneficial influence on the Garrick children, in particular Gilbert Walmesley, already mentioned.

Among the friendships formed early on in Lichfield was that between David Garrick and Samuel Johnson (1709–84). Because they were so often and so long together, there was little need for them to write, and only very few letters between them have come down to us, and they are in any case rather impersonal in tone. One cannot rely on the correspondence, therefore, in this case, to give us an intimate picture. We have to rely on the recollections of people such as Mrs Thrale, James Boswell and Fanny Burney.

In 1735, Johnson opened his short-lived school at Edial, just outside Lichfield, and David and George Garrick were two of the very few pupils. The school was a failure, and since Garrick could not afford to go to university, he set out with Johnson for London on 2 March 1737. Gilbert Walmesley had written to John Colson, headmaster at Rochester School and the son of a Lichfield vicar-choral. The idea was that Garrick would study with him as a private pupil for about two or three years before joining the Temple and so make a career at the Bar. Colson agreed to take on Garrick. As for Johnson, as Walmesley wrote again to Colson on the same day that the two men set out from Lichfield: 'He and another neighbour of mine, one Mr Johnson, set out this morning for London together. Davy Garrick is to be with you early the next week, and Mr Johnson to try his fate with a tragedy and seek to get himself employed in some translation, either from the Latin or the French. Johnson is a very good scholar and poet, and I have great hopes will turn out a fine tragedy writer.'[8] Johnson spent only about three months in London on this occasion before returning to Lichfield for the summer, but Garrick enrolled in Lincoln's Inn on 9 March and then went on to Rochester. His stay there was not even one year, however, for his father died that same month of March, and though one might assume that he stayed with John Colson for the rest of the spring and summer, Colson left to take up a chair at Cambridge, and in the late summer Peter Garrick came up to London, where the two brothers used their inheritance to set up in the wine trade — in Durham's Yard, off the Strand.

For the next four years it was David who remained based in London, whilst Peter went to and from Lichfield, and there is a gap in the correspondence. On 10 June 1741, however, Peter finally settled in their home town, and though he could have had little conception of exactly what his brother was up to, David was taking the first steps that would eventually lead to his embracing the acting profession once and for all. Had Peter thought about it in retrospect — and indeed he must have done so — David already had strong connections with the theatrical world of London. Moreover, Peter himself knew Charles Fleetwood, manager of Drury Lane; and Johnson, who was at that time trying to make his mark with his tragedy *Irene*, had read it to Peter in the Fountain Tavern in London in the autumn of 1737.

Then as early as 15 April 1740, David's popular entertainment *Lethe* had been produced at Drury Lane for Henry Giffard's benefit, who played Esop in the play, and on 30 November 1741 *The Lying Valet* was to be put on at the theatre known as Goodman's Fields.[9] *Lethe* was subsequently (1756) to provide Garrick with one of his favourite parts — Lord Chalkstone — which he wrote into it, and one of the chief characters — Lord Ogleby — in *The Clandestine Marriage*, which he wrote in collaboration with George Colman ten years later (1766). There

was, however, all the difference in the world between writing for the stage, which was a perfectly acceptable thing for civilized people to do, and acting on it. Indeed, there were so many clergymen playwrights pestering London managers that one wonders when they ever found time for religion. The acting profession itself, however, was decidedly not what anyone who had aspirations to gentility might be expected to enter, and one of Garrick's greatest achievements, as we shall see, was that he substantially altered society's attitude in that regard.

By 1740, then, David was well and truly in the theatrical milieu of the capital and, as mentioned above, trying to drum up support for the actor and manager Henry Giffard (1699–1772), who ran the Goodman's Fields theatre, which had been closed in 1737 by the strict application of the Licensing Act of that year. Giffard was now evidently trying to re-open the theatre, and Garrick was helping him. Permission had to be granted by the Lord Chamberlain, at that time Charles Fitzroy (1683–1757), second Duke of Grafton, who held the office for over thirty years, from 1724 until his death. In the event, Giffard failed to obtain a licence, though in October of 1740 he was given permission to open the theatre for concerts, for which admission was charged, and then give a play and afterpiece gratis, as the filling in a musical sandwich.

One of David's reasons for helping Giffard is stated in a letter to Peter,[10] namely, that it was through Giffard that the Garricks had obtained the custom of the Bedford Coffee-House in Covent Garden. According to David, it was one of the best in London, and therefore useful for their wine business. It also happened to be a favourite gathering place for those with literary and theatrical connections and aspirations. It was, nevertheless, as a wine dealer that David Garrick was officially in the habit of frequenting the Bedford Coffee-House, but we find him in a letter of 4 September 1740 actually asking his brother for orders from Lichfield.[11] Business was not exactly flourishing, and no wonder, for David's mind cannot be said to have been entirely on his job. Indeed, he was more concerned with the plan to erect a monument to Shakespeare in Westminster Abbey than in selling his wares. Of more immediate concern in this letter, however, was the health of their mother, who died that same month, and was buried on 28 September, as we know from the Lichfield Cathedral registers.

As a sign of the times — certainly as far as the evolution of literary taste was concerned — it was decided to erect a monument to

(see opposite page)
A portion of a linen and cotton wall-hanging, plate-printed in blue, showing scenes from Garrick's play Lethe, which may have been produced to commemorate the command performance of the play given at Drury Lane on 23 January 1766. The figure of Lord Chalkstone was taken from Zoffany's portrait of Garrick in the role, which also dates from 1766. (Victoria and Albert Museum, London)

Shakespeare in Westminster Abbey in 1740, and to this end money was raised by public subscription, and that meant also from the clientele of the London coffee-houses. Obviously David Garrick was by now well suited to being one of the promoters of this scheme, since he had on the one hand a wide acquaintance in the coffee-house milieu — especially in Covent Garden — and on the other his involvement with the theatre, and his devotion to Shakespeare in particular.

It is almost impossible to point to any particular moment or incident at which Garrick espoused the cause of Shakespeare, and it is more likely to have been a gradual process, with knowledge of at least some Shakespeare being imparted in childhood, and then increasing familiarity with his works on stage as David was drawn more and more towards the theatre. For there was certainly a growing interest in Shakespeare — there was in existence a Shakespeare Ladies' Club, for example — and the process of re-editing his works and bringing the plays to the stage had been gathering momentum since the Restoration. The first critical edition had been that of Nicholas Rowe (1709). Subsequently, Alexander Pope had published his six-volume edition in 1725 — though it was a flawed one — and there were regular performances of the plays, even in mangled versions, at the time Garrick made his début in London. Garrick was not responsible for the revival of Shakespeare, then, as has often been suggested, though he did indeed take up the cause in a way that virtually no one else had done hitherto. That did not prevent him from doing his own mangling, especially with *Romeo and Juliet*, for example, but at the same time he brought back to the stage plays such as *Antony and Cleopatra* and *The Taming of the Shrew* that had not been seen for many years. It seems, then, that as an actor, Garrick felt in himself an instinctive response to Shakespeare that was certainly profound, if not unique in his day. Certainly it seems to have been more deeply felt than in any of his theatrical contemporaries. Moreover, through his generous practice of allowing scholars to use his extensive library, and particularly his collection of early plays, he subsequently contributed greatly to the establishing of accurate texts of not only Shakespeare, but other dramatists of the period.

With so much devotion to matters theatrical on the part of the London partner, it is perhaps not surprising that the Garricks' wine business did not prosper, though it dragged on for more than a year longer as a partnership. However, in June 1741 David had crossed the Rubicon, though writing to his brother Peter on 11 July that year, he made no reference to the fact that he had already made his début as an actor.[12] From the substance of the letter itself — all talk of stage machinery — one might have had strong suspicions. In fact, David Garrick appeared with Henry Giffard's Norwich touring company as Aboan in Thomas Southerne's *Oroonoko*, in a theatre at Ipswich, in June 1741, though he took care not to appear under his own name, but took that of Lyddall, the maiden name of Giffard's first wife. It was not until after David had made his London début in the autumn of the same year, however, when he opened with Giffard (albeit anonymously) as Richard in *Richard III* on 19 October, that he made a clean breast of the matter to his brother Peter. As ever, he was most circumspect in the way he unfolded his tale: 'I received my shirt safe and am now to tell you what I suppose you may have heard of before this, but before I let you into the affair 'tis proper to premise some things, that I may appear less culpable in your opinion than I might otherwise do. I have made an exact estimate of my stock of wine and what money I have out at interest, and find that since I have been a wine merchant I have run out near four hundred pounds, and trade not increasing, I was very sensible some way must be thought of to redeem it.'[13] In fact, there were several other things he might have done before going on the stage, if he were simply looking for an alternative way of making a living, but he was quite correct in stating that he would make more of a success of acting than he had of the wine trade. Interestingly he went on to maintain that he had from an early age been drawn to the theatre, and that he was virtually suffering from what today we would describe as a psychosomatic illness because he was prevented from pursuing his chosen career: 'My mind (as you must know) has been always inclined to the stage, nay so strongly so that all my illness and lowness of spirits was owing to my want of resolution to tell you my thoughts when here. Finding at last both my inclination and interest required some new way of life, I have chosen the most agreeable to myself, and though I know you will be much displeased at me, yet I hope when you shall find that I may have the genius of an actor without the vices, you will think less severe of me and not be ashamed to own me for a brother.' He then went on to make practical proposals for winding up the London end of their partnership, though could not help breaking in with what must have been for him the most exciting moment of his life so far: 'Last night I played Richard the Third to the surprise of everybody, and as I shall make very near £300 per annum by it, and as it is really what I

The theatre in Tankard Street, Ipswich, where David Garrick made his first appearance on a public stage in a speaking role, during the summer of 1741. The company on that occasion had been brought together by Henry Giffard, manager of the Goodman's Fields Theatre in London, whilst the theatres in the capital were closed. In this way Garrick hoped that if he were a failure, he might fail in the convenient obscurity of the provinces. As an added precaution, however, he took the name of Lyddall, Giffard's wife's maiden name. (*Mansell Collection*)

October 19th, 1741.

GOODMAN'S FIELDS.

At the late Theatre in Goodman's Fields, this Day will be performed,

A Concert of Vocal and Instrumental Music,

DIVIDED INTO TWO PARTS.

TICKETS AT THREE, TWO, AND ONE SHILLING.

Places for the Boxes to be taken at the Fleece Tavern, near the Theatre.

N.B. Between the Two Parts of the Concert will be presented an Historical Play, called the

LIFE AND DEATH OF

King Richard the Third.

CONTAINING THE DISTRESSES OF K. HENRY VI.

The artful acquisition of the Crown by King Richard,

The Murder of Young King Edward V. and his Brother in the Tower,

THE LANDING OF THE EARL OF RICHMOND,

And the Death of King Richard in the memorable Battle of Bosworth Field, being the last that was fought between the Houses of York and Lancaster; with many other true Historical Passages.

The Part of King Richard by A GENTLEMAN,

(Who never appeared on any Stage),

King Henry, by Mr. GIFFARD,   Richmond, Mr. MARSHALL,

Prince Edward, by Miss HIPPISLEY,   Duke of York, Miss NAYLOR,

Duke of Buckingham, Mr. PATERSON,   Duke of Norfolk, Mr. BLAKES,   Lord Stanley, Mr. PAGETT,

Oxford, Mr. VAUGHAN,   Tressel, Mr. W. GIFFARD,   Catesby, Mr. MARR,   Ratcliff, Mr. CROFTS,

Blunt, Mr. NAYLOR,   Tyrrel, Mr. PUTTENHAM,   Lord Mayor, Mr. DUNSTALL.

The Queen, Mrs. STEEL,   Duchess of York, Mrs. YATES,

And the Part of Lady Anne, by Mrs. GIFFARD.

WITH

Entertainments of Dancing,

By Mons. FROMET   Madame DUVALT,   and the Two Masters and Miss GRANIER.

To which will be added a Ballad Opera, of One Act, called

The Virgin Unmask'd.

The Part of Lucy, by Miss HIPPISLEY.

Both of which will be performed Gratis, by Persons for their Diversion.

———

The Concert will begin exactly at Six o'Clock.

dote upon, I am resolved to pursue it.' There was also a postscript: 'I have a farce (*The Lying Valet*) coming out at Drury Lane.' In the event, as we have seen, it came on at Goodman's Fields on 30 November, and not at Drury Lane, but it was well received, and remained a popular item in the repertoire for several years.

Peter, however, was not so easily swayed. Indeed, there were some very good reasons why he should fail to share his younger brother's feeling of euphoria. Unfortunately, the letter in which he expressed his initial reaction has not survived, and we can therefore only read between the lines of David's reply as to what it was. [14] In the first place, it seems, Peter had objected because their uncle, Louis la Condé (married to their father's sister Jane), had assumed that Peter had been a party to David's intentions beforehand, and had consequently upbraided Peter as well. But the main force of his objection seems to have been the general low esteem in which actors tended to be held at that time. To this David replied that in general the stage deserved the censure it received, but he also pointed out actors and people of the theatre who had been successful, and had been 'admitted into, and admired by, the best companies'. In other words, the social standing of actors was not what Peter wanted his brother to descend to. As an indication of what this might be, there is a passage in Fanny

(see opposite page)
The playbill for *Richard III*, dated 19 October 1741, when David Garrick — 'a gentleman, (Who never appeared on any Stage),' — made his London début at the Goodman's Fields Theatre. It is here described as the 'late theatre' because the application of the Licensing Act of 1737 had removed its licence for plays. The evening was therefore described as 'A Concert of Vocal and Instrumental Music, divided into two parts'. *Richard III* was therefore given between the two parts, and was — in theory at least — 'performed Gratis, by Persons for their Diversion'. (*Mansell Collection*)

E. I. Portbury's engraving of William Hogarth's depiction (1745) of Garrick as Richard III awaking from his dream at Bosworth Field. The original is in the Walker Gallery, Liverpool. The impact of this performance was the greatest the London theatre had known for many years, and quickly became the main topic of conversation in circles well beyond those directly concerned with the stage. (*Mansell Collection*)

Burney's *Diary and Letters* for 1779, the year of Garrick's death, that indicates what certain members of Brighton society, almost forty years after the start of his brilliant career, were capable of saying: 'Ay, ay . . . that Garrick was another of those fellows that people run mad about. Ma'am, 'tis a shame to think of such things! An actor living like a person of quality! Scandalous! I vow, scandalous! I like all these people very well in their proper places; but to see such a set of poor beings living like persons of quality — 'tis preposterous! Common sense, madam, common sense is against that sort of thing. As to Garrick, he was a very good mimic, an entertaining fellow enough, and all that kind of thing; but for an actor to live like a person of quality — oh, scandalous!'[15] The emphasis on persons of quality has a loud echo of Mrs Heidelberg's obsession with the 'qualaty' in *The Clandestine Marriage*. One might add, however, that the person in Fanny Burney's diary had little higher opinion of musicians, either. They were dismissed as so much 'catgut and rosin', and in view of the profession of Fanny's father, that was hardly tactful, to say the least.

To this sort of objection David opposed his talent and genius as an actor. The letter to Peter of late October ends on a rather poignant note, with Garrick patently torn between his artistic destiny and his genuine affection for his family. As he had said at the outset of the letter, he had been prepared for Peter's disapproval, but not, perhaps, for the fact that it was to last so long. On 16 November he again wrote to Peter in much the same vein, though with much greater tokens of success — Pitt and the Prince of Wales are mentioned.[16] Even this letter, however, failed to impress Peter, who was, nevertheless, impelled to add to one of his replies that, although he did not approve of the stage, yet David would always be his affectionate brother.

David felt that that the ending of this latest letter was sufficiently well meant for him to take as a handhold, and so launch into his next letter of 24 November, leaving the door slightly open by saying that he was 'very near quite resolved to be a player', when there can have been no doubt whatsoever in his own mind. We learn, incidentally, that Peter had expressed the fear that David might hurt him by his decision. David refuted this strongly, with a profession of generosity which, as we know from his subsequent career, was no hollow gesture where his nearest and dearest were concerned: 'As to hurting you in your affairs, it shall be my constant endeavours [*sic*] to promote your welfare with my all. If you should want money and I have it, you shall command my whole, and I know I shall soon be more able by playing and writing to do you service than any other way.'[17]

There was, nevertheless, the social stigma attached to the description of his chosen profession as that of 'player', as we have seen. In the early days, therefore, his family were understandably hurt, and Peter referred to the rumour that David had played a Harlequin. In a letter of *circa* 29 December 1741, David answered this charge: 'As to playing a Harlequin, 'tis quite false. Yates last season was taken very ill and was not able to begin the entertainment, so I put on the dress and did two or three scenes for him, but nobody knew it but him and Giffard. I know it has been said I played Harlequin at Covent Garden, but it is quite false.'[18]

Another rumour which also had to be scotched was that of his impending marriage, as we see in the letter of 30 January 1742 to Peter.[19] Here, as in the previous case, there was some substance in the rumour, but this time it was potentially more serious. David was, in fact, amorously involved with none other than the actress Peg Woffington (?1714–60), and it is a pity that we know so little of the nature of their relationship. The conjunction of two such talents and personalities must have been stimulating, to say the least, but glamour on the stage is very rarely carried over into private life, and it seems that for all Woffington's professional accomplishments, she would never have been a suitable partner for the fastidious David Garrick. Nevertheless, as colleagues they established an extremely good working relationship on the stage, and were very popular.

It was customary at this time for actors to go over to Dublin when the London season had ended, and so fit in a second one before resuming in the autumn. Garrick set out for Ireland, then, in early June 1742, for what turned out to be a very successful engagement at the Smock Alley Theatre in Dublin, along with Peg Woffington and the dancer Barberini. On the 23rd of that month he wrote a letter to his brother Peter announcing his safe arrival and initial success — but not much more — with a promise to write again.[20] In the event, only one further letter has survived from this Dublin visit, by which time Garrick's affairs were 'quite finished . . . and with great success.'[21] This was written on 22 August 1742, and he had ended his season in Dublin with a performance of *The Recruiting Officer*, in which he acted Captain Plume to Mrs Woffington's Silvia on 19 August. He had, however, also played Hamlet; and Handel, who was in Dublin for the first performance of *Messiah*, is said to have been present at the time. It is unfortunate that no record of the composer's impressions

A portrait of Peg Woffington, engraved and published on 1 June 1740 by John Brooks of Skinner Row, Dublin. The accompanying verses leave no doubt as to the reputation Woffington enjoyed at the time, and why Garrick fell in love with her.

> Roll on fair Sun and let the
>   World admire,
> We feel your warmth and
>   share your gentle fire,
> But when your Rays in
>   brightest splendour play,
> Blush you at morn or smile
>   with evening ray,
> Confess, fair Sun, and own
>   a sweeter red
> Is on fair Woffington's soft
>   lips o'er spread,
> Or if your Noon-day
>   Glory's [*sic*] dare compare
> Look on her eyes, you'l [*sic*]
>   find your rivals there.

(*Mansell Collection*)

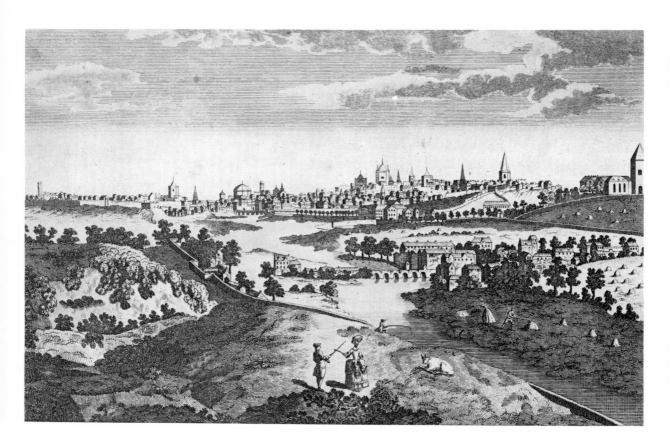

An engraving, by Cary, of Dublin in the eighteenth century, when the city enjoyed a rich social and cultural life that revolved around the person of the Lord Lieutenant in Dublin Castle. In 1742, however, when Garrick first acted there, the city was not yet the splendid, elegant place that it became later in the century, and it has been asserted that poverty was even more extreme there than in London. (*Mansell Collection*)

has come down to us. From one who was as much a man of the theatre as Garrick himself — though, of course, in a very different part of it — Handel's opinion would have been worth having. *Messiah* had had its first hearing there on 13 April that year, which in itself speaks volumes about the quality of artistic life in Dublin at the time. It also shows how small the world was in those days. John Boyle, Earl of Orrery (1731) and Cork (1753), a friend of Swift, Pope and Johnson, and a relative of the Burlingtons, wrote letters to all the noblemen and gentlemen that he could think of, so that Garrick described him as a demi-god, and declared that as a result of Boyle's efforts he was 'more caressed' in Dublin than he was in London. [22]

The focus of this society was, of course, the vice-regal court, and the Lord Lieutenant at this time was William Cavendish (1698–1755), third Duke of Devonshire. His son, also William, Garrick came to know extremely well through his wife and her patrons, the Earl and Countess of Burlington, whose daughter William Cavendish married in 1748.

The Irish visit was not the first time that David Garrick had worked with Woffington. He had seen her act at Covent Garden during the season of 1740–41, and then when he played Lear at Drury Lane on 28 May 1742 — followed by Richard III on 31 May — he had her opposite him as Cordelia. In the wake of their success in Dublin it was not entirely a surprise, therefore, that when Garrick returned to London for the season of 1742–3, for which he had already agreed with Fleetwood at Drury Lane, he should set up house with Woffington and Charles Macklin in Bow Street. This was not as scandalous as might at first seem, since Macklin was married with an eight-year-old daughter, and his wife also appeared on the stage of Drury Lane.

Almost inevitably, however, the arrangement came to grief, possibly over finances, which must have been complicated, to say the least, in such a household. But though they no longer kept house, Garrick and Woffington went on to act together for three successive seasons at Drury Lane, and towards the end of May 1745, Garrick spent some time at Teddington, where Woffington had now established her home. Despite his denial of any such intention to his brother Peter at the beginning of 1742, it does seem that in the summer of 1745 Garrick, perhaps in a final attempt, was seriously considering proposing to Woffington, and either did so and was turned down, or had second thoughts, so that they had no further intimacy. This did not prevent them from acting on the same stage, however, which they did both during the 1745–6 season at Smock Alley, Dublin, and the 1746–7 season at Drury Lane. Once Garrick became co-manager at Drury Lane, however, in April 1747, he ceased to act with Woffington, and indeed did not engage her for the theatre after that season. She appeared thereafter at Covent Garden and in Dublin.

It is a pity that we have no record of Garrick's inner feelings at the time of their parting, though there is a letter of 23 October 1745, written by Garrick to his friend Somerset Draper, in which he was preparing to go to Ireland again, and the letter has all the rush and excitement relative to the preparations:[23] 'If I resolve for Dublin, I shall send for my wigs, and some jewels in the bookcase drawers, and, I think, for a suit of cloaths [*sic*] . . . but I will give you further notice . . . *Woffington*, I am told, shows my letters about; pray have you heard anything of that kind? What she does now so little affects me that, excepting her showing my letters of nonsense and *love* to make me ridiculous, she can do nothing to give me a moment's uneasiness: *"the scene is changed — I'm alter'd quite"*.'[24]

Faber's engraving of Reynolds' portrait of William Cavendish, third Duke of Devonshire (1698–1755). The Duke was Lord Lieutenant of Ireland at the time of Garrick's first visit to Dublin in 1742. Horace Walpole remarked that 'his [the Duke's] outside was unpolished', and indeed the Duke was not noted for his patronage of the theatre. Nevertheless, his son came to be a close and esteemed friend of David Garrick. (*Mansell Collection*)

The fact that Woffington even bothered to show Garrick's letters to others would seem to imply that it was not entirely a matter of indifference to her that she had lost him. For his part, Garrick had been affected, despite his bravado to Draper. It is all the more regrettable, therefore, that nothing of their correspondence has survived. There is, however, quoted by William Cooke in his *Memoirs of Charles Macklin*, a long poem in a hand that has not been identified, and which was probably not published. It refers not only to Peg Woffington's affair with Garrick, but with other lovers also:

> I know your sophistry, I know your art
> Which all your dupes and fools control;
> Yourself you give without your heart —
> All may share *that* but not your soul.[25]

It may well have been that Garrick remonstrated with Woffington during the time he was with her at Teddington, and asked her to give him some sort of undertaking that she would renounce the seemingly endless succession of lovers — referred to in the rest of the poem — for which she was notorious, and, in the words of the *Book of Common Prayer*, 'forsaking all other, keep [herself] only unto him', but that she was evidently not prepared to do. In view of the uxorious man that Garrick turned out to be, however, one cannot imagine a union with even a reformed Woffington being a very enduring one, and the devotion that existed on both sides between Garrick and the woman he eventually married indicates that he was one who believed in, and elicited in return, complete fidelity.

However, the experience taught Garrick a great deal, one feels, about dealing with women, and especially the women of his own profession. He never had any serious problems, even when established queens of the stage had their inevitable fits of the vapours, as happened with Kitty Clive and Mrs Abington. Garrick liked to have matters sorted out and loose ends tied up. When he broke with Woffington, therefore, he sent back her presents and letters to him, retaining only a pair of diamond buckles which she had given him, and which he wore as long as he lived. He had, however, sown his wild oats. Now he could embark on his chosen career with single-minded dedication.

CHAPTER TWO

'UNCOMMON
APPROBATION'

(see previous page)
A portrait traditionally thought to be that of David Garrick at the age of 23 or 24, attributed to Jean-Baptiste van Loo. The fashionable clothes of the sitter, as well as the books and writing-materials, would be appropriate for the early career of Garrick in London before his stage career began in 1741. However, considerable doubt has been cast upon the identity of the sitter, despite the fact that no alternative identification has yet been advanced for it. (*The Maugham Collection of Theatrical Paintings, National Theatre, London*)

Garrick as Bayes in *The Rehearsal*, one of his most successful roles. The play became a vehicle for Garrick's views on acting, and inspired him to write a prelude, *The Meeting of the Company*, in 1744, which had as its sub-title 'Bayes's Art of Acting, or the Worst equal to the Best'. (*Victoria and Albert Museum*)

ARRICK did not lack advice in these early stages of his acting career, much of it communicated in epistolary form, not only by friends and acquaintances, but also by persons unknown to him. For example, he received several letters from another native of Lichfield, Thomas Newton (1704–82), subsequently Bishop of Bristol (1761). In a letter written towards the end of December 1741 to brother Peter, Garrick said that he had had 'several pretty letters', and that Newton had been to see him act several times.[1] Then there was another friend, Joseph Smith (1697–1781), who was also a native of Lichfield and a clergyman, who regularly attended the theatre. Smith's rather abrasive character seems to have been similar to that of Johnson, and he was said to have lost many of his friends as a result. On 25 January 1742 he wrote from New Bond Street to Garrick, after seeing him act at Goodman's Fields on more than one occasion: 'You surpass all whom I ever remember to have seen upon the stage, though I have some faint remembrance of Booth [Barton Booth (1681–1733)] and Wilks [Robert Wilks (?1665–1732)]. Booth could never fall into the easy character, nor Wilks rise into the great; Chamont [in Thomas Otway's *The Orphan*] showed how admirable you are in both. I was charmed in particular with your sudden starts into passion, and quite in raptures at your fine recovery out of it. But you are not made for tragedy only: the sock becomes you as much as the buskin.'[2]

Quite often those who have known an artist in his or her early career are more critical and exigent than those on whom the talent falls as a revelation. A whole party of Lichfield people turned up to see Garrick as Bayes in the Duke of Buckingham's play of 1671, *The Rehearsal*, which turned out to be one of David's most successful parts from the very beginning, as he wrote to his brother Peter on 6 February 1742, three days after his first performance: 'The night before last I saw Mr Sudall, who with more Lichfield people came to see *The Rehearsal*. I have the greatest success imaginable in the part of Bayes, and instead of clapping me they huzza, which is very uncommon approbation — and though the town has been quite tired out with the play at the other end of the town [meaning Drury Lane and Covent Garden] yet I have the great satisfaction to see crowded audiences to it every night.'[3] It was in this letter and the next, incidentally, that David finally wound up his side of the wine business in London from the next quarter day, 25 March 1742.

Despite David's somewhat superior references to Drury Lane and

Covent Garden, and the fact that the more humble Goodman's Fields was doing better business, inevitably, as the established homes of plays (and indeed officially the only two so recognized in London at that time), the other houses had the prestige which no budding talent might ignore. David had said as much in his letter of 30 January (1742) to his brother Peter, and that he had fixed his mind on Drury Lane, but that it was a secret still.[4] He also intimated that the Earl of Essex had made an approach to him which he assumed was to try and engage him with John Rich (?1682–1761) at the other house of Covent Garden. In a subsequent letter of 19 April, however, he told Peter that it was still not fixed, though it would 'certainly be at the other end of the town', and that he would be offered 500 guineas and a clear benefit, or part of the management.[5]

Garrick was now truly on the crest of a wave. He had supped twice with William Murray (1705–93) the future Earl of Mansfield (1776), who was going to introduce him to Alexander Pope. When the latter saw Garrick act for the first time he is reputed to have said that 'he was afraid the young man would be spoiled, for he would have no competitor'.[6] Then there was George Lyttelton, whom Garrick described as 'the Prince's favourite', where he 'met with the highest civility and complaisance. He told me he never knew what acting was till I appeared, and said I was only born to act what Shakespeare writ; these things daily occurring give me great pleasure.' The list continued. Lord Sandwich (who was to arrange dinner to meet Lord Chesterfield) and Lord Halifax both invited Garrick to dine; all of which is ample testimony to the fact that not only did people of taste — 'ingenious' was Garrick's adjective to describe Halifax and Sandwich — recognize that Garrick's talent was something quite new and unusual, but that he was eminently acceptable to them as a social acquaintance.

Though at this time the aristocracy were doubtless rather more civil in their behaviour, it is worth bearing in mind that, only relatively few years before, it was the same aristocracy who had supposedly resolved to teach Handel a lesson on the grounds that he had failed to observe the correct social niceties, and so had brought him to the brink of ruin. At least that was one of the chief professed reasons, and it is true that when it came to music, Handel was no respecter of persons. In reality, however, Handel was simply a convenient means whereby the Prince of Wales and his party might aim at the King, who supported the composer. In this case

A plaster bust of Alexander Pope (1688–1744), after Roubiliac. Pope was taken by Lord Orrery to see Garrick as Richard III, and was so impressed by his acting that he went twice more. When Pope had seen Macklin as Shylock, earlier in 1744, he was said to have been inspired to pronounce the concise couplet: 'This is the Jew/That Shakespeare drew.' On Garrick he was less concise and more effusive: 'That young man never had his equal and never will have a rival.' (*National Portrait Gallery*)

Handel's manners had virtually nothing to do with it. He was simply a victim of politics. Nevertheless, it shows that it was possible for people to mount this kind of campaign, and that there were a number of opera-goers prepared to give it their support.

Of course, the theatre — both opera and plays — generated much more passion and excitement in the eighteenth century, and the public loved pitting performers and composers against each other, even when the contest was a purely artificial one whipped up in the press. After making allowances for pure jealousy, however, at no point in Garrick's career is there evidence that any member of society who knew him properly, thought that he was getting above himself. However, those who envied his social and professional success devised a means of reminding him of his station in life, according to Joseph Cradock[7], by sending him notes, if he were staying in some grand house, addressed to: 'David Garrick, player'.

Be that as it may, for all his success and grand connections, Garrick never failed to look after those who had claims on him, however slight. On one occasion early in 1742 there was a misunderstanding about the name in which a box had been held at the theatre for a group of friends, and David explained to his brother what had happened: 'As to Mrs Brown's displeasure about the places, it was their own faults, for I put down the box in Mrs Dalton's name, and the footman asked for Mrs Brown's box, and I not being there, they were disappointed of it; such blunders of footmen make the unthinking part of the world angry when they should not be.'[8]

Eventually, then, David Garrick came to terms in 1742 to act for Charles Fleetwood, who in March 1734 had purchased five-sixths of the patent of Drury Lane. In all, Fleetwood managed the theatre for twelve years, though in such an indifferent way that it was a wonder he survived so long. Before taking David Garrick's theatrical career any further, however, it would be as well to take a look at the theatre of his day, so that one may appreciate better exactly why it was that he made such an impact, and brought about such a revolution in almost all aspects of the theatrical life of this country.

As a point of departure, one might take some lines written by a contemporary of David Garrick, Charles Churchill (1731–64). Churchill was a clergyman and a satirist, sometimes also known as 'the scourge of players'. Such praise was not bestowed lightly by Churchill, therefore, and is consequently all the more interesting. It comes from the eighth edition

32

(1763) of Churchill's satire on contemporary actors, *The Rosciad*, though the first edition was published in March 1761:

> If manly sense, if nature linked with art;
> If thorough knowledge of the human heart;
> If powers of acting vast and unconfined;
> If fewest faults, with greatest beauties joined;
> If strong expression, and strange powers which lie
> Within the magic circle of the eye,
> If feelings which few hearts, like his, can know,
> And which no face so well as his can show,
> Deserve the preference, Garrick! take the chair,
> Nor quit it — till thou place an equal there.

At this point Garrick did not know Churchill, and is said to have voiced the opinion that he painted such a glowing portrait purely so as to obtain the freedom of the theatre. In due course this came to Churchill's ears, and by way of retaliation he included a few lines of warning to Garrick in his *The Apology* of May that year (1761).

There was never a shortage of tale-bearers in the tightly knit world of the London theatre, however, and Robert Lloyd, a writer who had been at Westminster School with both Churchill and Colman, made sure that Garrick knew the background to the reference in *The Apology*. Garrick's reply was diplomatic, and opened in magisterial fashion: 'Whenever I am happy in the acquaintance of a man of genius and letters, I never let any mean, ill-grounded suspicions creep into my mind to disturb that happiness. Whatever he says, I am inclined and bound to believe; and therefore I must desire you not to vex yourself with unnecessary delicacy upon my account. I see and read so much of Mr Churchill's spirit, without having the pleasure of his acquaintance, that I am persuaded that his genius disdains any direction, and that resolutions once taken by him will withstand the warmest importunity of his friends.'[9] Under the cover of compliment and courtesy, one or two well aimed darts were nevertheless launched by Garrick, before he came down to earth and went straight to the point: 'In his *Rosciad* he raised me too high; in his "Apology" he may have sunk me too low.' Whatever the truth of the matter, Garrick and Churchill soon met, and a year or two later were on sufficiently intimate terms for the latter to feel able to ask Garrick for a loan. Moreover, Roscius, the name of the famous Roman actor, came to be one of Garrick's most frequently used nicknames. According to Arthur

33

Henri-Louis Le Kain (1728–78) won approval from Garrick when he saw him act in Paris in 1751, principally for his basic professional skill and ability to portray emotion. However, at the same time Garrick deplored the fact that 'he swallows his words, and his face is so ill made that it creates no feeling in the spectators from its distortions'. Some fifteen years later Garrick made the personal acquaintance of Le Kain and came to have considerable affection for him. (From F. Hedgcock: *A Cosmopolitan Actor, David Garrick and his French Friends*)

Murphy, it was first bestowed on him during his first Dublin season in 1742. The whole episode illustrates well the fact that the arrival of Garrick on the London stage was in itself sufficient of a phenomenon to rouse strong feelings, even in an age when people cared so much more about things which today would barely raise an eyebrow.

One must look beneath the verse, however, to see what it was that struck Garrick's audience as novel. 'Manly sense', and the linking of nature with art, means that Garrick brought emotions to the stage in a way that seemed more 'real' and compelling, more fresh and genuine, than anything else seen in living memory. Therefore it was, by implication, unusual that an actor should possess such a 'thorough knowledge of the human heart', and Garrick's powers of acting seemed, by comparison, 'vast and unconfined'. Faults he had, but fewer than most, and he had more 'beauties' in his acting than anyone else. Above all, his ability to show feelings through his facial expression seems to have been one of the most remarkable aspects of his acting, which is referred to time and time again by those who saw him, both on and off the stage. Samuel Johnson was moved to explain to Mrs Thrale that Garrick looked much older than he was: 'because his face has had double the business of any other man's. It is never at rest.'

Garrick's style of acting would probably seem quite normal to us today, but it was new and strange for his day. He overturned the previous French and English style, which John Hill wrote of in *The Actor* (1755), when describing the French actor Henri-Louis Le Kain (1728–78), though in fact based on Sainte Albine's *Le Comédien*: 'The principal comedian . . . has less action than any of the English players. He will stand in his place on the stage, with his arms genteelly disposed, and without once stirring hand or foot, go through a scene of the greatest variety. He will in this single posture express to his audience all the changes of passion that can affect an human heart; and he will express them strongly, so that tossing about of the arms and strutting from side to side of the stage is not the business'.[10]

From other accounts, it seems as if a markedly artificial kind of intonation — by modern standards — was used, certainly in tragedy, as acted on the English stage. Indeed, in the prologue that Samuel Johnson wrote for Garrick for the opening of Drury Lane in 1747, there is a reference to the state of affairs after the Restoration of the monarchy in the previous century:

> Then, crush'd by rules, and weaken'd as refin'd,
> For years the pow'r of Tragedy declin'd;
> From bard to bard the frigid caution crept,
> Till Declamation roar'd, while Passion slept;
> Yet still did Virtue deign the stage to tread,
> Philosophy remain'd, though Nature fled.

Of course, there were English critics, such as Theophilus Cibber (1703–58) in his *Two Dissertations on the Theatres* (1756), who felt that Garrick went too far the other way: 'His over-fondness for extravagant attitudes, frequently affected starts, convulsive twitchings, jerkings of the body, sprawling of the fingers, flapping the breast and pockets; a set of mechanical motions in constant use; the caricatures of gesture, suggested by pert vivacity; his pantomimical manner of acting, every word in a sentence, his unnatural pauses in the middle of a sentence; his forced conceits; his wilful neglect of harmony, even where the round period of a well-expressed noble sentiment demands a graceful cadence in the delivery.'[11] Of course, one might say that Cibber, as a fellow actor, was an interested party, and the reaction of James Quin (1693–1766) when he first saw Garrick act was: 'If this young fellow be right, then we have been all wrong.' It says much for Quin's character that he was able to accept the fact and become a close friend of Garrick. Something of the same attitude as Cibber's was also expressed by David Williams (1738–1816), a dissenting minister, in his *A Letter to David Garrick, Esq.*, of 1772, though perhaps less forcefully: 'Your perfection consists in the extreme; in exaggerated gesture, and sudden bursts of passion, given in a suppressed and under manner, where the extensive powers of voice are not required, you are inimitable. In the struggles and conflicts of contradictory passions; or in their mixture and combination; and when their effects are drawn by the author to a point of instant and momentary expression — there you are often excellent. But where the situation of the mind implies a continued agitation, you become defective. And in all simple, unmixed passions, in all the simpler degrees of expression; and in conveying the various proportion of pathos which various cases require; in these cases you are no longer yourself, the expression must be in extreme, or you are not Garrick . . . In all degrees below the extreme, your gesture, and every species of expression, is what the French call *trop chargé*.'[12] As it turned out, Williams was no less an interested party than Cibber, since he was attempting to promote the actor Henry Mossop (?1729–74?), but George

35

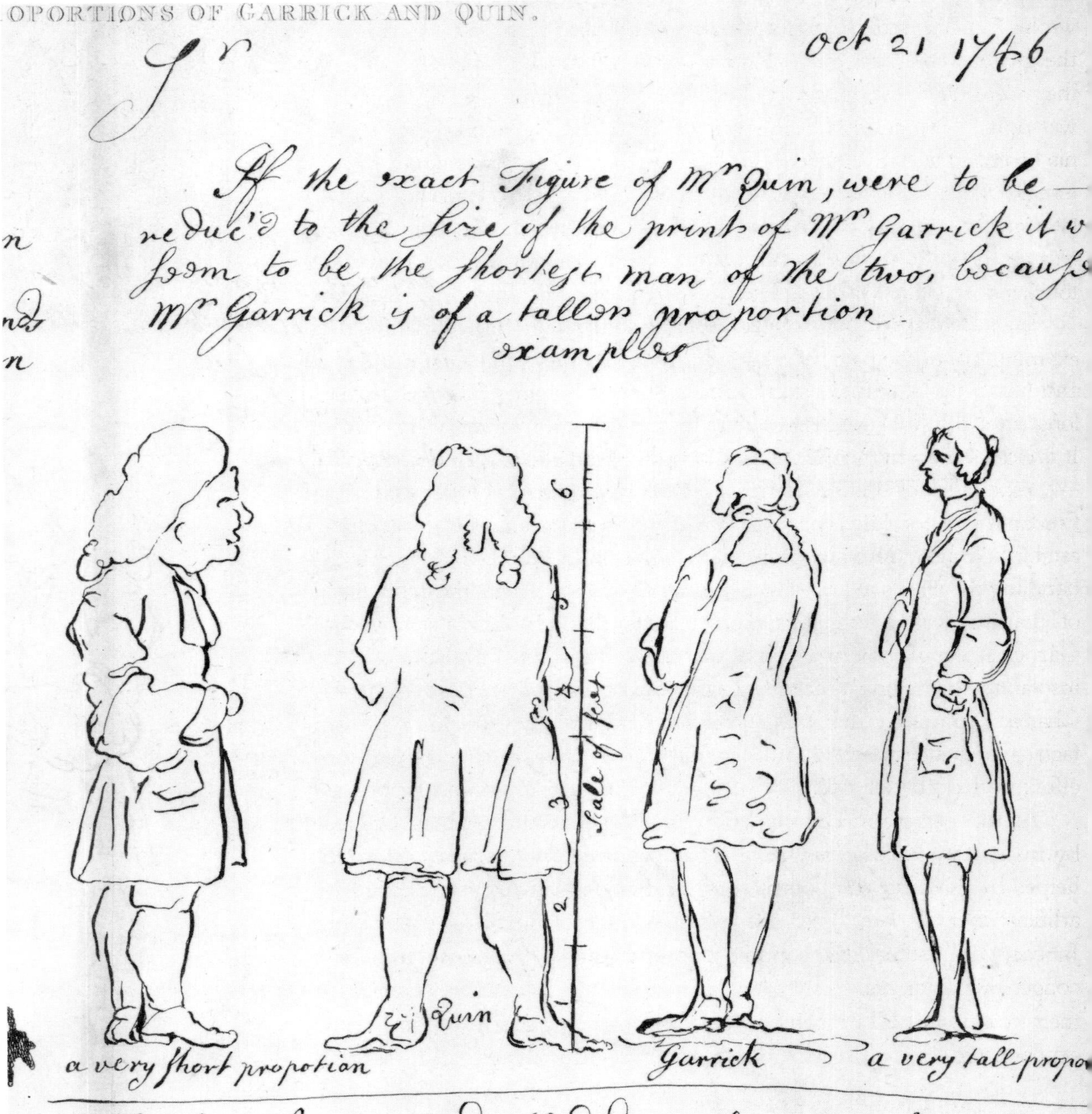

ROPORTIONS OF GARRICK AND QUIN.

Oct 21 1746

Sr

If the exact Figure of Mr Quin, were to be reduc'd to the size of the print of Mr Garrick it w seem to be the shortest man of the two, because Mr Garrick is of a taller proportion.

examples

a very short proportion   Quin   Garrick   a very tall propor

Let these figures be doubled down so as to be seen but on at once, than let it be ask'd which represents the Tallest man

36

Alexander Stevens (1710–84), in *The Adventures of a Speculist* (1788), wrote: 'Garrick, indeed, corrected the audience's taste: he taught them, by the greatness of his acting, to know those nice touches of nature, which they were till then strangers to. When he acted, the audience saw what was right.'[13] Stevens had been given a letter of introduction by Garrick to his brother Peter in Lichfield on 24 September 1773. Stevens had failed initially as an actor at Covent Garden in 1754, but he appeared much later at Drury Lane, on 12 May 1773, as Stephano in *The Tempest*. He was a pioneer of the monologue, and it was in this capacity that he was touring the provinces at the time.

Luckily for posterity, Garrick set out some of his own ideas — for example, about the parts of Abel Drugger in Ben Jonson's *The Alchemist*, and Macbeth — in his *An Essay on Acting* of 1744, and there is extant a long letter dated 24 January 1762 in which he replied to one of his critics. It is clear that Garrick had thought long and hard about the texts of plays — especially of Shakespeare — and how the text provided the fundamentals of the character and the motivation. Once he had established the motivation, however, he then applied his dramatic sense to handling the words in a way which some of what he called 'the gentlemen of the pen' found exaggerated. But when Cibber had written about Garrick's 'pantomimical manner of acting' he was in element correct, insofar as that manner of acting was founded on mime. According to Charles Dibdin, Garrick was able to stand completely still and, solely by facial expression, run the gamut of passion and emotion, moving from one effect to the other at will.

As we shall see, Garrick's eyes were felt to be particularly expressive by many of those who saw him, and there is no doubt that he was also helped by the strength of his features, and his bone structure, which took artificial lighting well. There appeared in the *London Chronicle* for 2–4 January 1772 some lines supposedly written by a young man who was congenitally deaf and dumb. He may well have had some assistance in their composition, but behind them lies the immediacy of first-hand experience:

> With ease the various passions I can trace
> Clearly reflected from his wondrous face;
> Whilst true conception with just action joined,
> Strongly impress each image on my mind:
> What need of sounds? when plainly I descry

Gainsborough's portrait of the actor James Quin (1693–1766), which remained unfinished at the artist's death. It was painted during Quin's retirement in Bath, though the full-length version was exhibited by Gainsborough at the Society of Artists in 1763. Garrick wrote to Quin on 20 June that year that Hudson, who had painted Quin previously, was annoyed by 'the much, and deservedly, admired picture of you by Gainsborough . . . there is merit sufficient in that portrait to warm the most stoical painter'. (*Royal Collection — Mansell Collection*)

(*see opposite page*)
Hogarth's caricature comparing and contrasting the figures of David Garrick and James Quin, contained in a letter. Garrick wrote an affectionate epitaph for Quin, his old rival: 'That tongue which set the table on a roar/And charm'd the public ear, is heard no more.' (*Mansell Collection*)

> Th'expressive features, and the speaking eye;
> That eye, whose bright and penetrating ray,
> Does Shakespeare's meaning to my soul convey.
> Best commentator on great Shakespeare's text!
> When Garrick acts, no passage seems perplext.

As Garrick well knew, the best way to be able to interpret Shakespeare's text was to know it inside out. As he wrote to his protégé the actor William Powell (1735–69): 'But above all, never let your Shakespeare be out of your hands or your pocket. Keep him about you as a charm. The more you read him the more you'll like him, and the better you'll act him.'[14] As for Garrick himself, he was lucky in that he possessed, in addition, 'the speaking eye'. We have Fanny Burney's testimony to the brilliance of Garrick's eyes in her *Early Diary*: 'I never saw in my life such brilliant, piercing eyes as his are. In looking at him, when I have chanced to meet them, I have not really been able to bear their lustre. I remember three lines which I once heard Mrs Pleydell repeat (they were her own), upon Mr Garrick, speaking of his face:

> That mouth that might Envy with passion inspire;
> Those eyes! fraught with genius, with sweetness, with fire,
> And every thing else that the heart can desire.'[15]

Fanny Burney also introduced a description of Garrick's acting in one of his most famous roles, that of Ranger in *The Suspicious Husband*, into her first novel, *Evelina*:

> Well may Mr Garrick be so celebrated, so universally admired —
> I had not any idea of so great a performer.
>
> Such ease! such vivacity in his manner! such grace in his motions! such fire and meaning in his eyes! — I could hardly believe that he had studied a written part, for every word seemed spoke from the impulse of the moment.
>
> His action — at once so graceful and so free! — his voice — so clear, so melodious, yet so wonderfully various in its tones — such animation! — every look *speaks*!
>
> I would have given the world to have had the whole play acted over again. And when he danced — O how I envied Clarinda. I almost wished to have jumped on the stage and joined them.
>
> I am afraid you will think me mad, so I won't say any more; yet I really believe Mr Garrick would make you mad too, if you could see him.[16]

L.Roberts del. Publish'd for Bell's British Theatre Sept 10th 1776. Thornthwaite Sculp.

Of course, Fanny Burney adored Garrick and he was an old friend of the family. *Evelina* is subtitled 'The history of a young lady's entrance into the world', and therefore presents all the excitements of London life as seen through the eyes of a young girl fresh from the provinces. It is therefore perfectly within the character of the girl as portrayed by the author that she should have been so impressed by what she had experienced at the theatre. So much so, in fact, that either by design or accident, a mistake appeared. Ranger does not dance with Clarinda at the end of the play, but with Mrs Strickland. By the time the book was first published in 1778, Garrick had already been in retirement for some two years, and he had played Ranger as one of his farewell performances at Drury Lane on 23 May and 1 June 1776. He did not long survive the publication of *Evelina*.

Garrick and Miss Younge in James Thomson's (1700–48) *Tancred and Sigismunda* (1744–5) which featured in no less than eighteen seasons at Drury Lane between 1747 and 1776, and five at Covent Garden during the same period. Although Garrick played the role as early as 1748, Thornthwaite's engraving, done for *Bell's British Theatre*, was not published until 10 September 1776. (*Mansell Collection*)

It comes as some surprise, perhaps, after all the raptures voiced by those who were lucky enough to see him act, that Garrick was only five feet four inches tall. There is an interesting account by Richard Cumberland in his *Memoirs*, when he saw James Quin as Horatio and Mrs Cibber as Calista in Rowe's *The Fair Penitent*. They were both of the old school in this play: 'It was so wanting in contrast, that, though it did not wound the ear, it wearied it.'[17] But when Garrick came on stage as Lothario, 'alive in every muscle and in every feature . . . it seemed as if a whole century had been stept over in the transition of a single scene'.

Garrick also brought changes to the use of costume, though this was a different problem, since contemporary clothes were usually worn. In this way, actresses might dictate fashion, and when the opera star Francesca Cuzzoni appeared in Handel's opera *Rodelinda* in 1725 in a brown silk dress trimmed with silver, she took London society by storm. Every lady of fashion copied her. The effect was not always the same, however. Tate Wilkinson told in his memoirs that when Kitty Clive saw Garrick in a 'silver spangled tissue shape' in *Barbarossa* (1754), she exclaimed: 'O my God! Room! Room! Make room for the royal lamplighter.' There were, however, some traditional, accepted conventions for costumes, known as 'shapes'. There was the Roman 'shape' for heroes of Classical antiquity, and the Turkish 'shape' for anything oriental. Both of these had a feathered headdress. There was also a Spanish 'shape', thought suitable for villains, and Old English, used in *The Jubilee*, for example. Both of these had slashed or puffed doublet, and knee breeches and cloak in the first case and hose in the second.

Garrick was determined to try and introduce more 'realism' into the use of costume, though the word may only be used in an approximate sense at this time, and his efforts were not always appreciated. In 1745, when he first played Othello, he appeared on stage with a black face, dressed in the scarlet coat of a Venetian general, and the whole topped off with a large turban. It was unfortunate, to say the least, that he unwittingly created for himself a direct comparison to one of the characters in Hogarth's set of pictures *A Harlot's Progress*. In one of them the lady deliberately upsets the tea-table so as to distract the attention of the current lover as a previous one is leaving. In the foreground of the painting is a small black servant, known at the time as a 'Pompey', bearing the kettle. At Garrick's appearance, Quin remarked audibly to Dr Hoadly: 'Here's Pompey, but where's the tea-kettle and lamp?' Arthur Murphy records that many years later, when Garrick was one day looking through his 'own choice folio of Horarth's prints', he came to the one in question and was bound to remark: 'Faith! It is devilish like.'[18] Othello was never a part that he took to, or had a great success with.

Whatever the reaction he inspired in the audience with his innovations — and as the *Othello* incident indicates, they were capable of having the opposite effect from what was intended — Garrick was determined not to capitulate to current taste simply in order to court popularity. He made as much clear when he pronounced his first prologue at the start of his management at Drury Lane. He was scornful of what he saw as mere pantomime, the spectacle and music of Rich, for example, at Covent Garden:

> 'Tis yours this night to bid the reign commence
> Of rescu'd nature, and reviving sense;
> To chase the charms of sound, the pomp of show,
> For useful mirth and salutary woe...

However, as a man of the theatre, he came to appreciate that what the author of *A Dialogue in the Shades* wrote in 1766 was quite true: 'The multitude are incapable of distinguishing; and if their ears are but tickled, and their sight gratified, they re-echo applause, and go away contented; so that [Harlequin], Doctor Faustus, or the Coronation in *Harry the Eighth*, will bring in a full house very often when *Hamlet* or *Othello* might be a losing play.'[19]

Garrick then found that his 'entertainments' were the answer to compete with the pantomime that Covent Garden offered. There had been a performance of *Henry VIII* put on to celebrate the coronation of George II in October 1727 at Drury Lane, at a cost of £1,000. In 1761, for the coronation of George III, both houses repeated the play, though Rich outdid Garrick on this occasion with his spectacle, even though Garrick opened up the stage onto Drury Lane, where a real crowd made merry around a real bonfire. It was a pity that the smoke was found to be a great nuisance to all and sundry.

For *The Institution of the Knights of the Garter* in 1771, Garrick spared no expense, and there was the successful resurrection of his Shakespeare celebration, *The Jubilee*, in 1769, which made up for the débâcle of what had happened at Stratford, as we shall see. For this, people were brought in from the street to appear as the stage crowd. There was also *A*

Christmas Tale of 1774, where Garrick sketched out for De Loutherbourg a synopsis of scenes. Some of its success came no doubt from the use of licopodium, which Garrick and De Loutherbourg introduced from France, for producing special pyrotechnic effects.

As to how quickly Garrick made his impact, we have the testimony of 'A student of Oxford', writing in 1750: 'Since Mr Garrick's management the stage is become the school of manners and morality; ribaldry and prophaneness are no longer tolerated. Sense and nature exert their influence; *Pantomime* daily declines; dancers are little encouraged; the *Burletta* performs to empty benches, and the *British* can now vie with the *Athenian* drama when in its severest state of purity.'[20] In fact, the author was wrong about the pantomime and dance, but he was right about most of the rest.

With all his new excitements as his career began to develop, however, Garrick was still not too busy to deal with his increasing correspondence — and indeed throughout his life he seems to have dealt with it with the same amount of application and dedication, even if he sometimes had second thoughts about sending some of the answers he had prepared. It was in one of those many letters that he summed up his philosophy, when he wrote to William Powell: 'Don't sacrifice your taste and feelings to the applause of multitude; a true genius will convert an audience to his manner, rather than be converted by them to what is false and unnatural.'

To return to the 1740's. After August 1742 there is, then, a gap in Garrick's surviving correspondence of rather more than two years, and when it resumes on 11 September 1744 there are two letters in connection with a performance of Dryden's *All For Love*, mounted by John Russell (1710–71), fourth Duke of Bedford (1732), and his friends at Woburn Abbey. Some detractors always maintained that Garrick was only too happy to put himself out for a member of the aristocracy, but at this relatively early stage in his career there is no reason to suppose that he was doing anything beneath his status as an artist or genius in dealing in 'fasces, asps and garlands' for aristocratic amateur theatricals.

What is more interesting with the resumption of the sequence of letters at this time is the one following, to Somerset Draper, dated 16 September 1744. Draper was a brewer, stationer and partner with the booksellers Jacob and Richard Tonson from 1743 until about 1753, some three years before his death. Garrick wrote to him from Eton, where he had gone with his friend William Windham the elder (1717–61), presumably to visit the latter's close friend, Dr Thomas Dampier. Windham was Garrick's benefactor and constant friend until the former's death. From Garrick's fulsome praise of him to Draper in this letter, one can see why: 'He is a most ingenious, worthy, knowing young gentleman, and I think myself very happy and honoured with his friendship; he has travelled and read to some purpose; and he has so much good-nature, honour, spirit, and generosity, that I am confident when he is possessed of a great fortune, and sits in Parliament, he will make an extraordinary figure.'[21] Whatever the promise of William Windham, it was much to the point at this time that he had taken Garrick's part in what had turned out to be the first crisis of any magnitude since he had embarked on his chosen career.

The trouble began when the previous season (1742–3) had ended at Drury Lane. Fleetwood was known to have gambled away his profits from the theatre at White's, so that when it came to paying the company, he simply did not have the funds to give many of the performers their full salaries. Relations between Garrick and Fleetwood had already been somewhat strained, but at that point they collapsed. Garrick and the actor Charles Macklin (1699–1797), who was Fleetwood's assistant manager, got together a group of the Drury Lane company with the intention of forming a new company, either at the Opera House in the Haymarket or any other theatre they could find. The problem was that the Lord Chamberlain would not grant them a patent, especially when he learned how much the actors were accustomed to earn, and in the end the rebels had to go back to Fleetwood, who took them all with the exception of Macklin. Despite their previous friendship, and time spent under the same roof together, Macklin naturally supposed that it was Garrick who had been the one to cause the group to capitulate, and therefore by implication isolate Macklin in that way. In fact, Garrick had offered to take a reduction in salary of £200 if Fleetwood would take Macklin back. He also offered to find Mrs Macklin an engagement at Covent Garden at £3 a week, and to give Macklin £6 a week until he could find work. However, Fleetwood would only take the actors back if Garrick went too, and Macklin was excluded.

Garrick published a defence of his actions in the *Daily Post and General Advertiser* of 25 November 1743. Macklin's next move was to create disturbances during performances at Drury Lane, and publish a pamphlet in which he set out his accusations against Garrick. The latter

Zoffany's portrait of Charles Macklin as Shylock, painted *circa* 1767–8, when Macklin played the role at Covent Garden. He had first played it in 1741, at Drury Lane, and did not relinquish it until 1789. Here, in the trial scene, Macklin is shown left centre. Portia is played by his daughter, Maria Macklin, and the judge on the extreme left is William Murray, Lord Mansfield, who may have commissioned the painting. (*Tate Gallery, London*)

replied to this with a further pamphlet, but it was a great pity that what had previously been a pleasant association had to end in this way. One of the things that rankled was that Garrick had actually gone back with an increase in salary, but he had not accepted the settlement easily, and it was largely his feeling of responsibility towards the other players, who had been led by him and Macklin, that induced him to do so. In his letter to Draper of 16 September 1744, Garrick gave his version of the reconciliation between himself and Fleetwood, the accuracy of which one has no reason to doubt, and it is evident that Garrick had little respect for the man and was far from keen to be on anything more than a square business footing with him: 'he invited me several times to dinner; but I would not go'.

It was all a sobering and salutary experience for Garrick, and it was as well for his subsequent career that it happened at such an early point in it.

As it happened, Fleetwood's affairs had now become so complicated that he was obliged to put up his patent for sale, and by the time Garrick wrote to John Hoadly on 29 December 1744, Fleetwood had sold to James Lacy (?1698–1744), who had opened Ranelagh Gardens in 1734, sold out, and was at this time assistant manager to Rich at Covent Garden. Garrick told Hoadly that he hoped to be able to sign himself 'Manager of Drury Lane'. That eventually came about, but not until 1747. Nevertheless, it was true that at this time Fleetwood had made an agreement with Lacy to sell Drury Lane, the money to be advanced by the bankers Green and Amber, and with Lacy himself, as manager, holding a third share of the patent.

Lacy then began negotiations with Garrick the following year, in early October, but at first Garrick's reaction to Lacy's approaches was that they were 'impudent' — or so he wrote to Somerset Draper from Lichfield in a letter of 10 October 1745. William Windham was called upon to help, and Garrick also wrote to Johnson for assistance in framing his reply to Lacy. Garrick was certainly not going to be put upon, but at the same time he was within sight of his goal, and his eventual association with Lacy was to last until the latter's death in 1774. As a writer in the *European Magazine* of April 1809 put it: 'This was the thing that, of all others, *Garrick* wished; yet being in wordly affairs endued with a proper portion of prudence, he, as the sailors term it, hauled his wind, and, pretending to consult his friends upon the occasion, lay upon his oars for a short period, before he accepted the tempting offer upon which he had long had his eye.' In fact, it was not quite a simple as that, since at first Lacy was only offering terms to Garrick to appear as an actor on stage, and there was the complication of another offer that Garrick had had from Thomas Sheridan to go to Ireland. Lacy knew of this, and had — according to Davies — written to Dublin and 'gave Mr Garrick great offence'.[22] From the very strong tone of Garrick's reply to Lacy, it is a wonder that they eventually became such good partners, or that their association should have lasted so long. The very opening paragraph is a fairly strong blast, and is indicative of the tone throughout the letter: 'Though I agree with you that our disputes are impertinent to the public and prejudicial to ourselves, yet as you have begun the attack in so ungentleman-like and unjustifiable a manner, I am constrained to defend myself, and as I have no reason to disguise the truth by metaphorical flourishes or oratorial scurrillity [*sic*], I shall only have recourse to plain matter of fact supported

Walker's engraving for *Bell's British Theatre*, dated 1 August 1776, of Thomas Sheridan as Cato. Like Garrick, Sheridan began his stage career in the part of Richard III, though at the Smock Alley Theatre in Dublin, on 29 January 1743, after Garrick's London début. Sheridan survived to assist his son at Drury Lane after Garrick's retirement, and though the arrangement did not last long, it was the cause of an exchange of letters between Garrick and the younger Sheridan. (*Mansell Collection*)

45

Thomas King as Lord Ogleby and Mr and Mrs Robert Baddeley (née Sophia Snow) in Garrick and Colman's play *The Clandestine Marriage*, first produced at Drury Lane in 1766, and playing no less than eighty-seven performances. The character of Lord Ogleby was developed by Garrick from his own Lord Chalkstone, a part he added to his play *Lethe* in 1756, and played himself. (*Garrick Club, London*)

by unquestionable evidence and written agreements, and let the world determine between us.'[23]

Garrick, as we have seen, always had responded to letters, no matter how seemingly unimportant they were, and he continued to do so when one might have thought that he could afford to worry no longer. He was jealous for his character, however, and this was at least one way of ensuring that he was not traduced. In fact, when writing to Somerset Draper about this same matter and at the same time, Garrick put his attitude in a nutshell: 'I shall very fully answer each paragraph and send it to you for your advice. It is a most weak, scurrilous performance, and writ *in terrorem*. I should not care to have any more controversy, but if villains will attack me, I must defend myself.'[24]

46

Garrick accepted Sheridan's offer in the end, and reached Dublin on 24 November 1745 to play a season at the theatre in Smock Alley. The company also included Spranger Barry (1719–77), Miss Bellamy and Mrs Furnival. At this time Somerset Draper was looking after Garrick's interests back in London, and there are several letters surviving from the period. It was the time of the Jacobite Rebellion, and Mrs Cibber had proposed to Garrick, before he left for Dublin, that they should, along with James Quin, give their services free at the Haymarket in order to raise money to enlist men to fight for the King. Until now Quin and Garrick had never acted together, and Garrick regarded him as something of a rival. Eventually they did act together, and that rivalry turned into a firm friendship. At this point, however, Garrick told Somerset Draper that he would feel much happier if Quin were engaged with Rich at Covent Garden — a stage on which Garrick had no urge to act: 'I am afraid of the house, and other things.'[25]

Garrick had also been told that the London theatres had been closed because of the Rebellion. This is evident from his letter of 1 December 1745 to Somerset Draper, and Prince Charles Edward did in fact reach Derby on 5 December, causing panic in the capital. It was not true about the theatres, however, and Garrick had been misinformed. Nevertheless, he was philosophical enough to feel that by the time his Dublin engagement was over in the following spring, things would be different: 'I am not uneasy at my situation, and do not doubt but theatrical as well as political affairs will wear a better face by March next, and I hope to find something settled to my hands at my return to England.'

One of the matters well to the front of his thoughts was the possibility of securing the patent at Drury Lane. Mrs Cibber had written twice to him about it, since things were reaching a critical point at that theatre. As David wrote to Draper, probably on 15 December 1745: 'If you can conveniently wriggle your little friend into the patent upon good terms, you make me forever.'[26] It was very frustrating for Garrick, being so far away at such a potentially critical time. It was a sad time too in that while he was in Dublin he received the news of the death of his favourite sister, Jane (buried in Lichfield Cathedral on 15 December). As he wrote to Draper in the same letter: 'She was the handsomest of the family, and a very good girl; but her life was made so uncomfortable by continued ill health, that the loss of her is less afflicting, as she was sickly and blameless. I am sure she is happy, and I'm not sorry she is released from the pain and

47

anxieties of this world: I believe the terrors and alarms . . . the country was under on account of the rebels hastened her death — but let her rest.'

Eventually Garrick left Dublin on 3 May 1746, and was in London a week later. Inexorably, it seemed, he was now moving towards his next prize, the management of Drury Lane.

CHAPTER THREE

ACTOR AND MANAGER

Cheltenham Wells, in a view published by J. Sewell in 1786 in the *European Magazine*. Garrick had visited Cheltenham some forty years earlier and, when his occupations permitted, evinced a taste for spa and resort life in common with his contemporaries. He moved on, however, to Bath, Tunbridge Wells and eventually Brighton. Such was the popularity of these resorts that Garrick's friend Richard Rigby engaged Robert Adam to turn his seat at Mistley in Essex into a spa — a project which, sadly, failed to materialize. (*Mansell Collection*)

GARRICK had not been back from Ireland a fortnight before he was writing to his brother Peter in Lichfield about their younger brother George, for whom David had secured a situation in a solicitor's office. This did not last for long, however, and from about 1750 until the end of David Garrick's theatrical career, brother George was destined to be his right-hand man at Drury Lane.

David Garrick took his filial responsibilities seriously and always tried to do his best for his family, to the extent of trying to placate Peter, who had been upset by their brother William, and generally pouring oil on troubled waters. On this occasion he was not particularly successful, however, since William, writing to George on 19 April 1747, continued to feel that Peter had given him 'ill usage and unbrotherly kindness'.[1] Human relationships were always important to David Garrick, and this concern is one of the explanations for the regard in which he was held by so many people throughout his life. A particularly revealing document in this respect is a letter he wrote to the artist Francis Hayman (1708–76) on 18 August 1746. Garrick had gone to Cheltenham to take the waters, which agreed with him well, though he found the place itself 'damned dull', despite the fact that there were balls twice a week, assemblies every night, and 'the facetious Mr Foote to crown the whole'.[2] Still, as he confessed to Hayman, his 'want of relish for the pleasures of Cheltenham' was probably due to the fact that he had a boil under the waistband of his breeches, rather than for any deficiencies in Cheltenham itself. Samuel Foote (1720–77), whom we shall meet again, had recently taken up the role of mimic in dissatisfaction with his success — or lack of it — as an actor.

Garrick then went on to explain to Hayman at length why it was that he had not rushed into a friendship with the artist. He was somewhat wary of Hayman's friends and acquaintances, who did not like Garrick. Since he was not a lukewarm person, he explained, but was rather 'open and impetuous', then he had to be prudent and shun company he was doubtful of; but as far as Hayman himself was concerned, Garrick made a direct and warm expression of friendship: 'I tell you what, Hayman, and I speak it from my heart, that no opportunity shall be slipped, or endeavours wanting on my side, to promote your welfare and interest to the best of my power, and though my abilities are but small, you must take the will for the deed.'

On another plane, the letter is interesting for the way in which it reveals Garrick's knowledge of Shakespeare, as he elaborated for Hayman an illustration to *Othello*. Hayman had started his career as a scene painter at Drury Lane under Fleetwood's management, and then on the latter's death Hayman married his widow. He established his reputation with the paintings he did for the alcoves at the Vauxhall Pleasure Gardens, and was the teacher of the young Gainsborough, as well as being one of the founders of the Royal Academy. He prepared a series of illustrations for a subsequent issue of Sir Thomas Hanmer's edition of Shakespeare's plays (1743–4) — which, in the event, were not used — though Charles Jennens, incorporating Garrick's suggestions, used them for *Lear* and *Othello* as frontispieces to his separate editions of the plays in 1770 and 1773. What is certain from Garrick's letter to Hayman of August 1746 is his understanding of the depth of tragedy in *Othello* in terms of human suffering and interplay of character. For Garrick there was no doubt at all in his mind that the most dramatic moment in the play was Emilia's discovery about the handkerchief and not, for example, the murder of Desdemona: 'The scene which in my opinion will make the best picture is

The duel scene in Garrick's *Miss in her Teens*, as drawn and engraved by C. Mosley, dated 29 January 1747 (in fact, the play had opened on 17 January at Covent Garden). The part of Fribble, seen here at left, was one of Garrick's most successful ones, and demonstrated his ability to excel in both comedy and tragedy. The engraving is also interesting for what it shows us of the theatres of the day. *(British Museum)*

THE MODERN DUEL.
Taken from Miss in her Teens, as it's now Acted at Covent Garden.

1. Miss Biddy Bellair   2. Mr Fribble   3. Capt Flash   4. Mrs Tag

that point of time in the last act when Emilia discovers to Othello his error about the handkerchief. . . . Here at once the whole catastrophe of the play is unravelled and the group of figures in this scene, with their different expressions, will produce a finer effect in painting than perhaps any other in all Shakespear [sic], though as yet never thought of by any of the designers who have published their several prints from the same author.'

The following theatrical season of 1746–7 Garrick did in fact play at Covent Garden — despite his reservations about the house — along with James Quin, Mrs Cibber, Mrs Pritchard and Henry Woodward. There was also the first performance in that theatre, on 17 January 1747, of Garrick's own farce *Miss in her Teens* (based on a French original), in which he played the part of Fribble.[3] As Mrs Delany wrote: 'Last Saturday [29 January] I went to . . . the new farce . . . composed by Garrick; *nothing can be lower*, but the part he acts in it himself he makes so very ridiculous that it is really entertaining. It is said he mimics *eleven* men of fashion.'[4] One must bear in mind that Mrs Delany was a lifelong devotee of Handel, and felt that his music was the highest art form possible. In the light of this, her opinion about Garrick and his play is remarkably complimentary.

For Garrick himself, the tide was now running strongly in his favour, and on 9 April 1747 he and Lacy finally became co-patentees of the Drury Lane theatre. Even before the new season opened, however, Garrick had to deal with professional jealousies amongst his proposed company. From a letter Garrick wrote on 11 July 1747 to William Pritchard, his treasurer at Drury Lane, someone had been putting around the rumour that although Mrs Pritchard had been invited to join the company, too, it was Garrick's intention to give her only minor parts, and the main ones to Mrs Cibber. As in similar situations, Garrick went to great lengths to allay Pritchard's fears, but at the same time gave him fairly to understand that if he did not accept Garrick's undertaking, he could go elsewhere: 'However, if you have any doubts about you, and you had rather chuse [sic] Covent Garden than Drury Lane, let me know it immediately (the very next post) and [I] will do my endeavours with Mr Lacy (for I will not let him know till then) to discharge you from any agreement that may make you and Mrs Pritchard uneasy.'[5] And then, in a touch that gives a brilliantly vivid glimpse into Garrick's doings and the excitement of those days: 'I am just com[e] from the house; we are in the midst of alterations and mortar so you must excuse this scrawl.'

(see opposite page)
Francis Hayman (1708–76), as painted by Reynolds. Hayman painted several of the supper–box decorations for Vauxhall Gardens in London, as well as scenes from contemporary theatrical productions, and a portrait of Garrick as Richard III in 1760. The actor had befriended the scene-painter early in their respective careers, and they remained friends throughout his life. (*Mansell Collection*)

Even when the season had opened, and one set of problems had been resolved, a new set arose. Garrick now had to deal with critics of his own acting style, whom he answered with remarkable forbearance. There is a letter from Garrick to the Reverend Peter Whalley, dated 15 March 1748, in which he accepts some of the criticism, but rejects the rest, making, *en passant*, the interesting observation: 'At my first setting out in the business of an actor I endeavoured to shake off the fetters of numbers, and have been often accused of neglecting the harmony of the versification from a too close regard to the passion, and the meaning, of the author.'[6]

Others, however, were more perspicacious, and when volume seven of Samuel Richardson's *Clarissa* came out in the autumn of 1748, it contained a great tribute to Garrick, apropos a revival of *Lear*: 'And yet, if it were *ever* to be tried, *now* seems to be the time, when an *Actor* and a *Manager*, in the *same person*, is in being, who deservedly engages public favour in all he undertakes, and who owes so much, and is gratefully sensible that he does, to that great master of the human passions.'[7] On 12 December 1748 Garrick wrote a suitably gracious letter of thanks to the author for the gift of the last three volumes, and three years later, when Richardson also gave a set to Garrick's wife, Garrick returned the compliment by composing some verses which he inscribed in the first volume. It is interesting, however, that for all his praise of Garrick, Richardson had not seen him act as late as 27 October 1748, when he wrote to Aaron Hill: 'I never saw him on the stage; but of late I am pretty well acquainted with him.'[8] When next we hear from Garrick's own hand it is on 18 July 1749, and his whole world has changed, for he is now a married man. As to how that came about, one must go back a little in time.

After the affair with Peg Woffington came to an end, Garrick had not been destined to be long out of love. On 11 March 1746 the playbills for the Opera House in the Haymarket announced that: 'Madem. Violette, a New Dancer from Vienna, will perform this day for the first time.' Though Garrick did not meet her immediately, in just over three years' time she was to become his wife. She was born in Vienna on 29 February 1724, and was a pupil of Franz Anton Hilverding (1710–68). Her stage name came from rendering her surname — Veigel — into French. She soon won aristocratic patronage, including that of Countess Rabutin, and Prince Eugen of Savoy asked her to dance at private receptions. It was even rumoured that she had caught the eye of the Emperor himself, and

(see opposite page)
A somewhat fanciful portrait (after Boucher) of the young Mrs Garrick which nevertheless captures what must have been the glamour of her persona in her early days in London. It is not too difficult to see the contrast between the elegance of Mrs Garrick and the less ethereal charms of Peg Woffington (see p. 25), and why it was that the fastidious David Garrick found his lifelong partner in Eva Maria Veigel. *(Mansell Collection)*

Maria Theresa expressed the wish that Violette should leave Vienna. At all events, she made her début in London in 1746, and on 5 June Horace Walpole was able to write: 'The fame of the Violetta increases daily.'[9]

Because of her situation, Violette travelled to England dressed as a boy, accompanied by her brother Ferdinand and a third person by the name of Rossiter. As with most of the passengers on the ship from Holland to Harwich, she was seasick. By chance there was also on board a young Scotsman by the name of Alexander Carlyle, who penetrated the disguise of the young lady and was of assistance on the journey from the port up to town, especially when dealing with the innkeepers.

Violette had been helped considerably in her entrée into London society by the fact that she had brought with her an introduction from the Stahremberg family to the Earl and Countess of Burlington, who took her under their wing, and whose house in Piccadilly became her home. Dorothy Savile (1699–1758), daughter of the second Marquis of Halifax, had married Richard Boyle (1695–1753), third Earl of Burlington, in 1721. Of the latter Walpole wrote: 'Never were protection and great wealth more generously and more judiciously diffused than by this great person, who had every quality of a genius and artist, except envy.'[10] In the autumn of 1746 Violette moved from the Opera House to Drury Lane, though at that time Garrick was at Covent Garden. Conversely, when he became manager of Drury Lane in 1747, she had moved to Covent Garden. We do not know exactly how or when they made each other's acquaintance, though it was probably in a social context rather than a professional one.

Garrick and Violette were two of the most popular persons on the London stage at the time, and it was inevitable that they should be invited to the same social occasions and should eventually meet. When the Duke of Richmond gave a party by the river for the Duke of Modena on 15 May 1749, Walpole noticed Garrick 'ogling and sighing the whole time' in the direction of Violette, and the feeling seems to have been reciprocated. However, Lady Burlington had rather grander ideas for her protégée. A nobleman might take an actress or dancer to wife without any difficulty as far as she was concerned, and there was the example of the Earl of Peterborough, who had been secretly married to Anastasia Robinson for years, but the idea that an actor — even a highly successful one — should aspire to the hand of her Violette was a different matter entirely.

Richard Boyle, third Earl of Burlington (1695–1753), whose involvement in and patronage of the arts become legendary, even if it was made fun of in certain quarters. Garrick's friend Hogarth, for one, deplored Burlington's patronage of the painter and architect William Kent, and was highly critical of the taste of the Burlington House circle. Indeed, an engraving of 1732 specifically ridiculed the whole concept of 'Taste', showing the word incised on the gateway to the house. (*Mansell Collection*)

It was, therefore, with considerable determination that Eva Maria Veigel and David Garrick were married on 22 June 1749, first in the Protestant chapel in Russell Street, Bloomsbury, and then later that same day in the Roman Catholic chapel of the Portuguese Embassy in South Audley Street. Lady Burlington had not at first encouraged the idea, as we have seen, of a liaison between her protégée and an actor, and indeed did much to discourage it. Love finally triumphed, however, and the match turned out to be one of the happiest. Lady Burlington gave a dowry, to which David Garrick also contributed, and the Garricks spent their honeymoon at Merton in Surrey.[11]

If the tone of the letters at this time from Garrick to the Burlingtons seems rather too fulsome, one must bear in mind that he had good reason to be grateful for their generosity in the first place, and also relieved that he had been able to impress the Countess with his personality to the

Burlington House, as engraved by Kyp and drawn by Knyff *circa* 1708. In those days the house lay open to the fields at the back, and provided a pleasant home for Mrs Garrick when she first came to London. Even after her marriage she remained a frequent visitor and she and her husband were able to take their friends on a tour of the house if they so wished. (*Mansell Collection*)

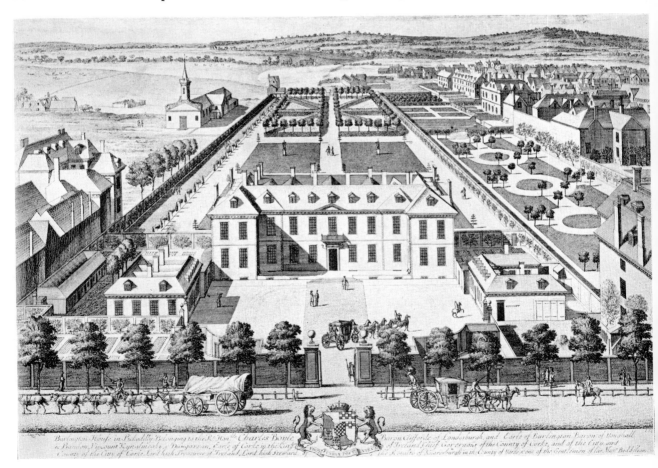

57

extent that he had overcome her objections to him as a person, and the way he had chosen to earn his living. As Burke wrote in an epitaph for Garrick which was never used: 'He raised the character of his profession to the rank of a liberal art.' Garrick wrote to Lord Burlington on 18 July from Merton: 'I have lately had the highest satisfaction in flattering myself that your lordship has now some hopes of Mrs Garrick and I being happy together; your former doubts proceeded from your esteem for her, and from a very just opinion you had conceived of the people in my profession. However, if it should be my good fortune to afford your lordship one exception to the general rule against us, I shall then gain the height of my wishes; for with such a wife and such friends, I can have nothing more to ask or to desire.'[12] A letter to Lady Burlington by the same post is slightly more jocular in tone, but he had good cause. Lady Burlington had been highly complimentary about him in a letter to Mrs Garrick, to which he responded: '. . . delicious flattery indeed! The two most delightful things in the world are to be praised by the person you most admire to the person you love.'[13] Garrick was well aware how crucial a role Lady Burlington had played prior to the wedding: ''Tis owing to you, madam, and you alone, that I am now the happiest of men, and in possession of Mrs Garrick. She has more than once confessed to me that though she liked me very well, and was determined not to marry anybody else, yet she was *as* determined not to marry *me* if Your Ladyship had put a negative upon me.' Such pressures seem intolerable to us today, but were perfectly common at the time, when patrons not only had the ability to exert them on their protégés, but did so on their own children as a matter of course.

Lady Burlington's own daughter, Charlotte Elizabeth (1731–54), had made a splendid marriage — even though she was Baroness Clifford of Londesborough in her own right — to William Cavendish (1720–64), Marquis of Hartington and heir to the dukedom of Devonshire. In the month of the Garricks' marriage — June 1749 — William's father (also William), the third duke, had retired to Chatsworth after a long period of public service, and the Burlingtons were paying a visit at the time. On 5 December 1755 the Duke died, and Hartington succeeded. The Garricks had indeed a grand friend in the fourth Duke of Devonshire.

On 25 July 1749, Mrs Garrick announced to Lady Burlington: 'Mr Garrick has bought the house in Southampton Street [number 27] for five hundred guineas, *dirt* and all; 'tis reckoned a very good bargain.'[14] It was to be their London home from October 1749 until they moved to the brand-new Adelphi Terrace in March 1772. When they went from Merton to see how work was coming on at Southampton Street, the Garricks were able to rest at Burlington House in Piccadilly, and they also visited Chiswick Villa, another Burlington property west of London. Even at this stage we see how much Garrick was immersed in Shakespeare, from a letter to Lady Burlington of 26 August 1749: 'I am afraid my madness about Shakespear [*sic*] is become very troublesome, for I question whether I have written a single letter without bringing *him* in, head and shoulders. I know Your Ladyship must admire him, and therefore I have been more forward to introduce him to you.'[15]

The new season opened at the theatre on 16 September 1749, and according to Garrick they had the fullest house for a first night in twelve years. He himself did not appear, however, until 28 September, when he played Benedick in *Much Ado About Nothing*, since he said that he found that 'the people are very impatient to laugh with me and at me' — as Benedick the married man. He chose the part deliberately, therefore, in

Chiswick Villa — more so than Burlington House — is a testimony to the Earl of Burlington's taste for the Palladian style, and is a direct imitation of Palladio's Villa Rotonda near Vicenza in Italy. For the interior the Earl employed William Kent, thus introducing a rich contrast to the somewhat austere exterior which Burlington designed himself. It was here that the Garricks spent a good deal of time in the first years of their marriage. (It is now known as Chiswick House.) (*Mansell Collection*)

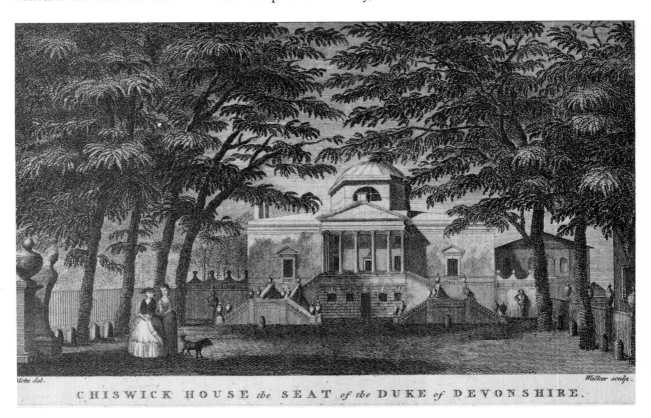

Dietz del.   *Walker sculp.*

CHISWICK HOUSE *the* SEAT *of the* DUKE *of* DEVONSHIRE.

anticipation of the barbs and darts of the writers of lampoons and epigrams that circulated in the London coffee-houses at that time. There are three letters at this point to Lacy, Lacy, and Foote, respectively, probably dating from January 1750. Though Lacy is only the presumed recipient of the first two, internal evidence almost certainly points to him. The letters concern a matter of little importance, though they are most useful to show how, in spite of a certain amount of mutual antipathy at first, Lacy and Garrick were in fact well suited to run the theatre jointly and as a result of this, Drury Lane enjoyed a success previously unknown there. As Thomas Davies put it: 'Mr Garrick and Mr Lacy divided the business of the theatre in such a manner as not to encroach upon each other's province. Mr Lacy took upon himself the care of the wardrobe, the scenes, and the economy of the household; while Mr Garrick regulated the more important business of treating with authors, hiring actors, distributing parts in plays, superintending of rehearsals, etc.'[16]

Garrick made his final appearance of the 1749–50 season at Drury Lane on 11 May 1750, and then he and his wife went to stay first at Hardwick Hall with the Marquis of Hartington, and then on to Chatsworth, from where he wrote to Somerset Draper on 2 June. From this letter, Garrick was evidently already planning ahead for the next season, as he wrote: 'I shall work this summer like a dragon; and, let what will happen, I shall be well prepared.'[17] Nevertheless, Garrick relied on correspondents such as Draper and James Clutterbuck (?1704–76), a London mercer, to keep him informed of events in town, send forgotten items such as books and rhubarb pills, keep an eye on Southampton Street, and generally act for him in his absence. From Chatsworth he went on with Lady Burlington to Londesborough Park near Market Weighton in Yorkshire, where Lord Burlington had built himself a house, to his own design, in the Elizabethan style. On the way they stayed with the Marquis of Rockingham at Wentworth Woodhouse, and despite a mishap with the coach en route, when a horse took fright, reached Londesborough safely. Even so, Garrick thought it best to write from there to Lord Hartington on 8 June in case he was worried by exaggerated reports of what had happened to the party. The Garricks spent their first wedding anniversary at Londesborough, but on the very same day, Garrick was able to write to Draper with ideas for engaging members of his company, especially the actress George Anne Bellamy (?1731–88) as a rival to Mrs Cibber at Covent Garden.

Garrick's letters from Londesborough to Lord Hartington have an immediacy and spontaneity which show how easily the Garricks fitted into this world, as well as their occupations during the very warm summer of 1750. For example, to Lord Hartington on 13 July: 'I murder a rabbit now and then, and have been fatal to the woodpeckers, but from a five years' cessation of arms, I really cannot distinguish between tame and wild pigeons; for unluckily I fired among a flock of 'em yesterday upon the wolds and incurred a penalty of twenty pounds by Act of Parliament — I shall look before I shoot the next time, for such mistakes have no joke in 'em.'[18]

Exactly a week later, to the same correspondent, Garrick gave an account of 'a disagreeable circumstance', which had their 'wit and humour' for five minutes: 'My Lord Langdale, who had eaten three plates of soup, two of salmon, one of carp besides the head, two dozen of gudgeons, some eels, with macaroni, omelet and raspberry tart, and adding to these, strawberries and cream, pineapple, etc, etc, etc, grew a little sick after the third bottle of Burgundy, and I believe had left the maigre compound upon the table he took it from, had not a handsome dram of brandy come to his and our relief. You may imagine we were damped for a few minutes, till my lord recovered his spirits again, and told us very seriously that *fasting* days never agreed with him.'[19]

July wore on, but despite this apparent immersion in matters inconsequential, Garrick had indeed been working 'like a dragon', and told Lacy from Londesborough on 27 July that he would be back 'in council' within a fortnight, and that he would soon be ready in *Romeo and Juliet*, opposite Bellamy. Garrick had doctored the play, so that — amongst other things — Romeo had only the one love. There was no mention of the earlier Rosaline. Garrick thought it much better that way. The whole letter breathes his urge to be back at work, for Lacy proposed opening the season on the first Saturday in September.[20]

There was fierce competition with Covent Garden, where *Romeo and Juliet* was also billed, and Garrick's deliberate policy was to get in first and pre-empt the rival house. In fact, he had coached Spranger Barry and Mrs Cibber in the leading roles for Drury Lane, opening on 29 November 1748. When they crossed over to Covent Garden, Garrick and Bellamy opened in the parts on 28 September 1750. On that same night both Garrick and Barry played Romeo, and so continued in competition until 12 October, when the *Daily Advertiser* published the following epigram:

Garrick and Miss (George Anne) Bellamy as Romeo and Juliet, as depicted by Benjamin Wilson and engraved by Ravenet in 1765. Initially Garrick had coached Spranger Barry and Mrs Cibber in the parts, but when they went over to Covent Garden he decided to play Romeo himself, and thereupon rehearsed Miss Bellamy as Juliet. The ensuing competition between the two houses during September and October 1750 made theatrical headlines, but its real significance lay in the fact that Garrick's text (reprinted every three years until 1787) and acting launched the play on its subsequent modern career. (*British Museum*)

'Well, what's to night?' says angry Ned,
　　As up from bed he rouses;
'Romeo again!' and shakes his head;
　　'Ah! Pox on both your houses.'

In the midst of this struggle, and returning from one of the performances of the play, in fact, Garrick still found time to write to Lady Burlington on 4 October: 'The battle between the theatres yet remains doubtful, though upon my word I most sincerely and impartially think that we have the advantage; our house tonight was much better than theirs, and I believe 'tis generally thought that our performance is best.'[21] When it was over, he wrote the very next day (13 October): 'I can give Your Ladyship the satisfaction, and I flatter myself that it will be so to you, of assuring you that the battle is at last ended, and in our favour — our antagonists yielded last Thursday night and we played the same play on the Friday to a very full house to very great applause; Mr Barry and Mrs Cibber came incog[nito] to see us, and I am very well assured they received no little mortification.'[22] Miss Bellamy had been a great success and had surprised everyone, according to Garrick. If he appears to crow or even gloat over his victory, one must allow that it was a normal part of London theatre life at this time — as we saw with the example of Handel — and the image of battle was never very long absent. The incident was closed, as far as Drury Lane was concerned, by Garrick's writing an epilogue for Kitty Clive to deliver on 11 October.

In the early part of the following year (1751) Garrick had an unexpected respite from the theatre. On 20 March, Frederick, Prince of Wales, died. The Prince was scarcely lamented, but nevertheless the theatres closed from 21 March to 8 April, and Garrick took the opportunity to visit Bath, where he arrived on Friday, 29 March, and stayed for about a week. There are two letters to brother George from Bath, one of them particularly touching, since in it David tells him how to write a letter to a lady, and it was either this year or the next that George married Catherine, daughter of Nathan Carrington. After that it was back to the round of London life, though the Garricks were able to spent time at Chiswick Villa when they felt like it, and also had leave to show friends round Burlington House, where Marco Ricci's decoration of the staircase was a great attraction.

The war of *Romeo and Juliet* had still one more skirmish, however. The Covent Garden season closed on 17 May with that play, with Barry once more in the lead, and it was repeated at the request of 'several persons of quality' on 21 May. By then, however, the Garricks were on the other side of the Channel, in Boulogne, having left London on Sunday, 19 May for a trip to Paris. Garrick wrote to tell Draper of his safe arrival on 21 May. The crossing had taken three and a half hours, and though Mrs Garrick had been a little sick, he was 'as hearty as the most stinking tar-barrel of them all'.[23]

From Garrick's diary of the trip it is quite clear that the first impression of France, formed on his experiences in Boulogne, was not a favourable one.[24] Things improved on the road to Paris, however, and though the inns were still bad, the people were civil and the wine good. Even more important, perhaps, the bill was very reasonable. The couple arrived in Paris on Thursday, 23 May. The very next day Garrick went to the Comédie-Française to see Molière's *L'Ecole des maris*, though since it followed the opening night of a new play the previous evening (*Zares* by Charles Palissot), none of the stars was appearing, and so Garrick's opinion of the performance was not high. The following evening it was the turn of the Comédie-Italienne, and though the acting was generally

better, Garrick declared that the dancing would have been hissed off the stage in England. The dancing was equally indifferent at the Opéra on the Sunday evening (26 May), and — as far as Garrick was concerned — the singing 'abominable'. Notre Dame, on the other hand, was 'the most splendid church' he had ever seen.

The sightseeing went on with great application during the week following. When he reached the top of Notre Dame, Garrick realized that the view from it was so fine largely because it was not obscured by the smoke from the chimneys, as it would have been in London. The exterior

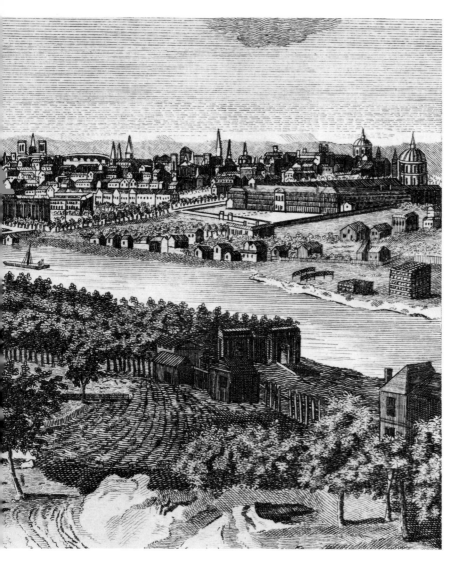

Paris in the eighteenth century, seen here from a point below the modern Etoile, possibly near St Pierre de Chaillot. What struck Garrick most forcibly during his first visit in 1751 was the general cleanliness of the place, and of the atmosphere in particular, so that he was able to see much more of the city than he could of London, for example, at that time. (*Mansell Collection*)

of the Hôtel de Soubise reminded him of Burlington House, though they were unable to go inside, since the family were at home and not at Versailles, which the Garricks were also due to visit. The weather became very hot, and the trip to Versailles was not a success. The view from the terrace to the lake was fine, but Garrick pronounced the palace itself 'inelegant'. They saw Louis XV return from Cressy. It was no magnificent spectacle, however, since the monarch went into the palace 'with great haste and a very dirty, dusty retinue'. A sight of the interior of the palace the following day elicited slightly more enthusiasm from Garrick —

'noble', 'fine' and 'magnificent' are used — and he saw the Royal family in the chapel. Even so, when the pair returned to their hotel they were 'more fatigued than satisfied'. The fountains barely matched up to the cascade and the *jet d'eau* at Chatsworth, Garrick remarked.

After various visits around Paris to St Germain-en-Laye, Marly, Meudon, Bellevue and St Cloud, the Garricks returned on Saturday 8 June, and the following Wednesday saw Mlle Clairon act for the first time. As Garrick noted: '[She] pleased me more than any actress I have yet seen.' On Friday evening he went by himself to the Opéra, liked it even less than before, was half asleep, got a headache, and so went home, and was in a bad humour all the evening. On this day and the next he sat for his portrait to Liotard, and there were to be several more sittings. By and large, Garrick came to the conclusion that none of the *hôtels particuliers* had as good a collection of pictures as there was at Chiswick, by comparison with which they were 'in general rubbish to 'em.'

On Wednesday, 19 June Garrick again sat for Liotard, but as he himself admitted, he 'did very little this day but idle and eat and drink', and the entry for the following day is the last of the diary. The Garricks were still in Paris on 30 June, however, for David wrote to brother George on that day. Exactly when they left Paris is a mystery, though it seems that Garrick may well have ceased his diary abruptly, and left in something of a rush, because he was under suspicion of trying to lure French dancers to London. Since they were officially servants of the Crown, this was a crime, and might well account for both the abrupt end to the diary and the sudden departure. There is, in the Arsenal library in Paris, a letter from the Provost of the Paris Merchants — who were responsible at that time for the direction of the Opéra — to one of the commissioners of police, dated 1 July 1751, which indicates that the authorities were on the alert, and were indeed hoping to catch Garrick red-handed. [25] He seems to have still been there on 12 July, however, from the diary of Charles Collé (1709–83), for he had dined the day before with Garrick, and the latter had played for the company the *Macbeth* dagger scene, which had become one of his party pieces. [26] By the end of July, however, Garrick was safely back at Chiswick, from where he wrote to brother Peter in Lichfield.

Despite his French ancestry, on his return from France Garrick wrote to John Hoadly that Paris had made him as true an Englishman as ever, but even so he was: 'much, very much pleased with my jaunt, and am ready and willing to take the same and for a month longer, whenever business will permit and I am called upon'.[27]

There was an invitation from brother Peter to go and visit him at Lichfield, though the claims of the Burlingtons took precedence, and brother George was deputed to take the gifts from France to Lichfield. Once again a large part of the summer was spent at Londesborough, and once again it was Draper who acted as Garrick's eyes and ears. When Garrick wrote to him on 17 August it was to take exception to the fact that, from what he had heard, the equilibrist Anthony Maddox had been engaged to appear on the stage of Drury Lane, though in fact there is no record that he ever did so. All the same, the very prospect filled Garrick with dismay: 'Have you seen the *Great Lacy* lately? I wish, when you have that pleasure, that you would hint your great surprise and dislike to *Maddox's* rope-dancing upon our stage. I cannot possibly agree to such a prostitution upon any account; and nothing but downright starving would induce me to bring such defilement and abomination into the *house of William Shakespeare*. What a mean, mistaken creature is this par[tn]er of mine! Has *George* told you that he has signed a memorandum with *Maddox* for double the sum he told us that he had engaged him for? What can be the meaning of this? Oh, I am *sick, sick, sick of him!*'[28] If nothing else, the outburst reveals what Garrick's aspirations for Drury Lane were, and that he was 'working and studying . . . like a horse' in order to prepare for the coming season, when *Coriolanus* and *All's Well that Ends Well* — along with plays by other authors — were to be in the repertoire, though Garrick never played in the first of these. He was still at Londesborough on 25 August when he wrote to Lady Hartington — the last of some three dozen letters, he claimed, that he had written in a fortnight — but already he was looking forward to the new season of 1751–2, which was to open on 7 September.

From the point of view of Garrick's acting career, one of the most important aspects of it was his revival, on 29 November 1751 at Drury Lane, of Ben Jonson's *Every Man in his Humour*. As with many of these revivals, it was a version doctored by Garrick, including a whole new scene in the fourth act, but his portrayal of the character of Kitely was one of his most successful. Reynolds subsequently recorded Garrick's appearance in the role, wearing a Van Dyckian costume, in a portrait which is now in the Royal Collection. There is also a copy in the National Portrait Gallery. The King was present for the second performance, and

A portrait of Garrick as Kitely in Ben Jonson's *Every Man in his Humour*, after Reynolds, dating from 1768. Four years earlier, Reynolds had been one of the founder members, along with Dr Johnson, of The Club, though Garrick was only admitted later. Nevertheless, the close association of three such giants in their respective callings was eloquent testimony to the way in which the arts had been established at the heart of English society. (*National Portrait Gallery*)

the production took London by storm. It is also only fair to say that Garrick had taken immense care in his preparations, so that the success was deserved.

Another production of this season was also the occasion for a painting, this time by Garrick's old friend William Hogarth (1697–1764). Garrick had met Samuel Foote during his trip to Paris, and Garrick agreed not only to mount Foote's comedy, *Taste*, at Drury Lane, but also to write a prologue for it, which he himself delivered, as an auctioneer, on the opening night, 11 January 1752. The play poked fun at those who went on the Grand Tour and bought up old masters and mutilated classical statuary. It was said that it was 'relished by the boxes only', but even so, there must have been several persons in the boxes who saw, in Lord Dupe and Mr Puff, caricatures of themselves and their assistants.

In Hogarth's charming painting, Garrick is seated at a table with the prologue to *Taste* in front of him, whilst his wife tries to snatch his pen from his hand from behind his right shoulder. It is said, however, that Garrick did not like the way the artist painted his features in the picture, and that he and Hogarth quarrelled over it. It remained unfinished at the artist's death, and might have been completed by another hand. His widow gave it to Mrs Garrick, and it remained in her possession until her death. The picture is now in the Royal Collection.

Taste had no great success, even for something that was ephemeral by its very nature, and the last new play of the season, *Eugenia*, which opened on 17 February, fared little better. Nevertheless, when the season ended on 12 May 1752, there was much that Garrick could look back on with a sense of satisfaction, and so encourage him to look forward to the next opening with anticipation.

During the ensuing summer Draper was not well, and so it was brother George who kept David informed of matters in London and carried out the errands for him. From a letter of 25 August it is evident that the Garricks were now thinking in terms of having a place of their own out of town, and George was to inspect a property at Ealing for them. The surviving correspondence for the 1752–3 theatre season is not extensive; in fact, only four letters survive for the whole of the period. And in many respects it was not very remarkable as far as the theatre was concerned. Consolidation was more the order of the day, and if the plays of that season were not especially memorable, Garrick and Lacy nevertheless did well enough to have the theatre repainted and regilded,

(see opposite page)
Hogarth's painting of Garrick and his wife, dating from 1752, remained unfinished at the time of the artist's death in 1764 largely, it was said, because of the way in which Hogarth had painted Garrick's features. Other observers expressed reservations about the portrayal of Mrs Garrick, too, concluding that the work did neither the sitters nor the artist much credit. The chair in which Garrick is seated was designed by Hogarth and made out of wood from Shakespeare's mulberry-tree (see p. 136) for Garrick to adorn his Temple at Hampton. Despite Garrick's reservations, the atmosphere of the picture conveys something of the early married bliss of the couple. (*Royal Collection*)

(see opposite page)
Garrick's house at Hampton, with the Temple of Shakespeare on the left. In 1770 Mrs Delany declared: 'The house is singular, and seems to owe its prettiness and elegance to her good taste. It has the air of belonging to a genius.' By then the couple had been in residence more than fifteen years, and had had ample time to impose their own taste on their surroundings. (*Mansell Collection*)

and order new scenery for the forthcoming season. And the endless search for suitable plays went on.

We next hear from Garrick on 18 June 1753, when he wrote from Chiswick to John Hussey Delaval about a play he had written. Garrick sent only a holding letter — though a very polite one at that — since he was off to Yorkshire for six weeks. He was still at Chiswick on 4 July, however, and still looking for a country property, for this time he wrote to brother Peter, since the property in question was at Ashbourne in Derbyshire. The inconvenience of that, however, would have been that it could only have been a holiday home, whereas what the Garricks really needed — as they came to realize — was somewhere within easy reach of London.

The Garricks do not seem to have arrived at Londesborough in 1753 until 16 July. From the letter that Garrick wrote to brother George on that day it seems that George, too, was once again involved in finding properties, the one in Ealing having come to nothing. Despite Lord Burlington's evident illness, Garrick tried to assure Lord Hartington in his letters that he was not in any manifest danger. However, Lord Burlington died in December that year.

On his return south, Garrick eventually found a house that suited him, and in January 1754 rented what was then known as the Fuller House at Hampton by the River Thames. On 30 August he entered into a contract to buy it from the owner, Lacey Primate or Primatt. A letter to his brother Peter dated 2 September, and probably from this year, shows that he was involved in finding staff in Lichfield for the new house. It was to figure largely in the lives of the Garricks for the rest of both their existences. From now on they had their town house, first in Southampton Street and then in the Adelphi, and when they wished for air and quiet, their elegant modern home by the river, some thirteen miles from Hyde Park Corner. The Royal family no longer favoured nearby Hampton Court Palace, but that might well have been a point in favour of Garrick's new home. He would be able to escape completely from the busy life of the capital.

Yet despite his preoccupations with his new property, Garrick found himself drawn into the most intimate family problems of the Burlington-Hartington connection in the aftermath of the death of Lord Burlington in the December of 1753. The Garricks had not spent the summer of 1754 at Londesborough as usual: there had been problems over Lord Burlington's will, and his widow felt that her son-in-law, Lord

Bed and wardrobe from David Garrick's villa at Hampton, probably part of the painted furniture supplied by Chippendale in about 1770. The painted cotton hangings were produced at Masulipatam, Madras, to the order of the East India Company, though we know from the correspondence that Mrs Garrick had difficulties with the Customs when bringing the hangings into the country. (*Victoria and Albert Museum*)

Hartington, could have been more helpful in the matter. In her later life Lady Burlington was regarded as eccentric by some, in an age when eccentricity was by no means uncommon, but the Garricks had only become friends of the Hartingtons through her. It put them in a delicate situation, and Garrick felt it best, in a sequence of letters, to keep Lord Hartington fully informed of what Lady Burlington had said. Her general state of mind was not helped by the death of her daughter, Lady Hartington, in December 1754.

To some extent the business sorted itself out in the spring of 1755, when Lord Hartington was made Lord-Lieutenant of Ireland on 27 March that year, and took up his duties on 5 May in Dublin. During his absence in Ireland his children were looked after at Burlington House, where the Garricks were now even more frequent visitors. However, just when the Garricks felt that they had poured oil on troubled waters, they themselves fell foul of Lady Burlington and were accused of trying to lure away one of her footmen. Garrick sent her a letter on 21 July, couched in remarkably strong terms for him, and yet his usual desire to justify himself, and cover all the possible points likely to relate to a matter, on this occasion took the upper hand.[29] He still felt obliged to keep Lord Hartington informed of all that happened, but for a while it seems that he made a point of seeing as little as possible of Lady Burlington, and it was his wife who brought him back news for transmission to Dublin. After all, he had a theatre and his career to run, and the autumn of 1755 saw his most daring, and most calamitous, innovation so far at Drury Lane.

CHAPTER FOUR

THE CHINESE FESTIVAL

(*see previous page*)
Mademoiselle Guimard in the
costume designed for her by
Boquet for *Castor et Pollux*.
(*Musée de l'Opéra, Paris*)

THE autumn of 1755 saw one of the few disasters that Garrick was to be held responsible for in his career, and even then it was not of his own making, though one could say that it was partly an error of judgment on his part. To set the matter in perspective one must go back in time, before his first visit to Paris in 1751.

In August 1748 Rich had invited the French theatre director Jean Monnet (1703–85) to bring a company of French players over to London, but when Monnet had asked — not unreasonably — for a formal contract to cover his own expenses and the salaries of his players, Rich refused. Monnet did not know Garrick at that time, but in his distress — for he had already engaged his company in France — he approached Garrick, who advised him to hire the Little Theatre in the Haymarket and put on a subscription season of French comedy, which raised £400. With that sum assured, Monnet went back to France, and the next year opened with his company in London on 9 November (1749),[1]

From a letter that Garrick wrote to the Countess of Burlington on 31 October 1749, we know that the prospect of the imminent opening of the French season was virtually the only topic of conversation in London society, and parties were forming for and against the company.[2] Such behaviour was extremely common, and perfectly innocent actors and

(*see opposite page*)
The theatre director Jean Monnet (1703–85) in a portrait by Cochin engraved by Saint-Aubin in 1765. After a disagreement between Monnet and Rich in 1749, Monnet appealed to Garrick, who at that time scarcely knew the Frenchman. However, when Garrick's help and advice proved efficacious, a long association began between the two, with Monnet acting as an agent in Paris for Garrick. (From F. Hedgcock: *A Cosmopolitan Actor, David Garrick and his French Friends*)

(*see opposite page*)
The French theatre season of 1749 was indeed seen by many as 'an invasion by French vagrants', and so hostile was the reception it received, that the Lord Chamberlain withdrew his licence and closed the theatre. In this engraving, Britannia declares that Lunn and Frible [*sic*] — meaning Garrick — were her 'only theatrical children', and that she would 'cherish no foreign vagrants'. (From F. Hedgcock: *A Cosmopolitan Actor, David Garrick and his French Friends*)

(*left*)
A demon from Boquet's designs for *Castor et Pollux*. There were some lasting results from Garrick's patronage of Boquet. One of the most spectacular was licopodium for lighting, as in the torches held by the demon. (From F. Hedgcock: *A Cosmopolitan Actor, David Garrick and his French Friends*)

musicians found themselves set up as rivals to persons they had often never even met, let alone wished to confront in any way. So far as Garrick himself was concerned, he did not care one way or the other, since the French company could not, in his estimation, affect Drury Lane. Even so, when the season began, anti-French feeling ran high among the more jingoistic members of the audience, and the Lord Chamberlain had to withdraw his licence and close the theatre. Monnet had to bear the full cost of the disaster, but the Lord Chamberlain gave him £100, and Garrick put on a benefit which produced one hundred guineas.

Monnet probably returned once more to France in April 1750, and though there is no mention of him in Garrick's diary of the first Paris visit, it would indeed have been surprising had they not met then, unless Monnet had been out of the capital for the whole duration of the visit. At all events, Garrick was definitely thinking of bringing some French actors and dancers over to England, as we saw earlier, and this might well have been the reason why he left Paris in such a hurry in 1751. Moreover, there are letters to Garrick from the English banker in Paris, Charles Selwin, dating from December 1754 and June 1755, in which he praised Mlle Clairon, whom Garrick had seen act in 1751 when she was still relatively a débutante.[3] It was Selwin who was also handling negotiations for Garrick at this time for engaging the choreographer Jean Georges Noverre (1727–1809) to come to London.

Noverre had already worked under Monnet, and in 1754 returned to his management in Paris, having spent some time in the French provinces and in Berlin. It was Noverre's *Les fêtes chinoises*, seen in Paris in the summer of 1754, after a tour of the French provinces, that was to cause such a stir in the French capital and ultimately cause riots in London. It would be as well, therefore, to give some account of it that appeared in the *Nouveau calendrier des spectacles de Paris* in 1755: 'The scene represents at first an avenue ending in terraces and in a flight of steps leading to a palace situated on a height. This first set changes, and shows a public square, decorated for a festival; at the back is an amphitheatre on which sixteen Chinamen are seated. By a quick change of scene, thirty-two Chinamen appear instead of sixteen, and go through a pantomimic performance on the steps. As they descend, sixteen other Chinamen, mandarins and slaves, come out of their houses and take their places on the steps. All these persons form eight ranks of dancers, who, by bending down and rising up in succession, give a fair imitation of the waves of a stormy sea.

The choreographer Jean-Georges Noverre (1727–1809) was one of Jean Monnet's recommendations to David Garrick, who thereupon began negotiations to bring Noverre's the *Chinese Festival* to London for the 1755 season. In much the same way as Garrick had brought a new realism and expression to the spoken word in the theatre, Noverre impressed his spectators with the way in which he made gestures and steps 'speak' in his choreography. (From F. Hedgcock: *A Cosmopolitan Actor, David Garrick and his French Friends*)

When all the Chinese have come down they begin a characteristic march. In this is to be seen a mandarin, carried in a rich palanquin by six white slaves, while two negroes drag a car in which a young Chinese woman is seated. They are both preceded and followed by a crowd of Chinamen, who play divers instruments of music in use in their country. When this procession is finished the ballet begins, and leaves nothing to be desired, neither for the variety nor for the neatness of the figures. It ends by a round-dance, in which there are thirty-two persons; their movements form a prodigious quantity of new and perfectly planned figures, which are linked and unlinked with the greatest ease. At the end of this round-dance the Chinamen take up their places anew on the amphitheatre, which changes into a porcelain shop. Thirty-two vases rise up, and hide from the audience the thirty-two Chinese. M. Monnet has spared nothing that could possibly assist M. Noverre's rich imagination. . . . The dresses were made from M. Boquet's designs.'[4] It was this spectacle, then, that Garrick was hoping to set before the London public in 1755.

Because of his great success, Noverre refused the £200 plus benefit at first offered, and asked for 350 guineas, with a performance in which Garrick himself was to act. In a letter of 11 January 1755, Selwin advised Garrick to accept, and pointed out that since Noverre was a Protestant from Lausanne, and therefore not tied emotionally to France, Garrick might be able to induce him to stay on in London, provided that he liked Noverre, of course, and wished to make it worth his while.[5] Selwin had not counted on the fact that other, quite extraneous, considerations would eventually determine that point. The contract was duly signed, but there were still problems over travelling expenses, because Garrick wanted to see Noverre in London. The ensuing exchange of letters lasted throughout February, March, April, and into May. By 24 May, however, Noverre was satisfied, and wrote so in glowing terms to Garrick.

Garrick was not blind, however, to the possibility of xenophobic intervention on the part of the London theatre-goers, so took the precaution of making it known through the press that Noverre was a Swiss Protestant, and his wife German, and that there were in fact very few French amongst the company. What actually happened when the ballet was first given on 8 November 1755 was described at length in a letter published in the *Journal étranger* in Paris the following month. It is even possible that it was written by a member of the company, perhaps

Noverre himself. Despite the presence of the King, there were audible cries of 'No French dancers', notwithstanding the fact that, according to the writer, the production was even more brilliant in London than it had been in Paris, and that there were no less than ninety executants on the stage. The next performance was on 12 November, and it ran for four successive nights, in increasing disorder. On Saturday, 15 November, because the nobility were absent at the opening of the opera, in the words of the writer in the *Journal étranger*: '*Les blagards* were victorious and made a horrible disturbance.' Seats were torn up and thrown into the pit, glasses and chandeliers were broken, and the mob advanced on the stage with the apparent intention of murdering the company on it. However, within three minutes the scenery had been removed, the traps were open, and if the invaders came further forward, there were armed men waiting in the wings. Finally, if the rioters still managed to advance, the tank behind the stage was ready to be filled with water so as to drown anyone who fell into the cellars. The riot went on until midnight, and Lacy had to promise that the ballet would not be given again.

On Monday, 17 November, the aristocracy were back at the theatre and demanded that the ballet be given. The pit and gallery demanded 'No French dancers.' Garrick himself had to come on stage, and finally the matter was put to the vote. The pro-ballet faction carried the day. The ballet was promised for the next evening. As might have been expected, Drury Lane was even more beset than before. The house was already full at three o'clock — a full three hours before the curtain was due to rise. One can well imagine what the atmosphere in the auditorium was like by the time the performance was about to begin. It was soon impossible to carry on, if only because of the dried peas and tin tacks that had been thrown onto the stage from the front of the house. When they were finally ejected from the theatre, the rioters went to Garrick's house in Southampton Street, broke all the windows, and would have set fire to it, had not Garrick asked for military protection. Such was the invincible stupidity of the rioters that credence was given to rumours that the dancers were in fact French officers, and Noverre none other than Prince Charles Edward himself. In the course of the riots Noverre's brother, Augustin, ran a man through with his sword, though luckily the man recovered. Unlike his more famous brother, Augustin found Drury Lane to his taste, and stayed there until 1761–2, and thereafter at some point retired to Norwich.

In the circumstances, Garrick could do no less than his best for Noverre, and gave him fifty guineas instead of the planned benefit. There had been an offer at one point that Noverre should complete three seasons in all in London (though at the time he had ignored it), and he was in fact to return for the season of 1756–7, though he only appeared on 1 December for a first night that should have taken place on 18 September. Since Garrick and Lacy stopped Noverre's pay for the missing performances, he and his wife returned to France in something of a fit of the vapours. Noverre's letter to Garrick on this occasion — though ostensibly aimed chiefly at Lacy — does not attempt in any way to conceal his feelings: 'There is in the world a race of beings whose only merit is that of possessing gold, and who, blown out with the pride of seeing themselves at ease, impudently insult the beneficent source which, in enriching them, has cleansed them from the filth in which they were plunged.'[6] Madame Noverre then wrote to Garrick, either late in 1757 or early in 1758, and his reply, written before 18 January 1758, which is the date of her next letter to Garrick, is a masterly refutation of her accusations: 'If I have been a little surprised that I have not yet received a letter from Mr Noverre, how much more am I that I have received one, and so extraordinary a one, from you, without date, or even mention where you are! You say that you have wrote several letters to me, without any answer. This is still more astonishing, for I have not received a single line from France, since your husband left us, with the name of Noverre to it before, and he himself makes mention in a letter to his brother of his intention only of writing to me. How is this to be reconciled, and what is the subject of the letter I am honoured with from you? A very lively and severe remonstrance against the injustice of the managers (which you'll permit me to say is entirely groundless), and not the least mention made of some other things, which I should rather have expected from your justice and your delicacy.'[7]

Garrick still remained well disposed to Noverre, however, and tried to bring him back to Drury Lane in 1767, though Lacy put his foot down in the face of what he considered were excessive demands, and again in 1775, though it was not until 1776 that Noverre apparently returned to London, where he took refuge again during the French Revolution. By that time, however, Garrick was dead.[8]

Garrick was destined to lose yet another of his friends in the Boyle-Cavendish family shortly after the disaster of the *Chinese Festival*, for

79

Tobias Smollett, in an engraved portrait by Aliamet, was not initially one of those who expressed unalloyed pleasure at the advent of Garrick to the London stage, though he certainly appreciated that a new era had begun, and that the old style of Quin, for example, which he described in *Peregrine Pickle* as 'a continual sing-song, like the chanting of vespers', had gone for ever. (*Mansell Collection*)

(*see opposite page*)
An engraving by Russell of Barrow's impression of Strawberry Hill, published on 1 November 1791. Although they were more or less neighbours when Garrick was at Hampton, he and Horace Walpole never became anything more than acquaintances. Walpole liked Mrs Garrick — 'her behaviour all sense, and all sweetness too' — but Garrick himself 'does not improve upon me'. (*Mansell Collection*)

there was a third death in that family in as many years when the third Duke of Devonshire died on 5 December 1755, and Lord Hartington succeeded to the title. On 10 May 1756, just over a year since he had arrived in Dublin, Hartington returned to England. Later that year, on 16 November, he was made First Lord of the Treasury, according to Garrick: 'Much against his will, but intreated to it by His Majesty.'[9] For some time Garrick had been trying to get some sort of sinecure for his brother Peter, and in August 1755 Lord Hartington, as he still was, had written to Garrick: 'If ever I have it in my power nothing can give me more pleasure than to serve any body that belongs to you, but at the same time I must inform you that I have very few things to give away.'[10] Eventually, however, Peter Garrick became Collector of Customs at Whitehaven, though remaining at Lichfield, and a deputy carried out his duties for him. One may well assume that his appointment was the new Duke of Devonshire's doing.

Meanwhile, the business of the theatre went on, and Garrick had not only to act and manage, but tactfully deal with a constant stream of persons submitting plays, often under the patronage of some grandee, which exposed him to abuse on occasion, or at the very least involved him in lengthy explanations to both writer and patron as to why he could not accept the offering in question. Tact was also required in his dealings with his company, and during the winter of 1756–7 there was a particularly difficult negotiation with Mrs Cibber, who had barely acted because of illness, and yet expected to be paid as usual. A similar situation arose with Madame Noverre in the wake of the *Chinese Festival* débâcle, as we have already seen, and in that letter of explanation to her, Garrick cited the example of Mrs Cibber in his defence.

Occasionally relationships improved as time went by. One such was with Tobias Smollett (1721–71), who for some ten years bitterly resented the fact that Garrick had refused to put on his play *The Regicide*. By March 1756, however, Smollett had forgiven or forgotten sufficiently to praise Garrick in his *Critical Review*, and when he revised *Peregrine Pickle* prior to its second edition, he took out the attacks it contained on Garrick. On 22 January 1757 Garrick produced Smollett's farce *The Reprisal*, and shortly afterwards James Rivington, the publisher, delivered to him Smollett's *History of England* on behalf of the author. In a gracious, if short, letter of thanks, Garrick wrote that he now knew how he was going to spend part of his vacation, thanks to Dr Smollett.[11]

One potential literary friendship that never blossomed, however, was that with Horace Walpole (1717–97). When Garrick bought his villa at Hampton, Walpole was a neighbour at Strawberry Hill, but in spite of this proximity, together with the fact that they had known each other for some time by now, and had several mutual friends, they remained cool, and eventually were openly hostile towards each other. Walpole's professed reason was expressed as follows: 'Garrick does not tempt me; I have no taste for his perpetual buffoonery, and am sick of his endless expectation of flattery.'[12] Of course, the first part of the reason was much the same as

Engraving by Cochran of the portrait of Horace Walpole, depicted in Venetian costume, by Rosalba Carriera (1675–1758), whose portraits, especially in pastel, became the rage of the European aristocracy and almost as obligatory a feature of the Grand Tour as sitting for one's portrait by Batoni was to become for Garrick and Lady Spencer in Rome. (*Mansell Collection*)

that expressed by Dr Johnson, and one of the reasons why, for years, Garrick was excluded from the select club, founded in 1764, that included Reynolds, Johnson, Burke, Nugent, Beauclerk, Langton, Chamier and Goldsmith. Garrick and Boswell were only elected in 1773. As far as the 'expectation of flattery' was concerned, however, apart from Goldsmith, Walpole is one of the few people on record as having noticed it, and one suspects that many of the subsequent accusations of this sort against Garrick came from this source. Walpole's aloofness did not force Garrick into submission, however, and when extracts from Walpole's edition of Hentzner's *Journey* were pirated, and suspicion fell on the printer Dryden Leach, Garrick was quick to inform Walpole that there was no evidence for accusing Leach. [13]

It is easy to see why Garrick may well have been thought a social climber by Walpole, however, for as early as August 1755, within a year of buying the Hampton property, Garrick wrote excitedly to Lord Hartington that the Duke of Grafton, Lady Holderness, Lord and Lady Rochford, the Marquis d'Abreu (the Spanish ambassador), and Walpole had all been to dinner. [14] Nor did Garrick hesitate to use his acquaintance with the aristocracy to gain favours for his family and friends — as did a great many other people, let it be said. We have already seen how he obtained a sinecure for his brother Peter, and there are also on record letters to the Duke of Newcastle on behalf of his brother George, to the Earl of Bute on behalf of Thomas Gataker, the surgeon, and to try and encourage the Prince of Wales to come to the theatre. On 4 September 1758 Garrick had no compunction in asking the Duke of Devonshire for a loan of £500 because of his expenses at Hampton. [15] He received the money within the week. On another occasion he wrote to apologize to Henry Fox for something he was supposed to have said. [16]

However justified the charge that Garrick was ingratiating, one cannot help but feel that there was with many members of the aristocracy a perfectly natural relationship, where neither side had to make any allowances. One of these friendships began round about 1759, when Earl and Countess Spencer visited Garrick at Hampton, and Lady Spencer in particular became a great favourite of Garrick's. He called her 'the most amiable of women', 'heavenly Lady Spencer', and she does indeed seem to have corresponded to his ideal of feminine perfection. The first extant letter is to Earl Spencer, but subsequently they were all to Countess Spencer.

Self-portrait by William Hogarth (1697–1764), painted *circa* 1757. The artist was one of Garrick's oldest friends in London, and had even aspired to follow the same profession as the actor, but had great difficulty in remembering his lines. Luckily he soon found his true and lasting vocation. (*National Portrait Gallery*)

Although Garrick complained on one occasion that he had been most unfortunate with his literary connections — which was only partly true — with painters he had more luck, and he numbered Hogarth, Reynolds and Zoffany among his friends.

Hogarth had been one of Garrick's oldest London friends, and he had actually tried to embark upon an acting career, but realized that he would never be a success in that field. For one thing, he had great difficulty in remembering his lines, and for another he was very short — barely five feet tall, though of course Garrick himself was no giant. In 1728 Hogarth eloped with the daughter of his teacher, Sir James Thornhill. They married the following year, and it was Lady Thornhill who had Hogarth's series of paintings, *A Harlot's Progress*, which he probably painted around 1731, put in the family dining-room. When her husband asked who the artist was, and learned that it was Hogarth, he observed that so

(see opposite page)
Terracotta bust of Hogarth by Roubiliac, *circa* 1741. As well as being one of the best likenesses of Hogarth, according to contemporary sources, this bust displays great freshness and wit, even to the addition of the rococo cartouche on the socle which incorporates a satyr's head and a palette, for the artist. (*National Portrait Gallery*)

(see opposite page)
An engraving of Hogarth's *Strolling Actresses Dressing in a Barn*, dating from 1738. The actresses are preparing for an evening performance of *The Devil to Pay in Heaven* at the George Inn, and this was their last performance before the Licensing Act of 1737 forbade drama outside the two royal theatres of Drury Lane and Covent Garden. (*Victoria and Albert Museum*)

accomplished an artist could well afford a wife who had no dowry. Luckily there was a reconciliation, and Hogarth's fame and success increased. At about the time that Garrick arrived in London, Hogarth painted *Strolling Actresses Dressing in a Barn*, which, although now destroyed, was engraved. It was painted in 1738, the year after the theatre licensing act had rung the death-knell for all but the most established companies for the time being, and 'strolling' became a way of life for many of the profession.

Hogarth painted Garrick in one of his most famous roles, that of Richard III, some four or five years after he first appeared in it on the London stage, and then, as we have already seen, one of the most charming portrayals of Garrick and his wife in the picture in the Royal Collection. It has changed hands only twice since it was painted. It was sold first at the sale of Mrs Garrick's effects in 1823 to Mr E. H. Locker of Greenwich, and in 1826 it was bought by George IV for the Royal Collection. John Hoadly wrote to Joseph Warton about it on 21 April 1757: 'Hogarth has got again into portraits, and has his hands full of business, and at an high price. He has almost finished a most noble one of our sprightly friend David Garrick and his wife; they are a fine contrast. David is sitting at a table, smiling thoughtfully over an epilogue ... Madam is, archly enough, stealing away his pen unseen behind.'[17] It was according to the Christie's catalogue for 23 June 1823 that it was established that Garrick is in the act of composing the prologue to Samuel Foote's play, *Taste*, which we know was produced on 11 January 1752. According to George Stevens (1710–84), however, Garrick so disliked the expression that Hogarth had given him in the picture that the artist actually blacked out the face and took it away. It was only after Hogarth's death that his widow sent it to Mrs Garrick as a gift.

In about 1754 Hogarth completed the set of four pictures known as the *Election* series. He had spent some three years on them, but was saddened to find, once they were finished, that no one was willing to pay the asking price of two hundred guineas. Consequently, he decided to raffle them. Garrick put his name down for tickets, but had second thoughts, and bought all four pictures. They were hung on each side of the fireplace in the Bow Room of the villa at Hampton.

Some ten years later, when Garrick was in Paris on his second visit, it was from a letter written to him by George Colman that he learned of the death of Hogarth, and there is no doubt that it came as a considerable

84

blow. When Hogarth's friends wanted to erect a monument to him in Chiswick churchyard in 1771, it was to Garrick that they turned for the epitaph to be engraved upon it, and he complied at the request of Hogarth's widow. It is touching that the only letter that has come down to us from Garrick to Hogarth, dating from 8 January [year conjectural but probably 1757 or 1763], is one of concern at having neglected the latter: 'It may be so, though upon my word I am not conscious of it, for such ceremonies are to me mere counters, where there is no remission of regard and good wishes. . . . Montaigne, who was a good judge of human nature, takes notice that *when friends grow exact and ceremonious, it is a certain sign of coolness, for the true spirit of friendship keeps no account of trifles.* We are, I hope, a strong exception to this rule . . . Could I follow my inclinations I would see you every

Garrick between Tragedy and Comedy, by Reynolds, exhibited at the Society of Artists in 1762. Horace Walpole wrote of it: 'the thought [is] taken by Garrick from the Judgement of Hercules ... Tragedy is a good antique figure but wants more dignity in the expression of her face, Comedy is a beautiful and winning girl — but Garrick's face is distorted and burlesque.' (*Mansell Collection*)

day in the week. . . . I am yours, dear Hogy, most sincerely, D. Garrick.'[18]

Sir Joshua Reynolds (1723–92, knighted 1769) did not get to know Garrick until the early 1750s, but in the course of their friendship he painted several portraits of the actor. As with Hogarth, there are few extant letters — in this case two — because they saw each other so often, and eventually they were both members of The Club. It was all the more difficult for Garrick, therefore, when Reynolds sent him a play by his nephew Joseph Palmer, in August 1774, and Garrick was unable to accept it, on the grounds that he already had more plays than he could put on.[19] Reynolds interpreted this as a refusal and asked for the play to be returned, though he subsequently accepted Garrick's explanation. From a

letter to George Colman, however, written from Bath on 15 April the following year (1775), it would appear that Garrick did not think much of the play, and rather wished that Colman had seen it, and so confirmed Garrick's opinion of it: 'I hate this traffic with friends.'[20]

Possibly the most famous portrait of Garrick by Reynolds is that of him depicted between tragedy and comedy, exhibited in 1762 and engraved that year. It is now in the collection of Lord Rothschild. Another excellent portrait is the half-length of Garrick in costume as Kitely in Ben Jonson's *Every Man in his Humour*, painted in 1768, and now in the Royal Collection. It was supposed to have been given by Reynolds to Burke, and then bought for the Prince Regent at Burke's sale in 1812. The National Portrait Gallery now has another Reynolds, of Garrick with his wife, painted in 1773, which has a rather muted, even autumnal quality. Some maintain that Reynolds was not at all that fond of Garrick, but then the artist had his critics and enemies, too, like the actor.

The third artist, Johan Zoffany (1734–1810), had originally been engaged to paint backgrounds and draperies for Benjamin Wilson, but Garrick took note of him, and offered to sit for him for *The Farmer's Return*, exhibited at the Society of Artists in 1762. Wilson, who later informed Garrick about neglecting Hogarth, was apparently somewhat jealous, as well as anxious lest he lose his assistant, and so called on Garrick to get Zoffany 'to fulfil his engagements and act, if he can, like an honest man'.[21] Once again, Garrick had to write a firm letter. Zoffany broke his engagement, and Garrick bought out the remainder of his time.

During the summer of 1762 the artist went on to paint a pair of conversation pieces at Hampton which hung in the dining-parlour of the Adelphi house. Then in the autumn of that year he was commissioned to paint a companion-piece to *The Farmer's Return*, this time showing Garrick with Mrs Cibber in *Venice Preserv'd*. These two pictures also hung in the Adelphi dining-parlour, on the wall opposite the fireplace. As an overdoor there was a view of Hampton House and the garden, in which Garrick is writing. For Hampton itself, but once more in the dining-parlour, Zoffany later painted Garrick as Sir John Brute in *The Provok'd Wife* (1763–5). After this, portraits of Garrick in other roles followed — Lord Chalkstone in *Lethe* (1766); Macbeth (with Mrs Pritchard) in 1768, and Abel Drugger in *The Alchemist* (circa 1769–70). The last belonged to Reynolds, incidentally, who paid a hundred guineas for it, and then sold it to Earl of Carlisle for the same sum, on condition

A detail from Zoffany's painting of Garrick as Sir John Brute in Vanbrugh's *The Provok'd Wife*, dating from *circa* 1765. Garrick first played the part in 1744, at Drury Lane, thus displacing Quin, and went on to play 95 of the 97 performances of the play given at the theatre between 1747 and 1776. The painting was commissioned by Garrick himself, and records a performance that took place on 18 April 1763, before Garrick left later that year for the Grand Tour. (*Mansell Collection*)

Wren's drawing of Drury
Lane theatre which he had
designed in 1674 and which
had remained essentially
unchanged at the time that
Garrick took it over in 1747,
though the seating capacity
had been increased from
about 700 to somewhere in
the region of 1,000 over the
intervening period.
(*Codrington Library, All Souls
College, Oxford*)

that he gave the additional twenty guineas he was offering Reynolds for
it to Zoffany.

Garrick's eye for paintings and décor was by no means confined in its
scope to his own homes. In the summer of 1762 he had Drury Lane
modified inside, chiefly so as to increase the seating capacity and repair
some of the ravages of previous seasons. Precisely what was done on this
occasion is unfortunately not documented. The theatre he had taken over
in 1747 was substantially that designed in 1674 by Sir Christopher
Wren, which probably held no more than about 700 people, though
Christopher Rich — according to Colley Cibber — had enlarged it
before 1700 by taking four feet from the front of the stage, thus gaining
more room for benches in the pit, and replacing the first set of stage doors
with boxes. There may well have been further modifications during the
early part of the eighteenth century with a view to gaining yet more
seating capacity, so that by 1747 the theatre probably held around one
thousand people. Even this was not sufficient to make a reasonable profit,
however, and the 1762 alterations — though there seem to have been
some in the intervening period, too — raised the potential sum for a

capacity house to £350, implying an audience of more than two thousand. It is all the more frustrating not to have precise details, therefore, though we know that Garrick enlarged the pit and the boxes by taking away one of the side lobbies, extended the galleries, and added slips along the walls of the upper tier.

The irregular island site of the Drury Lane theatre had always been a difficult one, bounded as it was by Bridges Street on the west, Drury Lane on the east, and Russell Street on the north, and that in itself dictated severe restrictions on the amount of room for manoeuvre. To add to the problem, however, other properties abutted on all sides, so that patrons entering from Bridges Street had to go down a passage before they reached the lobby. Other entrances from Drury Lane and Vinegar Yard had similarly to be made along passages. It was not until the centenary of the theatre approached in 1774 that Garrick decided to engage Robert Adam to provide the fine new entrance from Bridges Street and redecorate the interior of the auditorium, though it is interesting that the alterations on this occasion did not increase the capacity of the house itself.

That was more than ten years away yet, however, and what ensued in the course of the 1762–3 season must have taken Garrick by surprise, and brought back unhappy memories of the *Chinese Festival* riots of 1755.

For many years it had been accepted practice that, once the main play was over, or after the third act, patrons might enter the theatre at half price, and in this way see whatever afterpieces were on the bill for the evening. Garrick had for some time felt that the custom ought to be abolished, though for the theatre-goers it was not so much a custom as a right, as he was to discover to his cost. For Tuesday, 25 January 1763, therefore, when *The Two Gentlemen of Verona* was scheduled, along with a pantomime, it was stated quite clearly at the bottom of the playbills that: 'Nothing under Full Price will be taken.' This provoked a certain Thaddeus Fitzpatrick to take up the cause of the playgoers and their lost 'rights'. Despite the fact that for the first five performances people had paid the full amount no matter what time they had arrived at the theatre, Fitzpatrick issued posters addressed to 'The Frequenters of the Theatres', and signed 'An Enemye of Imposition', in which he drew the public's attention to the loss of its rights, and during the course of the sixth performance he caused a disturbance in the house. Garrick now met the opposition head on. Their demand, according to Genest, was as follows: 'A set of young men, who called themselves The Town ... consulted

Riot at Covent Garden Theatre. in 1763. in consequence of the
to admit half-price in the Opera of Artaxerx

The riot at Covent Garden on 24 February 1763 during a performance of Thomas Arne's opera *Artaxerxes*, when damage to the theatre was so great that it had to be closed whilst repairs were carried out.

It was the instigator of this riot, Thaddeus Fitzpatrick, who had previously created similar trouble for Garrick at Drury Lane over admission prices. (*British Museum*)

90

together, and had determined to compel managers to admit them at the end of the third act at half price, to every performance, except during the *run of a new pantomime.*[22] Garrick came out front to speak to the audience, but was unable to get a hearing. 'The Town' and their supporters began to break up the chandeliers, pit barriers and boxes, and the play could not continue. Only the prompt action of the actor John Moody prevented the scenery from being set on fire. But on that night Garrick did not give in.

The following evening, therefore, although the damage had been repaired, it was with a great deal of apprehension that the evening's show began. When Garrick came on stage 'The Town' shouted: 'Will you, or will you not, give admittance for half price, after the third act, except for the first performance of a pantomime?' Garrick now gave in, but this only roused the mob to more demands.[23] They demanded also that Moody come on stage and apologize for his anti-incendiary measures of the previous evening. In a broad Irish accent he did so, begging their foregiveness for 'displasing them by saving their lives in putting out the fire'. This would not do, and they now demanded that he should go down on his knees. 'I will not, by God,' he replied, and walked off. It is said that Garrick, waiting in the wings, welcomed him with open arms, and vowed that while he had a guinea, Moody should receive his salary. Even so, Garrick had to go back on stage and agree that Moody would not appear again. The theatre was saved, and Moody continued as a member of the company until after Garrick's death. The cost to Garrick, however, had been a heavy blow to his self-esteem.

In September 1770, writing from Hampton in a letter probably destined for Pierre Jean Grosley, since he was the author of *Londres* (published in Paris that year) and Garrick was correcting some of the mistakes in it relative to himself, he explained his intention now that the dust had settled: 'I never wanted to receive the full price as they do at Paris, but only for new plays, and for those we revived with new scenes and habits, which my predecessors always received. We had performed our best plays to what we call half-price, which is, taking the half-price at the end of the third act for the two last acts and the petite-piece. It was no innovation on our part. There certainly was a great riot in the theatre — and the money was returned without finishing the play: but giving up the dispute on the second night, I was received with great applause, without the least murmur or even hint of asking pardon; nor did I discontinue playing till my health obliged me to go abroad in the year sixty-three for

ers refusing

1763

two winters; and at my return to England, I returned to the stage, and am still upon it.'[24]

In the aftermath of the Drury Lane riots it is somewhat surprising that John Beard at Covent Garden should willingly go through the same experience the following month, unless it was an act of belated solidarity, or that he felt he would succeed where Garrick had failed. At all events, Beard also tried to charge full price, and during a performance of Thomas Arne's opera *Artaxerxes*, a similar riot broke out. The damage to his theatre was so great, however, that it had to be closed whilst repairs were carried out. Four days later the *London Chronicle* carried a notice to the effect that henceforth Covent Garden would charge the same prices as Drury Lane.[25] Beard took the opportunity to let it be known, however, that he had 'received several anonymous threatening letters'. He was 'ordered by one to add a farce to *Love in a Village*, or the house should be pulled about his ears'. Such was the potential strength of the voice of the London theatre-going public, and for the rest of Garrick's life it continued to make itself heard in this manner whenever it disapproved of the way the theatres were being run. That in itself was not necessarily a bad thing, but the system — such as it was — was often simply a means for the jealous and the disappointed to cause trouble for their rivals or enemies.

CHAPTER FIVE

THE GRAND TOUR

THE riots at Drury Lane and Covent Garden were evidently unpleasant and even unnerving to Garrick, now in his forty-seventh year. Concern for his health — a recurring preoccupation in his letters as time went by — first makes its appearance round about this time, and there is no doubt that he had made great demands on his mental and physical resources over the years. Now that Drury Lane was working according to plan, he would permit himself a holiday. After all, he had always hankered after another trip to Paris, and then, why not further afield? Many of his friends among the aristocracy had done the Grand Tour in their time, so why not Mr and Mrs Garrick?

First, however, during the summer of 1763, the Garricks went for a long holiday at Chatsworth with the Duke of Devonshire. Garrick wrote to his brother Peter on 7 July to inform him that he, too, would be welcome, and he repeated the invitation in a second letter, two days later.[1] The atmosphere was extremely warm and friendly. Indeed, such was the Duke's generosity and regard towards Garrick's family that not only was Peter invited, but Garrick's sister and brother-in-law, Mr and Mrs Docksey, also. In the event, David and his wife had to leave Chatsworth sooner than either they or the Duke had intended, because the Duke of Cumberland decided to pay a visit.

The summer relaxation was a considerable tonic for Garrick, but there seems little reason to doubt that what he wrote to Mrs Cibber towards the beginning of September was substantially true: 'I have been advised by several physicians, at the head of which I reckon Dr Barry, to give myself a winter's respite. I have dearly earned it, and shall take it in hopes of being better able to undergo my great fatigues of acting and management.'[2]

Of course, there were those who maintained that Garrick only went away in order to prevent audiences growing weary of him, so that, in the belief that absence makes the heart grow fonder, he would be all the more welcome on his return. In the precarious world of the theatre, that is far from true. Absence often merely makes people forget. Furthermore, after almost ten months away, Garrick wrote to Colman that he had no longer contemplated his return to the stage with joy.[3]

In September the Garricks went to Italy. Technically, as a member of the Royal Household, Garrick had needed the Lord Chamberlain's permission to absent himself, which was why his departure had, in theory at least, been kept fairly secret until quite late. However, the granting of

(see previous page)
By June 1764, Garrick was in Venice, where he bought pictures and books, though the city itself did not draw from him any of the raptures that Rome, for instance, had elicited — despite the fact that Venice already had a rich theatrical history, and had long been celebrated in paintings, such as this detail from a view of the Doge's Palace — from the studio of Canaletto — in the Wallace Collection, London. (Mansell Collection)

the permission was little more than a formality, so it had been announced in the *St James's Chronicle* for 9–11 August, and Garrick himself referred to it in the letter to Mrs Cibber mentioned above. Obviously he could not have simply left the theatre to its own devices from one day to the next, and his own preparations for such a long journey were considerable. Happily for us there survives a fascinating sequence of letters, starting with one to George Colman, presumably from Paris, on 8 October 1763. One follows to George Garrick, dated 10 October, from Montmélian in Savoy, and the next one is to Colman again, from Turin on 18 October. There is a good and vivid description of the theatre there, which is corroborated by accounts of such visits from other travellers: 'The people in the pit and boxes talk all the while as in a coffee-house, and the performers are even with them, for they are very little attentive, laugh and talk to one another, pick their noses, and while they are unengaged in singing, they walk up to the stage boxes (in which the other actors and dancers sit dressed in sight of the audience), turn their backs, and join in

Garrick in Florence in 1763, as depicted by Thomas Patch, with the then resident, Sir Horace Mann, whose caricature can be seen in the pictures on the walls. Prior to Garrick's arrival, Walpole told Mann to expect: 'the famous Garrick and his once famous wife. He will make you laugh, as a mimic, and as he knows we are great friends, will affect great partiality for me; but be a little on your guard, remember he is *an actor!*' The italics are Walpole's. (*Royal Albert Memorial Museum, Exeter*)

A view of Turin by Bernardo Bellotto (1720–80), showing a bridge across the Po. Although the artist left Italy in 1747 to work abroad, the appearance of Turin had probably altered little by the time Garrick visited it. (*Mansell Collection*)

the laugh and conversation of their brethren, without the least decency or regard to the audience.'[4]

Garrick's arrival in Turin was overshadowed by his being shown two issues of the *London Chronicle* from the month of September in which were certain acerbic remarks about his departure, including the suggestion that he was to be made a peer in the kingdom of Ireland: 'A circumstance very far from improbable, as so many comical people are

daily raised to coronets in that kingdom.'[5] He wrote to Colman in the letter referred to above that he 'read their malignity with as much sang-froid as Plato himself would have done'. He maintained that what he regretted more was the fact that the Duke of Devonshire's name had been mentioned in the same context. He took, he said, comfort from the fact that the Duke was 'above feeling their nonsense', but in view of the way Garrick reacted to such treatment throughout his life, it must have made its mark.

The Italian countryside was much appreciated, but the inns less so: 'The travelling through Savoy and Piedmont to this city [Turin] is the most romantic and delightful with regard to the scenery that can be imagined, but the nastiness in the inns, the peculiarity of the nastiness, is likewise as much above conception.' There is then a letter to the Duke of Devonshire from Florence, dated 30 November, and to Colman again from Naples on 24 December. In this last, Garrick confessed that initially Rome had been a great disappointment: 'I hardly slept the night before I arrived there with the thoughts of seeing it — my heart beat high; my imagination expanded itself and my eyes flashed again as I drew near the *Porta del Popolo*; but the moment I entered it, I fell at once from my airy vision and utopian ideas into a very dirty ill looking *place* (as they call it), with three crooked streets in front, terminated indeed at this end with two tolerable churches — what a disappointment! My spirits sank and it was with reluctance that I was dragged in the afternoon to see the Pantheon — but my God, what was my pleasure and surprise! I never felt so much in my life as when I entered that glorious structure: I gaped, but could not speak for five minutes. It is so very noble that it has not been in the power of modern frippery, or popery (for it is a church, you know) to extinguish its grandeur and elegance... Though I am pleased, much pleased with Naples, I have such a thirst to return to Rome as cannot possibly be slaked till I have drunk up half the Tiber. . . . It is very strange that so much good poetry should be thrown away upon such a pitiful river.'[6] He was to go the next day with Lord and Lady Spencer to Herculaneum, and the following week to the top of Mount Vesuvius.

But Garrick was interested in more than sightseeing in Italy. He was there to observe contemporary institutions as well, and especially — in view of the way in which Italy had provided so much musical inspiration for the rest of Europe — the nature and quality of musical life in Naples, which at that time had taken over the role of Venice as the foremost seat of

The effect of the Pantheon, seen here in an engraving by Schenck, did more than enough to dispel Garrick's initial doubts about the splendour of Rome, and although Naples pleased him subsequently, he could hardly wait to back to the Eternal City. (*Mansell Collection*)

(*below*)
The Piazza del Popolo, Rome, as engraved by Parr, where Garrick first set foot inside the city of Rome. His disappointment was profound when he saw what he described as a 'dirty, ill-looking place', though he conceded that the churches were 'tolerable'. (*Mansell Collection*)

the art in Italy. It is not surprising, then, that Charles Burney (1726–1814) is first referred to in the extant letters, on 24 December 1763, in one from Garrick to George Colman, from Naples. Garrick and Burney were lifelong friends, and possibly met first in Fulke Greville's house. Still from Naples, on 2 January 1764, but this time to George Garrick, Garrick told him that he would be writing to Mr Burney to 'let him know the present state of music in Italy'. Burney was to receive his doctorate of music in 1769, and publish his *The Present State of Music in France and Italy* in 1771. On 31 January (1764), again to George Garrick, David Garrick asked what had become of Burney's musical entertainment — presumably *The Cunning Man*, which was an adaptation of Rousseau's *Le Devin du Village*. It was eventually produced, with only moderate success, at Drury Lane on 21 November 1766.

In a letter of 27 June 1766 from Garrick to Burney, written after his return from his tour, and presumably as he was about to go off to Mistley in Essex, one wonders whether the reference to Burney's 'amiable daughter' is to Frances — Fanny Burney (1752–1840). There was an older sister, Esther (1749–1832), who had been in Paris since 1764, but it was Fanny who gave us such vivid glimpses of Garrick as a private person. As an indication of the relationship the Garrick and Burney families enjoyed, there is a passage in her diary dated 26 January 1772: 'Mr Garrick is this moment gone. Unfortunately my father was out, and Mama not come downstairs; yet to my great satisfaction he came in. Dick ran to him, as the door was opened. We were all seated at breakfast. "What, my bright-eyed beauty!" cried he; and then flinging himself back in a theatrical posture, "and here ye all are — one — two — three — four — beauties all." He then came in and with a great deal of humour played with Dick. How many pities that he has no children, for he is extremely, nay, passionately fond of them.'[7] No wonder, then, that for the father of this family Garrick was more than happy to collect what information he could in order to help him in his work when he himself was in Italy on his Grand Tour.

As a souvenir of the time spent there, Garrick followed the example of many other English visitors, including Lady Spencer herself, and sat for his portrait by Pompeo Batoni. Lady Spencer's portrait, with the Coliseum in the background, is still at Althorp. That of Garrick is in the Ashmolean Museum in Oxford. His suit of dark purplish brown velvet

A view of Naples from the West, drawn by James Hakewill and engraved by George Cooke, published on 1 May 1818. It was whilst Garrick was in Naples in 1763 that he went with Lord and Lady Spencer to Herculaneum on Christmas Day, and a month later they were still in Naples in each other's company. Although Garrick later managed to offend Lady Spencer, the rift was healed, and they remained on good terms for the rest of Garrick's life. (*Mansell Collection*)

In Rome, Garrick sat for
Pompeo Batoni (1708–87),
and the portrait was seen,
together with that of Lady
Spencer, in Batoni's
showroom by another English
tourist, James Martin, on 6
March 1764. Garrick is
pointing to an edition of
Terence's comedies which
George Colman was then
translating, and indeed
Phormio in this version was
dedicated to Garrick by
Colman. (*Ashmolean Museum,
Oxford*)

— carmelite is the name of the colour — is still in existence in the
Museum of London, and he is shown leafing through an illustrated
volume of Terence, whose comedies Colman was then translating. The
feeling of the portrait is definitely conservative in flavour, though that may
well have been Garrick's own desire. What can only be laid at Batoni's
door, however, is the lack of any real insight into Garrick's character in the
portrait, or the facial animation — especially in the eyes — so often
commented on by others, and certainly captured by Reynolds, for
example, in his paintings of the actor.

Garrick also commissioned portraits in Italy from Nathaniel Dance, Angelica Kauffmann, Alessandro Longhi, and the bust by Joseph Nollekens at Althorp. Nor was his activity limited to commissioning pictures. There is an interesting passage in the letter to George Colman dated 12 June 1764, from Venice: 'I have been buying pictures and books, and am scarce able to hold my pen with fatigue. I have no joy now in thinking on the stage, and shall return (if I must) like a bear to the stake — and this baiting, my good friend, is no joke after forty.'[8] He was in fact turned forty-seven at this time, and did not act his final season until 1775–6. He had offered to buy things for the Duke of Devonshire, but the Duke replied that he had no money. He did, however, ask Garrick to get him all the prints by Francesco Bartolozzi (1727–1815) that he could. Bartolozzi, who had been invited to engrave from the Guercino drawings at Windsor, was appointed Engraver to George III this same year.

The Garricks had expected to be back in England by August 1764, but that meant not going via Paris, and a combination of Mrs Garrick's rheumatism, then Garrick's own illness in Munich, and the charms of society in Paris once they arrived there, all conspired to delay their return until April 1765. Certainly from the letter that Garrick wrote to his brother George from Munich on 23 August 1764, he had been critically ill, and though he was told that his health would be the better for it, he confessed to George: 'I almost gave myself up for gone.'[9]

In fact, illness or sickness overshadowed the central part of their tour, though not all of it was quite so critical. On 31 October 1764, Garrick wrote to James Clutterbuck with a recipe for pile ointment that he had intended including in his previous letter but had forgotten: 'The manager of the theatre at Strasburgh was so affected with the piles that he could do no business for several weeks, and he was obliged to creep upon his hands and knees on a carpet, and the easiest posture he could find was leaning upon his elbows, for he could not bear to lie upon his side. He tried all kinds of remedy, leeches, lancet, etc . . . when a Monsieur Renaudin, who was my physician, and a very clever fellow, gave him ease in two hours, and cured him without return by the following recipe: '*For the Piles.* Six grains of opium. Forty grains of white lead in fine powder with a piece of very fresh butter, as large as a nutmeg, they must be well mixed together, and spread upon a piece of linen that will cover the part affected, and remember to put it on cold or at most just and barely warm." I am persuaded of the efficacy of this simple thing, and hope you'll try it when you are very bad.'[10]

Shortly before he returned to Paris on 10 November (1764), Garrick wrote to Voltaire from Nancy, explaining why he could not accept the invitation extended through M. Camp, a Lyons banker, and go to Ferney: '... had it been in my power to have followed my inclinations, I should have paid my respects at Ferney long before this time, but a violent bilious fever most unluckily seized me upon the road and confined me to my bed five weeks at Munich and now my affairs are so circumstanced that I am obliged to go to Paris as expeditiously as my present weak state of health will permit me.' At the same time he used the occasion to press home to Voltaire his championing of Shakespeare: 'You were pleased to tell a gentleman that you had a theatre ready to receive me; I should with great pleasure have exerted what little talents I have, and could I have been the means of bringing our Shakespeare into some favour with Mr Voltaire I should have been happy indeed. No enthusiastic missionary who had converted the Emperor of China to his religion would have been prouder than I, could I have reconciled the first genius of Europe to our dramatic faith.' There was then a P.S.: 'Though I have called Shakespeare our dramatic faith, yet I must do my countrymen the justice to declare that, notwithstanding their deserved admiration of his astonishing powers, they are not bigoted to his errors, as some French journalists have so confidently affirmed.'[11]

As some indication of what Voltaire thought about Shakespeare, one may cite a letter of his dated 4 December the following year (1765): 'As far as the English are concerned, I cannot reproach you for mocking Will Shakespeare somewhat. He was a savage with imagination. He wrote a lot of pleasant verse, but his plays can only please in London or Canada. It is not a good sign for the taste of a nation when that which it admires only succeeds on home ground.'[12] At the opposite end of the scale — certainly in Garrick's opinion — a similar view was expressed by Abbé Jean Bernard Le Blanc (1707–81): 'It is a pity that he [Shakespeare] so often falls into the low and the puerile. One has as much pleasure in seeing an extract from one of his tragedies as one would have difficulty in reading one of them from beginning to end.'[13]

When Garrick reached Paris one of the first things he did was to write to George Colman on 10 November. He was still suffering from the after-effects of his illness, but emotional stress had been added to physical weakness. At last he had heard of the death of the Duke of Devonshire, kept from him by his wife. The Duke had actually died at Spa on 3 October, only a few weeks after the Garricks' visit there: 'I am a little the worse for wear, and was so altered a fortnight ago, that I was not known till I spoke; but now, my cheeks are swelling, my belly rounding, and I can pass for a tolerable looking Frenchman; but my nerves, sir, my nerves. They are agitated at times; and the Duke of Devonshire's death had very nearly cracked them. They kept his death from me by the management of the best of women and wives, till I was better able to struggle with such a heart-breaking loss. He loved me to the greatest confidence, and I deserved it by my gratitude, though not by my merits. I must not dwell upon this subject, it shakes me from head to foot. I can't forget him, and the blow was as dreadful to me in my weak condition as it was unexpected.' But more was to come, and this time Garrick had learned it from Colman himself: 'I heard nothing of Hubert and Hogarth before your letter told me of their deaths. I was much affected with your news; the loss of so many of my acquaintance in so short a time is a melancholy reflection. Churchill, I hear, is at the point of death in Boulogne. This may be report only — he is certainly very ill. What a lust of publishing has possessed him for some time past. The greatest genius, no more than the greatest beauty, can withstand such continued prostitution. I am sorry, very sorry for him.'[14]

One death which did not touch David so closely by any means, however, was that of Colman's uncle, William Pulteney (1684–1764), Earl of Bath. Colman's mother was the sister of the Countess of Bath, whose son, Viscount Pulteney, had died at Madrid in February 1763. Lord Bath had always said that Colman was his second direct heir, but when he died on 8 July 1764 he left the estate to his brother, General Harry Pulteney (died 1767), and 900 guineas a year to Colman, subject to the General's pleasure. It may well have been thanks to the influence of Mrs Elizabeth Montagu, queen of the blue stockings, that this happened, because she disliked Colman, and during the last four years of his uncle's life she had great influence over him. As Garrick wrote: 'Had Lord Bath behaved to you as he ought, and not suffered himself at the last to be flattered by a learned lady and her flatterers, I should have *dropped a tear*, too, but my nerves bore the news of his death without agitation. Madame la précieuse [Mrs Montagu], I hear since, has been disappointed, and has acted her part for a pair of ear-rings only. I hope 'tis true, from my soul.' In fact, the *St James's Chronicle* reported on 10 July: 'His lordship, among other legacies, has bequeathed a ring and a pair of diamond ear-rings to Mrs Montagu, wife of Edward Montagu, Esq, for Huntingdon.'

The idea of returning to the theatre — either as actor or manager at this point — did not fill Garrick with much enthusiasm, as he told Colman in this same letter: 'You wish me in Southampton Street, and so do I wish myself there, but not for acting or managing, but to see you, my dear Colman, and other friends. The doctors all have forbid me thinking of business. I have at present lost all taste for the stage. It was once my greatest passion, and I laboured for many years like a true lover. But I am grown cold. Should my desires return, I am the town's humble servant again, though she is a great coquette, and I want youth, vigorous youth, to bear up against her occasional capriciousness.'[15]

The actor William Powell had written to Garrick on 30 March 1764, though the latter did not find time to reply until 12 December that year. Garrick's letter contains some good advice on acting, and Powell had turned out to be a great success during Garrick's absence. Inevitably, Shakespeare was advanced as the most important influence an actor could expose himself to, and Garrick ended by putting one of the most fundamental elements in his philosophy of stage management: 'One thing more, and then I will finish my preaching; guard against *the splitting the ears of the groundlings who are capable of nothing but dumb show* [s], *and noise.* Don't sacrifice your taste and feelings to the applause of the multitude. A true genius will convert an audience to his manner, rather than be converted by them to what is false and unnatural.'[16] The quotation from *Hamlet* is obviously very appropriate at this point, and Garrick must have been pleased with his efforts, for he later asked Powell for a copy of this letter for a book he was contemplating 'on our profession'.

In an attempt to help his friend Jean Monnet, and give a puff to his *Anthologie françoise ou chansons choisies*, Garrick landed himself in an embarrassing situation at this time. He wrote to Colman on 27 January 1765, suggesting that he might have something inserted in the *St James's Chronicle* by way of a letter from Paris, which would mention Garrick and then go on to Monnet.[17] Colman did this, but somewhat overstepped his brief in his zeal. True, Garrick was not entirely modest when he suggested that he might begin: 'Our little stage hero looks better than he did . . .' but he went on : 'If you think it right, speak of me as you please, gravely, ludicrously, jokingly, or how you will, so that I am not suspected to write it.' Nevertheless, this caused Colman's son to comment: 'Oh, Garrick, Garrick! That any man, of true talent (whether fully aware of his established fame or not), should forget the dignity of genius, and descend to this !!!'[18] In fact, Colman's father had not helped matters, either, because in the press extract he had written: 'If I am rightly informed, you are in the woeful want of him [Garrick] in London, both as Actor and Manager.' None of which can have been calculated to endear Garrick to the members of his profession, and certainly not those of his own theatre. When he saw the piece he was duly abashed, and wrote to Colman: 'My dear Colman, you frightened me with the "Extract of a Letter from Paris". I am very sorry that you mentioned the *woeful want of me as Manager and Actor*. They will suspect it came from me, and I have no right to say so much, as I have been taking my pleasures and left the theatre for a time. It appears ungenerous and ungrateful in me: which hurt me much. I beg that you will do all you can to make them not think the paragraph mine, if I am suspected. I never in my life praised myself knowingly, except a little matter in *The Fribbleriad* [see note on p. 210], which always pinched me. Perhaps I am too sensible about this delicacy, and nobody thinks about me or the extract.'[19]

But Garrick's letters were passed around, and already one that he had written about his reception by the Duke of Parma had found its way into the *London Magazine*, and it was obvious to Garrick from what Colman put in the *St James's Chronicle* extract that he had had access to a letter Garrick had written from Munich on 15 September 1764 to William Arden, tutor to Lord Spencer, whom the Garricks had met in Italy. As Garrick wrote to Colman: 'I desired you to say something *against* me, and you stuck your pen in your heart and wrote as you felt. I wish from my soul that you had not.' Well, that was not entirely true, and Garrick had brought it upon himself.

By 8 March, Garrick was beginning to think seriously about his return, for the lease on his apartment in the Rue Nicaise was to expire on 1 April, with fifteen days' grace for clearing up. He hoped to be met at Canterbury, and told Colman that if he could bring Notre Dame upon his back for him, he should have it. Two days later he was again writing to Colman, and was wondering whether, after all this time, he was still the darling of the London theatre-goers: 'I must entreat you to be very sincere with me. Do the town in general *really* wish to see me on the stage? Or are they (which I rather think the truth) as cool about it as their humble servant? I have no maw for it at all, and yet something must be done to restore our credit. That I may be able to play, and as well as ever, I will not deny; but that I am able to do as I have done, wear and tear, I neither must or [*sic*] can, or will.'[20]

The Garricks eventually arrived home on the afternoon of Thursday, 25 April 1765. There was much to catch up with, and Garrick told people that he still had not made up his mind about returning to the stage. There were friendships to be renewed, and there is one of the very few surviving letters to Samuel Johnson at this point, dated 31 May 1765: 'My brother greatly astonished me this morning by asking me, "if I was a subscriber to your Shakespeare?" I told him, yes, that I was one of the first, and as soon as I had heard of your intention; and that I gave you, at the same time, some other names, among which were the Duke of Devonshire, Mr Beighton, etc . . . I hope that you will . . . not think me capable of neglecting to make you so trifling a compliment, which was doubly due from me, not only on account of the respect I have always had for your abilities, but from the sincere regard I shall ever pay to your friendship.'[21] Johnson had issued a proposal, and begun collecting the names of subscribers, as early as 1756, and had promised publication before Christmas the following year. However, J. and R. Tonson did not publish the eight-volume edition until October 1765 — hence the reason, no doubt, for George's question to his brother, and his brother's letter to his friend Johnson, whom he always tried to support in whatever way he could. Garrick always felt rather conscious of the fact that he, who was less learned and 'worthy' than Johnson, should have so much more success and popularity.

In the first summer after their return, and for many years following, the Garricks went to stay at Mistley Hall in Essex, the seat of Richard Rigby (1722–88), said to have been one of the most unscrupulous politicians of his day. The visit became an annual event, nevertheless, and Garrick never imagined that his admiration for Rigby might have been mistaken. On one visit there occurred one of the few recorded instances of Garrick's being put in his place. A local clergyman, the Reverend Doctor Maurice Gough, was of the party, and Garrick noted his huge appetite, and amused the company with some jests at Gough's expense. Summoning all his dignity, Gough addressed the company when the

PARSONS's EDITION OF SELECT BRITISH CLASSICS.

SAM! JOHNSON, LLD.

Engraved for J. Parsons, Paternoster Row Feb. 1. 1793.

A portrait of Samuel Johnson engraved for Parsons's edition of *Select British Classics* and published on 1 February 1793. Dr Johnson was ambivalent, to say the least, in his pronouncements on his old friend David Garrick. He was capable of dismissing him out of hand, and then almost without having drawn breath, praising him to the skies. For his part, Garrick always felt slightly guilty that he, as a less worthy being, enjoyed the material success that seemed to elude Johnson. (*Mansell Collection*) laughter had subsided: 'Gentlemen, you must doubtless suppose, from the extreme familiarity with which Mr Garrick has thought fit to treat me, that I am an acquaintance of his; but I can assure you, that, till I met him here, I never saw him but once before, and then I paid five shillings for the right.' As the author of the passage added: 'Roscius was silent.'[22] It was tantamount, after all, to addressing him as 'David Garrick, player.'

It was a royal command that finally brought Garrick back to the stage of Drury Lane for the first time since the spring of 1763, playing Benedick in *Much Ado About Nothing*. As he wrote to his brother George on 9 November 1765: 'His Majesty has desired me to appear again to oblige him and the Queen. I shall obey their commands, but only for a few nights. My resolution is to draw my neck as well as I can out of the collar, and sit quietly with my wife and books by my fireside. If I could receive any great pleasure from the eager desire of all sorts of people to see me again, I might have it at present; for indeed their violent call for me is as general as it is particular — thinking people afraid of mischief the first night, and I wish from my soul that it was well over.'[23] In the event, he was given a warm and enthusiastic welcome by a packed house.

On 13 February 1766, Garrick wrote to Samuel Foote in an act of condolence. Despite professional collaboration, they had never been friends, and indeed on occasion were deeply at enmity. At this particular time, however, there is no doubt that Garrick's expressions were sincere. Foote had been paying a visit to the Earl of Mexborough at Cannon Park in Hampshire, where the Duke of York was also visiting. The Duke had a spirited mount and, egged on by other guests, Foote, who freely admitted that he was no rider, mounted the Duke's horse and was duly thrown, breaking his leg so badly that it had to be amputated — without anaesthetic, of course. If the accident was not actually to be regarded as the result of a practical joke played by the Duke, then at the very least he condoned it. It was said that, by way of compensation, Foote was granted a life patent in July that year to present plays from May to September at the Little Theatre in the Haymarket (now the Haymarket Theatre), and call it a theatre royal. Garrick had intended visiting Foote —at his invitation — at Cannon Park on his way to Bath in early March (1766), but failed to do so. However, in a letter of 21 March, he promised to call on the way back at the beginning of May, when he said that he would have only Clutterbuck with him.

Another person of Garrick's acquaintance makes his first appearance in the correspondence at this time, though they were already old friends. Isaac Bickerstaffe (?1735–1812) was a playwright of Irish origin who produced more than a score of pieces, mostly comic operas, between 1760 and 1771, for both Covent Garden and Drury Lane. His *Love in a Village* (1762) and *The Maid of the Mill* (1765) had been especially successful with the public, and in the latest season of 1765–6, his *Daphne and Amintor* had been given at Drury Lane. On this occasion Garrick was using Bickerstaffe as the bearer of a letter to Marie Jeanne Riccoboni, whom Garrick had met in Paris, and with whom he developed a firm friendship. After an unsuccessful career as an actress she had turned to writing novels, and her works were published in London by Becket. In sending the letter with Bickerstaffe, Garrick spoke highly of him to her.

Unfortunately, Bickerstaffe's career was to be brought to a swift and ignominious end, as we shall see later, when he had an encounter with a marine and had to flee the country in 1772. He had in any case been dismissed from the marines under something of a cloud before he embarked on his career as a dramatist. Even the friendship of such people as Garrick, Johnson and Goldsmith could not have prevented the prosecution for what was then a capital offence, and a rapid and self-imposed exile was seen as the only way out. Foote, too, one might note, fell under a similar sort of cloud when accused of making proposals to his coachman, but Foote elected to stand trial and was acquitted. In Bickerstaffe's case, however, the evidence was too strong, and even if Garrick and other friends had wished to rally round, it is unlikely that they would have been able to achieve much.

What was as regrettable for Garrick as the loss of Bickerstaffe's friendship was the fact that the affair was used as a means of getting at Garrick himself, by implicating him with Bickerstaffe, as we shall see, and the matter had to subside gradually, more in sorrow and regret than in anger on Garrick's part. When Mr Thrale mentioned the matter to Johnson, the latter's reply was restrained but firm: 'By those who look close to the ground, dirt will be seen. I hope I see things from a greater distance.'

In 1766, however, all was still light-hearted and happy, and the season had been a good one for all concerned, and for Garrick himself not only as actor and manager, but also as playwright, since *The Clandestine Marriage* had had such a success with its first night on 20 February 1766. The collaboration on the play between Garrick and Colman was,

Reynolds' portrait of Samuel Foote, now in the Garrick Club, as engraved by W. Greatbatch and published on 1 March 1837. Despite showing genuine concern and sympathy for Foote when he was injured in a riding accident, Garrick never felt at ease with his sometime rival, and for his part, Foote wasted no opportunity for ridiculing what he saw as the less satisfactory aspects of Garrick's career and personality. (*Mansell Collection*)

The Duke of York had allowed Foote — goaded by others — to try and ride his spirited horse when the latter was clearly incapable of doing so, and Foote was thrown so badly that he had to have part of a leg amputated. As a way of making amends for the disaster, the Duke obtained for Foote the patent of the Little Theatre in the Haymarket and he was allowed to call it a theatre royal — the forerunner of today's Theatre Royal on the same site. (*Mansell Collection*)

however, a source of irritation between the two men, and indeed Colman on occasion denied that Garrick had ever had any hand in it at all. So Charles Favart, writing to Garrick on 24 July 1766, asked him for his opinion of a comedy which Colman — 'the author' — had given him.[24] Madame Riccoboni knew slightly better, writing at much the same time, and congratulated Garrick for his part in it: 'The finger you put in the pie has certainly made it very tasty.' In his reply, in the letter carried by Bickerstaffe, Garrick good-humouredly wrote: 'I shall not be ashamed that I have had a finger in the pie.'

At this point, however, relations between Garrick and Colman had not turned sour. In fact, Colman had gone to Paris, where he had arrived by 30 June 1766, when Garrick wrote to him there. The affectionate way in which Garrick wrote of Colman's son — 'your sweet boy' — indicates that the Garricks' apparent inability to have children was, as Fanny Burney maintained, a positive source of regret to them, and that they would have been fond, if not adoring, parents, had they been so blessed.[25] The next letter is addressed to 'My dear Coley', and is dated from Hampton on 15 July. In the meantime Garrick had had a letter from Colman, via Esther Burney, from which it was evident that his first letter had miscarried. Again, there was much of the Colman son, but in view of future developments, perhaps the most interesting piece of news was the fact that Beard and his associates were going to sell the Covent Garden patent for £60,000. Garrick did not know to whom, but declared that when he did, 'there will be the Devil to do'.

On 18 July, Garrick wrote to the translator and writer Jean Baptiste Antoine Suard, who had married in January that year (1766) Amélie, the sister of the Parisian bookseller Joseph Panckoucke. The letter began, therefore, by way of offering congratulations on Suard's marriage, but soon turned to the matter of Shakespeare: 'I will venture to prove that there is not one French author, from their highest *Voltaire* down to their lowest *Abbé Le Blanc*, who understand[s] accurately any three speeches together of Shakespeare; and yet these are the gentlemen from whom the nation in general take their ideas of our theatre. The absurd blunders of the Abbé are not worthy of criticism, but it will be much to the honour of Shakespeare, and to our stage in general, that the willful [*sic*] and other mistakes of such a genius as Voltaire should be published, and I will not rest in my bed till his injustice and want of candour be exposed.'[26]

To a large extent Garrick was wasting his time, since Suard was a confirmed disciple of Voltaire, and persisted in expressing his contempt for Shakespeare, even after such a letter as this. And in the event it was Mrs Montagu, and not Garrick, who took Voltaire to task in her *Essay*, which though not published until 1769, was being prepared at this time. However, such was Garrick's reputation abroad that many people were inspired to think again about Shakespeare, and his contacts in Paris — renewed and extended as a result of his Grand Tour visit — in turn inspired Garrick to champion Shakespeare at every opportunity. Soon he was to be given a marvellous occasion for even greater service to 'the god of his idolatry', when the borough of Stratford decided to honour its most famous son and the nation's greatest actor at one and the same time. The result, as we shall see, was the curious Shakespeare Jubilee, held at Stratford in 1769, on which Garrick lavished all his loving tender care.

CHAPTER SIX

FAMILY AND FRIENDS

David Garrick had always been a family man, and after his family came his friends. Doubtless much of this affection and concern would have been absorbed by his children, if he had had any, but even so, one suspects that there would still have been room for certain particular favourites, and the distance separating him from the Lichfield members of his family meant that he would always be able to spare a thought for them. At times, however, it seems to have been little more than a thought, since business — or the claims of grand friends — often caused him to defer or abandon plans to pay a visit to the city where he was brought up. Nevertheless, out of sight was not out of mind, and Garrick's concern for his immediate family extended to nieces and nephews as well.

He always tried to keep his brother Peter informed about his life, and such an occasion was that of 18 August 1766, when a new gardener, sent by Peter, arrived at Hampton. Garrick also took the opportunity to make a little boast about his guests: 'We are in such vogue that last week the Duke and Duchess of Marlborough came to see us and drink tea, with Lord Charles Spencer and his lady. There was likewise a Miss Beauclerk who asked much after George and his babes. She lives, or did live, in Somerset House.'[1]

With brother George, on the other hand, Garrick was often rather crude in his letters. He wrote in something of a flutter on 8 February 1767 because the King had expressed the desire to see him as Oakly in *The Jealous Wife*. This was the first time that he played it since his return from the European trip. George had sent him the wrong part, and what he wanted was the prompter's book, for he said that he had forgotten it all: 'This damned Oakly is a crust for me indeed. I wish it don't prove too hard for my teeth, and rub my gums. Pray let me have it as soon as possible, the part I mean ... I have not played Oakly these three years. Sick, sick, sick, and Mrs P[ritchard] will make me sicker. Great bubbies, noddling head and no teeth. Oh! sick, sick, spew.'[2] In a reference to the actor William Powell, who had played King John the night before, and whose popularity undoubtedly incensed Garrick, he became positively gross: 'Sick, sick. King John beshit. Bouncing, strutting, striding, straddling, thumping, grinning, swaggering, staggering, all be shit. No matter. The more turd the more stink. I hold my nose, you leave in a morning. I lick my paper and am as clean as a whistle.'

Things had definitely become somewhat strained between Garrick and

(see previous page)
A portrait of Garrick by Gainsborough, painted around 1770 at Bath, which was later given to Albany Wallis, an executor of Garrick's will. Mrs Garrick always felt that Gainsborough had produced the best likeness of her husband in the portrait he painted the year previously for the Corporation of Stratford-upon-Avon to hang in the town hall — a painting which was destroyed by fire in 1946. (*National Portrait Gallery*)

Colman by this time, as we see from a letter to John Wilkes of 17 March, in which he wrote: 'My friend Colman, or rather *your* friend Colman (for I have lost him).'[3] And then on 5 April to brother George: '*Colman* and *Changuion* are arrived. We pulled off our hats, but did not smile. Our friends here will stir heaven and earth to bring us together. Make the best of it, it will be but a darn.'[4] Not only was there the trouble over the authorship of *The Clandestine Marriage*, but in addition, Garrick doubtless already knew by this time that Colman was interested in acquiring the Covent Garden patent, for on 28 April he again wrote to George: 'Now to the *grand* affair. Pray return my best respects to my partner, and tell him, if you think proper, that the news of the sale of the other house gives me not the least uneasiness. It is impossible that it should hurt us; and if P[owell] is to be a director, we have reason to rejoice, for he is finely calculated for management. What a strange affair! We shall know all in time. I am satisfied, be the news true or false. I shall most certainly keep the secret.'[5] On 31 March, in fact, William Powell, George Colman, John Rutherford and Thomas Harris had signed an agreement to purchase the patent of Covent Garden. The first two named were to raise £20,000, and the last two £40,000. Two days later, 30 April 1767, when Garrick wrote to George again, Colman still had not told Garrick himself: 'Colman has told me that he has an affair to open to me, but we have always been interrupted by somebody or another, so I have not yet had the whole, and which he has some qualms in bringing out. However, I am prepared, and he will be surprised at my little concern and ease upon this occasion. I am sure there is something in it, and yet the more I think of it, the more I am puzzled. Who finds money? What is the plan? Who are the directors? Damn me if I comprehend it but I shall know more.'[6] Garrick then went on to propose a meeting between himself and George and Lacy at the latter's house at Isleworth, which would mean that Garrick would only have to go over from Hampton, and George and Lacy only go from London to Isleworth.

One aspect of the matter which was not without significance for Colman was the discretion left to General Pulteney under the terms of Lord Bath's will, for indeed the General strongly disapproved of the whole venture, and as a result cancelled the section of the will settling the succession to an estate on Colman. Garrick went to Bath on 1 April 1767, where he stayed until 3 or 4 May. On 2 May, Colman finally unburdened himself to Garrick, who wrote forthwith to George with the news: 'I have this moment heard the whole affair and C[olman] is now in my room, so that I can only say that the thing is so. I received the news very calmly, and I believe surprised him. You shall know all when I next see you . . . C and I are well together'.[7] Even so, from a letter of 17 August, Garrick was very edgy with Colman, and there is a gap in the correspondence until the end of 1774. It was Powell, his former protégé, who most came in for Garrick's wrath, and the latter declared that he could not forgive him.[8]

As Garrick grew older and more secure in his role in life, he could be devastating in his directness. When the Duchess of Portland tried to wish an actor upon him, he replied on 29 October 1767 with a crushing description: 'If Your Grace will permit me to speak my mind, I think he has the most unpromising aspect for an actor I ever saw. A small pair of unmeaning eyes stuck in a round unthinking face are not the most desirable requisites for a hero, or a fine gentleman. However, I will give him a trial if he is unemployed at that time of year, and if he can be of the least service to me or himself.'[9]

Because of Garrick's long-standing friendship with Johnson, it would have been surprising if he had not come into contact with James Boswell (1740–95) at some point, and indeed they first met in 1760, but particularly during the year 1763–4 they had been in each other's company. The first extant letter from Garrick to Boswell, however, dates only from 25 November 1767. By this time Boswell had travelled on the Continent, and to Corsica, which was then struggling for independence. Garrick expressed the wish in his letter that he had had Boswell as a companion on his tour: 'Had I been happy enough to have met you in my ramble abroad, I should have had — I speak sincerely — a great addition to my pleasure there. I wanted now and then a man of fire to kindle up my fancy and set my electrical matter afloat. I have often been raised to rapture at the remains of antiquity, but the continuance of the fit can only be supported by social intercourse and, as our friend Johnson would call it, by an *animated reciprocation of ideas.*'

Boswell had been attracted by the idea of joining the Guards, but his father, who was a judge, wanted his son to follow him in the legal profession. In his letter, Garrick indicated that he agreed with the father's view — possibly with memories of his own father's life in the Army, though, of course, the Boswells were far more wealthy than Garrick's father had ever been: 'I most cordially wish you of having fixed at last to the *Law*, and that you have dropped your military spirit. Be assured, dear Mr

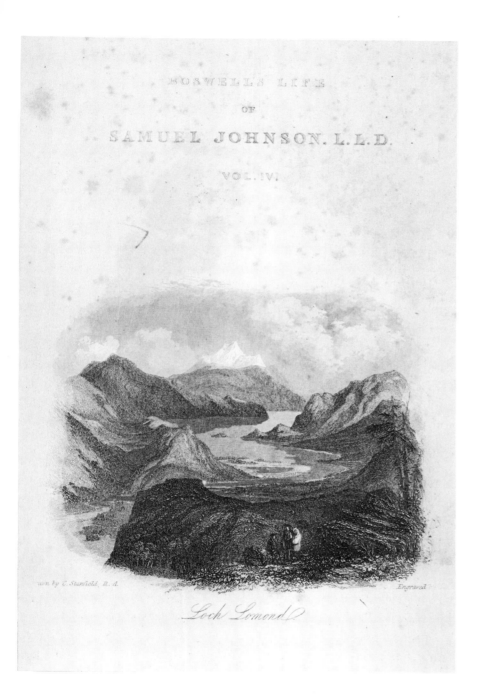

Loch Lomond

Reynolds' portrait of James Boswell, engraved by John Jones. The original was exhibited at the Royal Academy in 1787, but apparently was never paid for, and Reynolds wrote it off as a bad debt in 1791. Despite the fact that Boswell died at the relatively early age of fifty-five in 1795, he outlived Reynolds, Johnson, Goldsmith and Garrick. (*Mansell Collection*)

Loch Lomond, from the fourth volume of Boswell's *Life of Johnson*, drawn by C. Stanfield and engraved by E. Finden. When Boswell told Garrick of his trip to Forres with Johnson he wrote: 'I had great romantick satisfaction in seeing Johnson upon the classical scenes of Shakespeare in Scotland; which I really looked upon as improbably as that "Birnham Wood shall come to Dunsinane".' (*Mansell Collection*)

Catherine Clive, seen here in a Faber engraving of the portrait by W. J. Alais, was one of the few people among Garrick's theatrical contemporaries and/or colleagues who fully appreciated his qualities. As she herself wrote: 'I . . . was a living witness that they did not know, nor could they be sensible of, half your perfections . . . the public was entertained; they thought they all acted very fine — they did not see you pull the wires.' (*Mansell Collection*)

Boswell, when your youth and extraordinary vivacity subside a little, and thought and prudence take their turns, you will be happy in your most comfortable and honourable establishment, and have an additional satisfaction that you have made your father happy by the choice. Then, realizing that he had perhaps gone a little too far, Garrick recalled himself with: '. . . but my moralizing is impertinent. I am not to talk to you *now* as I did formerly, so you will excuse me and my honest intentions, and be assured no one takes more delight in your welfare.'[10]

When it came to dealing with matters such as property, Garrick now had marked confidence, particularly when dealing with the aristocracy. There is a letter to the Earl of Pomfret, who had his seat at Sunbury, near Hampton, and who wanted to purchase land at Hampton and split it with Garrick. The latter made no bones about the fact that he felt the asking price was far too high, in a letter of 7 December 1767, following on two from Pomfret that Garrick had received the month before.[11] The tone did not alter later, either, in a further letter of 17 June 1770, though the Earl's reply was courteous enough, even flattering, on the second occasion.

There were always people to criticize Garrick's acting, as we have seen, throughout the whole of his career, and it must have required considerable forbearance, as he grew older, always to react with equanimity on such occasions. In February 1768 it was the actor and dramatist Arthur Murphy (1727–1805), with whom Garrick had not enjoyed good relations in the past, and indeed it would be more accurate to say that the general tone of their relationship was bad, with occasional periods of friendship. This happened to have been one of their better periods, and Garrick was appropriately gracious: 'You have flattered me much by your very obliging letter, and I shall profit by your criticisms this evening, if I should happen to be in order. I am an old hunter, touched a little in wind, and somewhat foundered, but stroke me, and clap me on the back, as you have kindly done, and I can make a shift to gallop over the course. Once more I thank you for your letter, and am most truly . . .'[12]

Then there were also the actors and actresses to handle, and as she came to the end of her career, Kitty Clive (1711–85) became no easier to deal with. She had become a member of the Drury Lane company in 1747, and apart from one brief period remained there until her retirement in 1769. She often tried Garrick's patience, but she had genuine talent, especially as a comedienne, and though she was difficult and temperamental at times — he termed her 'fussocky' on one occasion — he had genuine affection for her, and called her 'Pivy'. In an undated letter he called her 'my dainty Kate', but in February 1768 she was being difficult, so she was 'Dear Madam'. With the confidence of well-tried friendship, he went on to be very straight with her: 'You always chuse [sic] to have some quarrel at your benefit, and without reason, but I do not. I am surprised that you have not thanked the managers for their kindness, instead of writing so peevish a letter. Your benefit is now settled, upon the best day in the week, and six days sooner than you were last year. This was meant kindly for you, and everybody must see it in that light. I shall be sorry *that you will not accept of that day* (as you are pleased to say) because I wish you well, and it will be of great service to you. Therefore if you will not advertise and fix your play, your folly be upon your own head. I cannot do more than I have done for you, and your friends must blame you.'[13] Pivy was not to be easily persuaded, however, and in her reply of 19 February wrote: 'Anyone who sees your letter would suppose I was kept at your theatre out of charity.' This stung Garrick to reply the following day: 'Dear Clive, How can you be so ridiculous and still so cross to mistake every word of my letter; that I could have so low a thought as what you suggest about *charity*, and which I am ashamed to read in yours. *The insignificant part* [of Lady Fuz in Garrick's own play *A Peep Behind the Curtain*], which you said you acted to oblige me, is very insignificant indeed, as well as the piece it is in. So you have endeavoured to be rude to me without effect. You speak of these things just as you are *in* or *out* of humour, so it shall stand for nothing. However, I have still such a regard for you that I promise you for the future that you shall be no more troubled with any nonsense of mine. . . You will find in your present humour objections to any day, but we really meant you *kindly* in giving you your own day, that you might avoid opera nights and have nobody to come immediately before or after you. This I did not do out of *charity*, but out of that respect which I ever pay to genius; and it is not my fault that Mrs Clive will not be as rational off the stage as she is meritorious on it.'[14]

They did, for a time, rather lose contact, but a friendship founded on mutual esteem was unlikely to die, and it was renewed in later years. Garrick truly admired her, and she, for her part, had stood in the wings once watching him act, and was heard to mutter: 'Damn him, he could act a gridiron.'

Later that year (1768), in April, Mrs Pritchard was to retire, and Garrick wrote an epilogue for her to deliver after her last performance, which was Lady Macbeth. It is perhaps more of interest in that it was yet another occasion for Garrick to propagate his gospel of the theatre:

> And may the stage, to please each virtuous mind,
> Grow every day more pure, and more refined;
> Refined from grossness, not by foreign skill,
> Weed out the poison, but be *English* still.

> Merits you have, to other realms unknown;
> With all their boastings, *Shakespeare* is *your own*![15]

120

At the time that the Covent Garden theatre changed hands, Garrick seems to have become nervous about his own standing with his partner Lacy from a legal point of view, and towards the end of 1767 consulted Charles Yorke, son of the first Earl of Hardwicke, who had been made Attorney–General in 1765. The letter is somewhat obscure, since the accompanying draft proposal is no longer with it, but Garrick seems to have been seeking to clarify the legal position of the two partners. [16] It was not the first time that Garrick had approached Yorke for such help. In August 1765 it had been about litigation with his neighbour at Hampton. From a letter of 8 April 1768 to Yorke, the affair with Lacy referred to above was either only resolved then, or had resurfaced. In fact, it may well have been the same matter, for in a letter to the writer and translator William Kenrick (?1725–79), dated 6 May 1768, Garrick stated that he was: 'Over head and ears in a law-matter.' [17] This prompted Kenrick to observe: 'Over head and ears in a law-matter! Law-matters, it seems, are common things with the litigious Roscius. Heaven send those a good deliverance that have to do with him!' These words were to be an accurate prophecy as far as Kenrick himself was concerned.

Certainly, Garrick had been made anxious by the sale of the Covent Garden patent, and he was prompted to find out exactly how he stood with Lacy. The advice from Yorke, then, as he wrote to brother George from Hampton, probably on 11 July 1768, was that he could sell tomorrow if he wished, and without Lacy's leave. [18] In the same letter he also said that he had 'had great inducements to quit Drury Lane'. The inducements were in all probability no more than irritations on Garrick's part at what he thought was Lacy's unreasonable behaviour. Lacy seems to have been suddenly inspired to deal with matters such as casting and rehearsals that in the past he had always left to Garrick, and there had been disagreement over a salary increase for brother George. Nor was it the first time that there had been tensions between Garrick and Lacy. A letter to the solicitor John Paterson, dated 5 March 1766, shows that there had been friction between them after Garrick's return from the Grand Tour, but the letter following this latest instance — also to Paterson, dated 21 August 1768 — shows that Garrick's ability to take such things in his stride had considerably diminished, and that what might have been out of the question before he went abroad — namely, that he should actually give up the theatre — was now more than a mere gesture: 'I have (and I believe you know it) withstood very great temptations to be easy at Drury

Lane, and to end my theatrical life there, but fate and Mr Lacy, who seems to be alone insensible of my merit and services, will drive me away ... Mr Lacy thinks and speaks very injuriously and unjustly of my brother, has very ill requited my services and has lately done some things which, I think, shows a spirit contrary to that of our articles, and the terms of our reconciliation settled before you. Therefore I will immediately prepare for my brother's retreat, and will most assuredly follow him. I will have no more altercations with Mr Lacy.'[19] In the event, of course, their association was ended only with Lacy's death in 1774, and they were to go on to still more theatrical triumphs together. And despite Kenrick's remark about 'the litigious Roscius', Garrick himself professed not to like lawsuits; as he wrote to James Boswell on 18 May 1768: 'a lawsuit is the Devil, and destroys all mirth, pleasure and goodfellowship'.

When it came to theatre accounts, however, or any other area where Garrick felt that he had no direct involvement, he kept well and truly out of it, as we see from a letter of 3 June 1768 to Spranger Barry about his salary: 'I must own that I am a very negligent attender to the accounts of the theatre, and depend upon the accuracy and justice of other people to do that business for me. I must therefore repeat what I said before, that the managers will immediately set to rights any articles of your account that may be wrong, and my brother will be ready to meet anybody for that purpose whenever you please to appoint him.'[20] One must appreciate, therefore, that in Garrick's own eyes, there were very clearly defined areas of responsibility in the administration of the theatre, and he expected those in charge to restrict themselves to those areas alone. He was lucky in having Lacy as his partner, and as his personal fame increased, he tended to overlook or ignore this fact. Not everyone would have been prepared to accept such autocratic behaviour in a partner, fed as it was by the adulation of a good many members of the nobility and important figures in London society. Lacy probably understood Garrick, and made allowances for him, to a much greater extent than Garrick realized. At the same time, the house prospered and went from strength to strength under Garrick's inspiration, and that was worth paying for.

Garrick's friendships with the noble and famous persons of his day have frequently brought the accusation that he was vain, a social climber, pretentious — and many other such epithets that one might easily apply in such circumstances. There are, of course, instances where he boasted mildly of his grand connections, but not in an absurd way, or one in which he made himself look ridiculous. But what it is all too easy to overlook is the fact that these people wanted Garrick's friendship, and thought that it was worth cultivating, or they would certainly not have taken the trouble to maintain the connection, or in fact solicit it, which sometimes happened later in life when he was well and truly established.

One such friendship was that with the statesman Edmund Burke (1729–97), whose unused epitaph for Garrick [see p. 58] was no small praise from such a pen! Burke had dined with Johnson and Garrick as early as 1758, and by the time that Burke was appointed private secretary to the Marquis of Rockingham, First Lord of the Treasury, in July 1765, the friendship was soundly established, and Garrick was able to send a

Edmund Burke in an engraved portrait by J. Chapman published on 15 December 1789. Burke became private secretary to the Marquis of Rockingham in 1765, and member for Wendover in the same year. Rockingham helped Burke financially from time to time, and directed that at his death the bonds should be destroyed. Garrick attended Burke's maiden speech in the House in 1766 on the American question, and became a close friend. (*Mansell Collection*)

warm letter of congratulation, and predict Burke's rise to fame. This appointment was indeed the turning-point in his career, and at the end of the year, Burke began his progress in Parliament as M.P. for Wendover in Buckinghamshire. Garrick was in the House to hear Burke's maiden speech — on the American colonies — which he delivered on 17 January 1766. Afterwards David wrote: 'I had the honour and pleasure of enjoying your virgin eloquence. I most sincerely congratulate you upon it. I am very nice and very hard to please, and when my friends are concerned, most hypercritical. I pronounce that you will answer your warmest wishes of your warmest friend. I was much pleased. I have much to say, which you will politely listen to, and forget the next moment; however, you shall have it.'[21] Such warmth was no fabrication, and such was Garrick's confidence in the closeness and genuine nature of the relationship, that when Burke sent him a play, possibly later in 1766, Garrick was able to pronounce it 'absolutely unfit for the stage'.

In April 1768, Burke bought the Gregories estate near Beaconsfield in Buckinghamshire, and invited Garrick to visit him there that summer. However, there was the annual visit to Mistley, which had special significance that year, since Rigby had been appointed Paymaster of the Forces on 14 June. As Garrick explained to Burke, in a letter from Hampton dated 17 June, Mistley had the prior claim. Nevertheless, Garrick said that he longed to see Burke, and Gregories, though even 'if you had a house in the fens of Lincolnshire, or on the swamps of Essex, where you were obliged to drink brandy, by way of small beer, to keep the ague out of your bones, I should long to be with you'.[22] After the visit to Mistley, however, Garrick told Burke: 'You may depend upon seeing my mahogany countenance ... Madam will rejoice with me to pay her respects to Mrs Burke, and we will be as happy as the day is long.'

It was a busy time for Garrick, however, for he had another visit to make, this time to Earl de la Warr, at Boldre Lodge in the New Forest, and that visit had been promised since the previous year. Then Lord and Lady Camden were to dine at Hampton, and there were the preparations for the visit of King Christian VII of Denmark (1749–1808, King from 1766), who had married Caroline Matilda (1751–75), youngest sister of George III. Garrick was to provide a dramatic entertainment on 18 August, which was to consist of Hoadly's *The Suspicious Husband*, and Bickerstaffe's *Daphne and Amintor*. We have a vivid account of that evening from Mrs Delany: 'Such a crowd as was in the pit I never heard

The Seat of the R.t Hon.ble Edmund Burke at Beconsfield Bucks.

of. They were so close and so *hot*, that every man pulled off his coat and sat in his waistcoat! Some had sleeves, more had none, and the various hues made a most surprising sight! When the King of Denmark came in, the clapping and noise was prodigious; the poor boy looked almost frightened, but bowed on all sides over and over. When Garrick came in, the house redoubled; his little majesty took it all to himself and redoubled his bows; many of the *men* fainted away — there were few or no women in the pit.'[23]

    Garrick's involvement in, and attitude to, this royal visit, was a source of ammunition for those who were irritated by him. Sir John Hawkins, for example, wrote in his *Life of Samuel Johnson*: 'The greatest of Mr Garrick's foibles was a notion of the importance of his profession: he thought that Shakespeare and himself were, or ought to be, the objects of all mens' [*sic*] attention. When the King of Denmark was in England, he received an order from the Lord Chamberlain to entertain that monarch with an exhibition of himself in six of his principal characters. In his way to London, to receive his instructions, he called on me, and told me this as

Gregories, the estate at Beaconsfield that Burke bought in 1768 at a period when his finances were reasonably sound. Garrick enjoyed visiting the house, though a year later he had to make Burke a loan of £1,000 which was never repaid, and even the payment of the interest on the loan fell into arrears. Such examples prove that the charges of meanness and greed that have been levelled against Garrick had little or no justification. (*Mansell Collection*)

A general prospect of Bath in 1752 and a view of the Circus after Thomas Malton, dating from around 1780. Bath was a favourite resort of Garrick and his friends (Quin described it as a 'cradle of age, and a fine slope to the grave'), and was endowed with many fine neo-classical buildings by John Wood senior (1705?–54) and junior (d. 1782). Under the 'rule' of Richard 'Beau' Nash (1674–1762), polite society frequented the Assembly Rooms, observed a code of etiquette and dress, and Bath became a focus of pleasure and intrigue. (*Mansell Collection*)

news. I could plainly discern in his looks the joy that transported him; but he affected to be vexed at the shortness of the notice.' [24] There is a letter from Garrick to Baron von Diede, the Danish Ambassador, dated 7 September 1768, in which he did in fact complain of the short notice he had been given — the command had been for the very next day — and declined to play Macbeth, though he offered instead Vanbrugh's *The Provoked Wife*, in which he had played Sir John Brute with great success, and his own *The Elopement*. Since the part of Macbeth took a great deal out of Garrick — he described it as 'so violent a character' — he felt that he could not put it on at a day's notice. This was not held against him, however, and on 12 September, after his visit to Hampton Court, the King of Denmark visited Garrick at Hampton. David did in fact play Macbeth for the King on 22 September (1768). His health, however, was again giving cause for concern. He had had gout earlier in the year, though it is recorded in the correspondence as troubling him as early as November 1765. On this occasion, however, it was more than gout.

As 1768 gave way to 1769, Garrick entered on the last decade of his life, and in illness, from a letter he wrote on 3 January 1769 to Helfrich

Peter Sturz, who had been in the Danish King's retinue: 'Though I can scarcely hold my pen in my hand, and am just risen from a sick-bed, yet I cannot delay a moment longer to answer your most friendly letter.'[25] Sturz had gone to Paris, and then written to Garrick about the acting he had seen there — especially that of Mlle Clairon.

The illness had been more serious than Garrick had probably ever known, and when he wrote to James Clutterbuck on 9 March 1769, he announced that he was off to Bath: 'I have had a very sad bout indeed with stone, gout, fever and jaundice. I must away for Bath directly and intend being there about Thursday next. The waters have the Devil and all to wash away. However, we must try, as I shall see you, my dear Clut, and that will be the best cordial I can have for my present low spirits. My wife, who has not been in bed these seven days, sends her love to you ... I literally cannot write more, so my love to the best part of you ... I am a perfect spectacle!'[26] A letter of thanks to the Earl of Halifax, probably written on 12 March, is in much the same vein, and Garrick said in it that he had suffered 'the martyrdom of saints for ten days past'.

The devotion of Mrs Garrick is evident here, and time did not diminish their attachment to each other. One of the reasons for rearranging his timetable the previous summer, as explained to Colonel Bernard Hale, had been that: 'If I do *not* return to Hampton, my wife would think one night's separation from her would break our matrimonial charm, that I should go to your Nancy Parsons, and she must think of a separate maintenance. To be serious with you . . .'[27] Annabella Parsons, despite being a notorious courtesan, became the second Viscountess Maynard in 1776.

Garrick's time at Bath was not destined to be all calm, however, since Samuel Derrick, the writer and dramatist, and Master of Ceremonies since 1763, had just died on 28 March (1769), and a successor had to be elected. A war of pamphlets ensued, in which Garrick played his part, and a fortnight later passions were running so high that there was actually a riot in the Assembly Rooms. In the end the three runners withdrew, and a Captain Wade was elected instead. By 29 April, Garrick was back in London, and about to embark on what ought to have been his greatest piece of showmanship, but which, thanks to the intervention of no human agency, but that of weather, turned out to be — at least initially — one of his greatest failures.

Sir John Hawkins' claim that Garrick thought that Shakespeare and himself ought to be the objects of all men's attention was soon to be given a good deal of substance, since what Garrick planned to embark upon next was certainly intended to make Shakespeare the chief object of attention, though in so doing, Garrick inevitably drew that attention directly to himself. Given the nature of the theatrical profession, it would have been hard to do otherwise, but one must not underestimate the degree to which Garrick had made the rehabilitation of Shakespeare a cause, and at this point any excess of egocentricity happily coalesced with that higher ambition.

CHAPTER SEVEN

THE SHAKESPEARE
JUBILEE

THE Jubilee is first mentioned in the correspondence on 29 April 1769 when Garrick, recently returned from a visit to Bath for his health, wrote to the politician and antiquary James West (?1704–72), whose town house in King Street, Covent Garden, was not far from Southampton Street. West had evidently written to the painter Benjamin Wilson (1721–88) — both were fellows of the Society of Artists — and it was this letter which had elicited Garrick's to West: 'I have seen your letter to Mr Wilson, and shall take the liberty of answering it myself. I shall remain in London and at Hampton for some time, I believe, till I shall be wanted to pay my duty to our immortal Shakespeare ... we will consult upon our intended Jubilee in memory and honour of Shakespeare. I shall be ready to do everything in my power to forward so laudable a work.'[1] We must go further back in time, however, for the origins of the Jubilee. There is, for example, a letter dated 28 November 1767, from Francis Wheler of Stratford, now in the New Place Museum there. Writing to William Hunt (1731–83), who became Town Clerk of Stratford in 1769, Wheler unveiled his strategy: 'It would be an ornament to our new town hall at Stratford if we could get from Mr Garrick some very handsome bust, statue or picture of Shakespeare.... In order to flatter Mr Garrick into some such handsome present, I have been thinking it would not be at all amiss ... to make Mr Garrick an Honorary Burgess of Stratford and to present him therewith in a box made of the Shakespeare's mulberry-tree.'[2] The idea obviously appealed to the Mayor and Corporation, and after more discussion a letter was eventually written to Garrick on 3 May 1769, informing him of his election at Stratford. His reply, dated 8 May, was suitably grandiloquent: 'Gentlemen, I cannot sufficiently express my acknowledgments for the honour you have done me in electing me a Burgess of Stratford upon Avon, a town which will be ever distinguished and reverenced as the birthplace of Shakespeare. There are many circumstances which have greatly added to the obligation you have conferred upon me. The freedom of your town given to me unanimously, sent to me in such an elegant and *inestimable* box, and delivered to me in so flattering a manner, merit[s] my warmest gratitude. It will be impossible for me ever to forget those who have honoured me so much as to mention my unworthy name with that of their immortal townsman.'[3]

The first public announcement of the Jubilee appeared in the *London Chronicle* on 11 May 1769. On 18 May, Garrick played his last part of the

(see previous page)
Detail of an impression of Shakespearian characters intended by Garrick as part of the Shakespeare Jubilee celebrations at Stratford in 1769. In the event, inclement weather prevented the procession from taking place, since James Lacy, Garrick's partner refused to allow the costumes to be rained on. The procession then became part of the stage version produced by Garrick for Drury Lane. (*British Museum*)

130

season as Archer in Farquhar's *The Beaux' Stratagem* for the Theatrical Fund, and for the occasion wrote an epilogue which he himself delivered, adding what he called 'a hint' about the forthcoming Jubilee. According to Garrick, in a letter to James West dated the following day, it was 'received with the loudest applause and approbation'. The relevant lines were as follows:

> My eyes, till then, no sight like this shall see,
> Unless we meet at Shakespeare's Jubilee!
> On Avon's banks, where flowers eternal blow,
> Like its full stream, our gratitude shall flow!
> There let us revel, show our fond regard,
> On that loved spot first breathed our matchless *Bard*!
> To him all honour, gratitude is due;
> To him we owe our *all* — to *him* and *you*![4]

Roubiliac's bust of Garrick gives a strong indication of the importance of the actor in his day. Roubiliac was very highly regarded by his fellow artists, and was the obvious choice of sculptor when it was decided to erect a monument to Handel in Vauxhall Gardens during his own lifetime. That Garrick should also have been a subject for Roubiliac is therefore elequent testimony to his standing. (*National Portrait Gallery*)

By 8 June, when Garrick wrote to Town Clerk William Hunt, he had decided that he ought to go down to Stratford and visit the site, which he proposed doing at the end of the following week, telling Hunt that he must be prepared to 'give up a day at least' to Garrick.[5]

The business of securing adequate lodgings for the players and musicians was already causing Garrick concern, but Lacy had a different one — the notorious English weather. Samuel Foote, who had not been slow to look for potential sources of disaster, and was to find ample material for satire when the Jubilee was over, reported Lacy as saying: 'Why, if the day should turn out, as you say, wet and windy, Garrick and his mummers may parade it as much as they please, but none of the clothes shall walk.'[6]

Garrick had turned his mind to an ode, which he was to write and, of course, deliver in the course of the proceedings. Its full title was: *Ode upon Dedicating a Building and Erecting a Statue to Shakespeare at Stratford upon Avon*. On 18 July, Benjamin Wilson wrote to William Hunt: 'I was with Mr Garrick this morning. He has wrote a most excellent *Ode* for the Jubilee, and which will do him honour. It is long, but not too long.'[7] The *Ode* was to be set by Dr Arne and, according to Garrick in a letter of 14 July to William Hunt, he 'works like a dragon at it. He is all fire and flame about it.'[8] Writing to the Earl of Hardwicke on 22 July, Garrick explained the 'experiment' he was trying out with the *Ode*. 'The recitative parts will be spoken by your humble servant, and the choruses and airs will at the proper times break in upon the speaker. I hope by [this] to avoid the dullest part of music, w[hich] is the recitative, and endeavour to supply [the] want with a warm, spirited declamat[ion].'[9]

Other doings were on foot that would have outraged people today. On 14 July, according to *The Gentleman's Magazine*, and with the permission of the Duke of Dorset, High Steward of Stratford upon Avon: 'Above one hundred trees were cut down near Stratford upon Avon, in order to enlarge the prospect against the approaching Jubilee in honour of Shakespeare.'[10] In return, Garrick 'Brought in a compliment (delicately) to the Duke of Dorset' in his *Ode*. There was also a reference to the proposed enclosing of common land, for which Garrick declared that he expected thanks after the performance. The thanks was duly forthcoming, and so on 26 September, when it was all over, the Corporation of Stratford wrote to Garrick: 'Our hearts, overflowing with gratitude, can never forget that attention and regard you have shown to our prosperity, in so elegantly expressing your abhorrence in your most incomparable *Ode*, of that cruel design to destroy the beauty of this situation by inclosing our open fields.'[11] It was evidently perfectly acceptable to fell more than a hundred trees, but not to enclose the fields.

More banal matters were to arise, however. The somewhat minor literary figure George Keate (1730–97) had written a poetical epistle to Voltaire entitled *Ferney* the year before (1768), in which he paid due tribute to Shakespeare. Doubtless in recognition of the service rendered, Keate was appointed by the Corporation of Stratford to present Garrick with the mulberry-box containing the freedom of the town. As a suitable memento of the occasion, the Corporation then decided to present Keate with an inkstand made from the same mulberry-tree. This was the cause of much jealousy among Keate's rivals, and so satirical articles on the Jubilee appeared regularly in the press.

An enterprising tradesman of Coventry produced a Shakespeare ribbon 'in imitation of the rainbow' on the theory that since it united 'the colours of all parties' it was 'an emblem of the great variety of his genius'. It was Boswell who wrote this up for the *Public Advertiser* on 16 September, and to it was added a quotation from Johnson's 1747 Drury Lane prologue: 'Each change of many-colour'd life he drew.' Boswell commented: 'I dare say Mr Samuel Johnson never imagined that this fine verse of his would appear on a bill to promote the sale of ribbands.'[12] Quite so!

To put the projected Jubilee more into perspective, as long ago as

1740, as we saw earlier, Garrick had been a member of the committee which arranged for a statue to Shakespeare in Westminster Abbey. William Kent designed it and Peter Scheemakers carved it. On that occasion the inscription chosen was from *The Tempest*:

> The cloud-capp'd towers, the gorgeous palaces,
> The solemn temples, the great globe itself,
> Yea, all which it inherit, shall dissolve;
> And, like this insubstantial pageant faded,
> Leave not a rack behind.

For the Stratford statue, however, Garrick wanted something different. This statue was to be an exact replica in lead, cast by John Cheere, of another statue by Scheemakers, but one which he had both designed and executed for the Earl of Pembroke the year before (1768). The new statue was to have its place in a niche on the new town hall at Stratford, and the presentation of it to the Corporation was to take place during the Jubilee. In his search for a new inscription, Garrick turned to his old friend Richard Berenger: 'I should have called upon you often had not the Stratford matters in honour of our immortal friend engrossed me wholly. Have you nothing to say about him? No song, epigram, frisk, fun or

Wood from Shakespeare's mulberry-tree was used to make the casket in which Garrick was presented with the document making him an Honorary Burgess of Stratford. The casket was carved by Thomas Davies of Birmingham, who took four months over the task. Shakespeare and the three graces appear on the front, Tragedy and Comedy on the sides, and Garrick as Lear on the back, based on the painting by Benjamin Wilson (see p. 145). (*British Museum*)

Garrick performed his *Ode* during the second day of the Jubilee celebrations, though none of Shakespeare's works was performed at all. (*Victoria and Albert Museum*)

flibbertygibbet upon the occasion? . . . pray think of some good inscription to be put upon a blank part of the pedestal of his statue which we shall erect to him . . . something relating to his own genius, immortality or what you please.'[13] In the end they settled upon some lines from *A Midsummer Night's Dream*, and it may well have been Berenger who suggested them:

> The poet's eye, in a fine frenzy rolling,
> Doth glance from heaven to earth, from earth to heaven;
> And as imagination bodies forth
> The forms of things unknown, the poet's pen
> Turns them to shapes, and gives to airy nothing
> A local habitation and a name.[14]

As the time approached, things became more and more silly. In a letter of 16 August to William Hunt, Garrick wrote: 'I heard yesterday to my surprise that the country people did not seem to relish our *Jubilee*, that they looked upon it to be *popish*, and that we should raise the Devil and what not.' He then said that he hoped that it was all a joke, and eventually treated it as such in the opening scene of the dramatic entertainment based on the Jubilee that he subsequently gave at Drury Lane. Nevertheless, he went on to Hunt: 'After all my trouble, pains, labour and expense for their service and honour of the county, I shall think it very hard if I am not to be received kindly by them.'[15]

Garrick was also worried that the locals would charge such exorbitant prices that the whole Jubilee would be affected, and there was the construction of the great octagonal building which was causing him concern.[16] He had nevertheless found time to read the *Ode* to the King and Queen and spent three and a quarter hours with them on that occasion, so he told William Hunt on 27 August. The building was described as follows: 'A very large and magnificent octagonal amphitheatre was erected upon the Bankcroft, close to the river Avon, and which, to please the prevailing taste, somewhat resembled Ranelagh Rotunda. It was capable of conveniently holding above one thousand spectators, and surely seldom was seen a more beautiful place. In the amphitheatre, which was supported by a circular colonnade of columns, of the Corinthian order, was built a noble orchestra, large enough to contain upwards of one hundred performers. From the centre of the dome was suspended an amazingly large chandelier, consisting of eight hundred lights, which had a beautiful effect.'[17] The chandelier, from Drury Lane, was never put in position, since it was a casualty on its journey from London.

The opening day of the Jubilee — Wednesday, 6 September — was to start with a public breakfast in the new town hall, commencing at 9 a.m. Garrick was there not long after 8 a.m., dressed as Steward of the Jubilee, and carrying his wand of office made — inevitably — from the mulberry-tree. Before the general company arrived, Garrick was presented with a medallion of Shakespeare, also carved out of wood from the mulberry-tree, and set in gold. A speech of welcome was delivered by the Town Clerk on behalf of the Mayor and Corporation. Garrick replied, and 'instantly fastened the medal to his breast'. In the portrait by Van der Gucht at Althorp, Garrick is shown contemplating the medal, with its rainbow ribbon, and he has his wand of office over his shoulder. Breakfast was taken to the accompaniment of a fife and drum band, playing favourite marches, outside the windows.

After breakfast there was a procession to the parish church for a performance of Arne's oratorio *Judith*, which had no particular connection with the occasion, it must be admitted. One of Dr Arne's nieces went with Mrs Garrick in her coach, and on arrival at the church a floral tribute was

Dr Thomas Arne, in a caricature by Bartolozzi, is now chiefly remembered as the composer of 'Rule, Britannia', but in his day was known as an expert in several musical genres, including opera and oratorio. Garrick commissioned him to compose the music for the *Ode*. (*Mansell Collection*)

placed below Shakespeare's monument. It appeared to one observer that the Bard, peering out from behind a bank of laurel, bore an uncanny resemblance to the god Pan. Both at the breakfast and the oratorio, there was a marked absence of many of the faces that had been expected. James Boswell, for one, arrived two hours late, having been unable to find a post-chaise at Woodstock, and having been obliged to ride six miles to the next stage — an occupation for which he was certainly not dressed.

From the church the procession was to make its way, led by the musicians, to the amphitheatre. It had, however, been an unusually wet season, and the river was very full, but the weather held, and once they were safely inside the building, some six or seven hundred persons sat down to dinner at ten shillings and sixpence a head. There were not sufficient waiters to serve food fast enough for the company, so they began to help themselves. Drink, however, was not in short supply, and the atmosphere soon improved. A band played, and soloists performed special songs. During the dinner Garrick was presented with a Loving Cup also made out of the wood of the mulberry-tree and lined in gold. In his reply he sang the Ballad of Shakespeare's Mulberry-Tree, which he had composed for the occasion.[18] After various toasts, during which the Loving Cup was passed round, the singing of *God Save the King* brought the meal to a close, and the guests left to prepare for the evening's ball, which was due to start at 9 p.m., but in the event began an hour late, and lasted until about 3 a.m. According to one person present, the ball was 'remarkable chiefly for the most elegant minuet I ever saw, or ever shall see, danced by Mrs Garrick. . . .'[19]

It had been decided that Thursday, 7 September would be the main day of the Jubilee, since people might arrive late on the Wednesday, and leave early on the Friday. It was a great disappointment, therefore, to wake up that Thursday morning to a 'hateful drizzling rain'. What was particularly crucial for Garrick was the fact that proceedings were to have begun with a pageant of characters from Shakespeare's plays, dressed appropriately, and this was really the only part of the entire Jubilee that involved any representation of the characters or indeed virtually anything from the plays themselves, and even then the players were not to act. In such conditions, however, it would have been foolhardy to insist on adhering to the programme. In any case, Lacy, with an eye on the money at stake, refused to allow the costumes to be used: 'Who the devil, Davy, would venture upon the procession under such a lowering aspect? Sir, all

The mulberry-wood medallion with a head of Shakespeare which Garrick wore as Steward of the Jubilee in 1769. The tree, said to have been planted by Shakespeare, grew at New Place, Stratford, but was cut down in 1756. Garrick bought some of the wood, which he had made into a chair, visible in the Hogarth painting on p. 69. (*Shakespeare Birthplace Trust*)

the ostrich feathers will be spoiled, and the *property* will be damnified five thousand pounds.' Apart from the weather, the day started badly for Garrick when, according to Joseph Cradock: 'The man who was to shave him, perhaps not quite sober, absolutely cut him from the corner of his mouth to his chin . . . the ladies were engaged in applying constant stiptics to stop the bleeding.'[20]

Procession or no procession, the amphitheatre was full for what was the most important part of the Jubilee celebrations, and Garrick's most personal contribution to it. His *Ode* was to be performed for the first time, with music by Dr Arne. There was a slight anomaly in that the building to be dedicated, as detailed in the full title of the *Ode*, was the town hall of Stratford, and not the amphitheatre; and the statue to be erected, which was here in the amphitheatre, was meant to be for the town hall. There it stood, in pride of place in the gallery — well, almost pride of place, for directly in front of the statue was Garrick himself in a high-backed gilt chair, which made it very difficult for him to throw appropriately reverent glances in that direction. He had hoped to have had Shakespeare's own chair for the occasion, but the owner, the satirist Paul Whitehead, had refused to part with it for such a purpose.

The Jubilee 'Booth or Amphitheatre' was modelled on the Rotunda at the Ranelagh pleasure gardens in London, and was intended to provide the setting for most of the important events during the three-day celebrations. Its idyllic position on the banks of the Avon proved to be a miscalculation of siting, however, since the river flooded the banks, and at one point almost cut off the amphitheatre from the town. (*British Library*)

137

Garrick had devoted a lot of time and energy to the composition of his *Ode*, and yet the decision to have Dr Arne set it to music presented considerable problems. The traditional pattern for such a work, familiar since the time of Purcell, was to have a succession of solo arias and choruses, and the arias might well be preceded by recitative. Garrick, however, was not going to deliver his words 'in what is called recitative'. Indeed, as he had told the Earl of Hardwicke, in his opinion, the recitative was 'the dullest part of the music'. Of course, Garrick was no singer, either, so if he was to deliver his own work, there could be no music. The solution devised was that he would declaim over Dr Arne's accompaniment instead.

The text began with three verses of extended interrogation:

To what blest genius of the isle
Shall gratitude her tribute pay,
    Decree the festive day,
Erect the statue, and devote the pile?

o'er step not the modesty of Nature.
Ham.

Garrick so devoted himself to the cause of promoting Shakespeare that he was bound to bring censure on himself from certain quarters. One relatively tactful admonition came from Isaac Taylor's engraving showing Garrick with the bust of Shakespeare, placed on top of an image of Diana of Ephesus, with a quotation from *Hamlet*, 'O'er step not the modesty of Nature'. Ophelia and Falstaff are among the characters represented. (*Mansell Collection*)

Finally the answer came, with a triple call of 'Shakespeare!', and the chorus joined in. An air followed to the words:

Sweetest bard that ever sung
    Nature's glory, Fancy's child;
Never, sure, did witching tongue
Warble forth such wood-notes wild!

This was the pattern for the rest of the work, though an extended section on the birth of Falstaff gave Garrick an opportunity for a portrayal of that character before the end.

But the end of the *Ode* was not the end of the affair, however, for the ladies and gentlemen present were then invited to say anything they felt for or against Shakespeare. It was an extraordinary idea, but was the cue for the actor Tom King (1730–1805) to rise from the audience, dressed in a blue and silver macaroni suit, to speak against the Bard. It took everyone completely by surprise, however, and as a result fell completely flat. Garrick then moved his Epilogue to the Ladies, in the course of which he mentioned most of the favourite female characters in Shakespeare. It was doubtless with no little relief that the audience rose to repair to dinner, for despite the attempts of many to praise the *Ode*, no one could claim that it was great poetry.

The evening was to be rounded off with a Grand Masquerade Ball, and a pyrotechnical display at 8 p.m. on the opposite side of the river. In the event, the fireworks did not materialize, and the ball itself was under considerable threat, for by now the Avon had overflowed its banks, and in view of the fact that Venetian masks had been called for that evening, gondolas would have been more appropriate conveyances to the amphitheatre than horses and carriages, which were in some two feet of water.

At noon on Friday it was still raining, and there was even less hope that the pageant would now be able to take place. There was, however, the Jubilee Cup horse-race with a prize of fifty pounds, though only five runners took part. As the day drew on, the rain finally eased, the fireworks that could be let off were sent up into the skies, and the final ball of the Jubilee began. Despite the initial difficulty in finding any beds at all in Stratford, by Saturday the guests had all departed, and the little town was left to mull over the recent events that had so disrupted its usual calm.

The London papers had a field-day, and Samuel Foote was certainly not slow to seize upon the more amusing possibilities of the affair, which he described as: 'A public invitation, urged by puffing, to go post without horses to an obscure borough without representatives, governed by a mayor and alderman who are no magistrates, to celebrate a poet whose works have made him immortal, by an ode without poetry, music without harmony, dinners without victuals, and lodgings without beds; a masquerade where half the people appeared bare-faced, a horse-race up to the knees in water, fireworks extinguished as soon as they were lighted, and a gingerbread amphitheatre which tumbled to pieces as soon as it was finished.'[21]

One of those who appeared barefaced at the masquerade was James Boswell. He went as a Corsican, because the freedom of Corsica was then very much his concern, and to appear, therefore, in a mask at a masquerade would not have been supporting the courage of the Corsicans in their struggle. Boswell had taken so many pains not only with his costume, but in getting to Stratford itself, because he was convinced that the *bon ton* would all be there. It would, therefore, be a glittering social occasion, as well as an excellent opportunity for airing his views on Corsica. He even took with him a poem that he planned to recite at a suitable moment, since odes were to be the order of the day. With no apparent sense of the ridiculous, he described himself thus in the *London*

An engraving by S. Wale of J. Miller's impression of Boswell in his costume for the Jubilee ball, when he was a strong supporter of Corsican independence. In the event, even the indefatigable Boswell realized that the Jubilee had failed to live up to its promise and he declared, 'I was in a little village in wet weather and knew not how to get away'. (*National Portrait Gallery*)

Magazine: 'He wore a short dark-coloured coat of coarse cloth, scarlet waistcoat and breeches, and black spatterdashes; his cap or bonnet was of black cloth; on the front of it was embroidered in gold letters *Viva la Libertà*, and on one side of it was a handsome blue feather and cockade, so that it had an elegant as well as a warlike appearance. On the breast of his coat was sewed a Moor's head, the crest of Corsica, surrounded with branches of laurel. He had also a cartridge pouch, into which was stuck a stiletto, and on his left side a pistol was hung upon the belt of his cartridge-pouch. He had a fusee slung across his shoulder, wore no powder in his hair, but had it plaited, at its full length with a knot of blue ribbands at the end of it.' Then, as if he had suddenly remembered that it was a Shakespeare commemoration, after all, and not a rally for Corsican independence: 'He had, by way of a staff, a very curious vine all of one piece with a bird finely carved upon it, emblematical of the sweet Bard of Avon. He wore no mask, saying it was not proper for a gallant Corsican.'[22]

Despite Boswell's attempt at glorifying the occasion, there was no doubt that it was Garrick's greatest débâcle since the *Chinese Festival*. Something had to be done, and Garrick began to turn things over in his mind. He said to Lacy: 'Be patient, my dear sir, I'll bring out a piece shall indemnify us.' Once back in London, however, he acted on the suggestion that was apparently put to him by Benjamin Wilson in the coach going back from Stratford, that the *Ode* and Jubilee should be brought to the London stage.[23] By 2 October, when Garrick wrote to Joseph Cradock, preparations were already in hand, though Colman had got wind of the scheme and was preparing his rival attraction at Covent Garden.[24] In the same letter Garrick expressed surprise at this, but after all, it was only what he had done to Rich over the rival productions they had mounted to celebrate the coronation of George III. Colman's piece, entitled *Man and Wife; or, the Stratford Jubilee*, opened on 7 October at Covent Garden, but ran for only eleven nights. Garrick's *The Jubilee*, however, opened on 14 October and ran for ninety-two performances.

Initially it was the *Ode* alone that had been announced for Drury Lane for 30 September, thus beating Colman by a week. Garrick gave it after a performance of *The Country Girl* that evening, 'to a crammed house . . . and indeed with astonishing success', as he wrote to William Hunt on 2 October 1769.[25] There were four performances in all, and then Garrick had a brilliant inspiration. There was no doubt that there had been many farcical aspects of the Stratford Jubilee, which Foote for one — as we have seen — had lost no time in exploiting. So be it. All would be grist to Garrick's mill. The result was *The Jubilee*, in which he was able to include 'the procession, as it was intended for Stratford on Avon'. Safe under the roof of Drury Lane, Lacy had no qualms about allowing the 'clothes' to walk now.

In the first scene, Goody Benson of Stratford is in her kitchen, discussing the projected Jubilee with her neighbour Margery Jarvis and Ralph, a country yokel. They voice all the fears and prejudices of the real Stratford folk as they faced the forthcoming invasion, and asked themselves what this 'Jubilee' might be. The scene then changes to a street in Stratford where, because of the shortage of beds, an Irishman has been obliged to spend the night in a post-chaise. Awakened by the noise and singing, he demands to know what it is all about, and at this point Garrick incorporated all the charges made by Foote against the Jubilee. With considerable dramatic skill, Garrick then builds up the pace from scene to scene, and for the third scene he moves to the yard of the White Lion Inn, where all the rooms have names of Shakespeare plays. The bustle on the stage is supremely well managed, and as Garrick himself noted: 'This is perhaps a scene of the most regular confusion that was ever exhibited.'[26] In the midst of all the uproar, hot rolls are to be sent to 'Julius Caesar', and Fribble orders jellies to be sent to 'Love's Labour Lost' [*sic*]. Two pedlars attempt to sell competing wares made from the famous mulberry-tree, and in the ensuing fracas it appears that neither has the genuine articles. This, however, is a cue for the mulberry-tree song, which in turn marks the start of the pageant of Shakespeare characters, 'with bells ringing, fifes playing, drums beating and cannon firing'. According to Garrick, this meant that 'in the procession, every scene in the different plays represents some capital part of it in action'. However, he knew too well that action would be very difficult to incorporate into a moving procession on stage, so we must assume that, for the most part, the characters simply walked in procession. In a contemporary engraving, the characters are shown with their most famous lines, or suitably characteristic ones, issuing from their mouths in speech balloons, rather as in children's comics, though this does not claim to be an accurate representation of what was meant to have taken place either at Stratford or at Drury Lane.

The end of the pageant is not the end of the play, however, though a succession of familiar characters and pleasing costumes and props must have delighted the audience. With sure dramatic sense, Garrick has a breathing space before the final piece of spectacle. The Irishman appears, only to find that the 'Pagans are all gone already'. He has spent too much time drinking, and now has to return to his homeland without ever having seen anything of the Jubilee. Since they have all gone to 'the great round house on the Meadow', however, he decides that he will try to see at least a glimpse before he departs. The last scene is, according to Garrick, in his own hand: '[A] magnificent transparent one, in which the capital characters of Shakespeare are exhibited at full length, with Shakespeare's statue in the middle crowned by Tragedy and Comedy, fairies and cupids surrounding him, and all the banners waving at the upper end. Then enter the dancers, and then the Tragic and Comic troops, and range themselves in the scene.' Finally: 'Every character tragic and comic join[s] in the chorus . . . during which the guns fire, bells ring, etc, etc, and the audience applaud.

> Bravo Jubilee!
> Shakespeare for ever!'

In Lacy's opinion, 'Davy is an able projector, sir. This was a devilish lucky piece.' Possibly, and it does sound rather like the finale of a good old-fashioned pantomime, but there is no doubt that Garrick, in the words of Sir Sidney Lee, with his Jubilee, 'gave an impetus to the Shakespearean cult at Stratford which thenceforth steadily developed into a national vogue, and helped to quicken the popular enthusiasm'. [27]

CHAPTER EIGHT

ADELPHI TERRACE

THE Jubilee left Garrick exhausted. As he wrote to the actress turned novelist and playwright Elizabeth Griffith on 15 September (1769): 'He was so much out of order that he was not able to attend the theatre but obliged to return directly into the country, where he continues very unfit for any kind of business.'[1] And as William Hunt wrote to Garrick on 28 September: 'I expect you'll burn every letter with a Stratford post-mark upon it, without opening it.'[2] In truth, there may well have been a good deal of licking of wounds going on at Hampton. Nevertheless, once Garrick had recovered, the *Ode* was duly published, and copies were sent to Jean Baptiste Antoine Suard, with a covering letter in which was the reference to Shakespeare as 'the god of my idolatry',[3] as well as to Voltaire: 'I have taken the liberty of offering my small poetical tribute to the first genius in the world. As nobody has written so well and so forcibly against the principles of intoleration as M. de Voltaire, I hope he will excuse the excess of zeal with which I have endeavoured to paint on this *Ode* the powers of our great dramatic poet, Shakespeare, who is both the founder and chief supporter of the English stage.'[4] This did not, however, prevent Voltaire from declaring: 'The taste [for Shakespeare in England] becomes a religion; and there are in that country many fanatics in respect of that author.'[5] Indeed, offerings such as Garrick's only tended to confirm Voltaire in his opinion.

At about the same time, i.e. October 1769, Garrick replied at great length to a letter from Charles Macklin criticizing the *Ode*. Despite going to such trouble, Garrick himself endorsed the letter: 'Critique of my *Ode* by Macklin. Answer by me. I might have spent my time better than supporting a foolish business against a very foolish man.'[6] But then Garrick always had to answer criticism, and anything that touched his reputation was usually replied to swiftly and exhaustively.

He put himself about for another cause towards the end of the year on behalf of the Reverend Evan Lloyd, who had a living in London as well as Wales, where he was being threatened by the local squire with prosecution for non-residence. The only way Lloyd could see to avoid this was by becoming chaplain to a nobleman, which would qualify him for legal dispensation from residence. Garrick thereupon approached Lord Verney, who was second Earl Verney and third Viscount Fermanagh in the peerage of Ireland. Thinking that he had already achieved their aim, Garrick wrote to Lloyd on 4 December 1769 and addressed him as 'My dear Chaplain'. Ten days later he had to write again to Lloyd to

(*see previous page and page 153*)
A view of the Adelphi (1768–74) from the Thames, showing the Royal Terrace, which eventually became Garrick's London home. (Durham Yard, demolished to make way for the Adelphi, was where David Garrick set up in the wine trade in partnership with his brother Peter in the late 1730s.) (*Mansell Collection*)

144

acknowledge that his efforts had been wasted.[7] Since the Verney title was an Irish one, the office of chaplain to Lord Verney would only carry dispensation from residence for Lloyd in Ireland. Garrick tried both the Spencers and the Wilmots: 'I have set my brain again to work for you, and will procure a British lord, if possible, for love or money. A Scotch lord would do, but I would much rather have an English one. I shall beat about, and have no doubt of starting some game.' In the event, however, Garrick seems to drawn a complete blank, though he continued for some time in trying to improve Lloyd's lot.

On 21 February 1770, Garrick played Lear for the first time since 1763. He described it as a 'laborious part' in one letter,[8] and then two days later, in a letter to the lawyer Edward Tighe dated 23 February, probably the same year, set down his thoughts on the character, which are most interesting: 'Lear is certainly a *weak* man, it is part of his character —

Garrick's portrayal of Lear, seen here in an engraving by McArdell of Benjamin Wilson's painting, was said to have been based on the observation from life of an old man whose tragedy was similar to that of Lear. Sir Joshua Reynolds was so moved by Garrick's last performance of the part that it took him three days to recover, and many other members of the audience in the house were moved to tears. (*Mansell Collection*)

violent, old and *weakly* fond of his daughters. Here we agree, but I cannot possibly agree . . . that the effect of his distress is diminished by his being an *old fool*. His weakness proceeds from his age (fourscore and upwards) and such an old man full of affection, generosity, passion and what not, meeting with what he thought an ungrateful return from his best beloved, Cordelia, and afterwards real ingratitude from his other daughters. An audience must feel his distresses and madness, which is the consequence of them. Nay, I think I might go farther and venture to say that had not the source of his unhappiness proceeded from good qualities carried to excess of folly, but from vices, I really think that the bad part of him would be forgotten in the space of an act, and *his distresses at his years would become objects of pity to an audience.'*[9]

Such a view is not at all surprising to us today, but it was obviously not a widely accepted one in Garrick's day. Samuel Johnson, for example, declared: 'I was many years ago so shocked by Cordelia's death, that I know not whether I ever endured to read again the last scenes of the play till I undertook to revise them as editor.'[10] In fact, although Betterton had used what was more or less Shakespeare's text in the post-Restoration period, after 1681 it was Tate's adaptation which was used for the next century and a half. Lone voices, such as Addison's in *The Spectator* for 16 April 1711, complained that in this version the play had lost half its beauty, and even Garrick, whilst discarding many of Tate's additions, still kept the interpolated love scenes between Edgar and Cordelia, along with the happy ending. Such was the climate of the age, and when Lamb attacked Garrick, he ought to have attacked public taste *tout court*: 'It is not enough that Cordelia is a daughter, she must shine as a lover too. Tate has put his hook into the nostrils of this Leviathan, for Garrick and his followers, the showmen of the scene, to draw the mighty beast about more easily. A happy ending! — if the living martyrdom that Lear had gone through — the flaying of his feelings alive, did not make a fair dismissal from the stage of life the only decorous thing for him. If he is to live and be happy after . . . why torment us with all this unnecessary sympathy? . . . as if at his years, and with his experience, anything was left but to die.'[11] But, of course, in some respects Lamb's attitude is equally unrealistic in terms of the drama when seen on stage. The audience's sympathy would not be made 'unnecessary' simply because Lear did not die at the end of the play. If a plausible character has been created, and the audience drawn into the drama, then the effect is not destroyed by the ending of the play. In any case, in terms of dramatic impact, the climax of Lear's development really comes with his total self-recognition in Act III, scene iv. Once he has crossed that momentous threshold, the rest is relatively less important. In his analysis of the character in dramatic terms, Garrick was entirely correct in his assessment of how and why the play worked on the stage, which hardly seems to have come into Lamb's estimate. But Garrick was a man of his time, and with all his love and knowledge of Shakespeare, there was a limit to how far he could have been expected to see the plays as subsequent generations have seen them, let alone take the audience of his day along with him.

Oddly enough it was *Lear* — or more precisely the description of the cliffs at Dover in the play — that came to mind on 7 June 1770, when Charles Burney set out on his continental tour. Garrick supplied him with letters — for example, to his Italian valet, Antonio Carara, who often travelled on the Continent, and to Suard[12] — though Burney had great difficulty in delivering them, certainly when he was in Paris, for the recipients never seemed to be at home; which caused Burney some unease: 'All this time I have not delivered one of Garrick's letters — of which I have four — and two of them full of commissions for him and Mrs G. which hang upon my mind and plague me more than all I have to do for myself. I have not been able, after many hours spent in vain every day almost to find M. Monnet, who was the first I wished to see, as from him I was to have an address to the rest. I begin to think I shall leave this place without delivering those letters which are written merely in my favour, as I shall not have time to avail myself of any civilities his friends may offer.'[13] But then Dr Burney had not gone for civilities. As he set down in a letter to Garrick from Naples on 17 October 1770, he quite clearly had two objects in view: 'The one to get, from the libraries to the viva voce conversation of the learned, what information I could relative to the music of the ancients; and the other was to judge with my own eyes of the present state of modern music in the places through which I should pass, from the performance and conversation of the first musicians in Italy.'[14] Garrick fully encouraged Burney in the project, not only giving help with letters of introduction where he could, but also giving advice as to how he ought to publish the fruits of his labours. Although Burney intended publishing his researches as part of his *General History of Music* eventually, he took the advice of Garrick and others, and published in advance the account of his tour in two volumes: France and Italy in 1771,

Charles Burney (1726–1814) as portrayed by Reynolds in 1781. Garrick was very fond of the Burney family in general and he, for his part, was a great favourite of the Burney children. Garrick helped Burney considerably when he was abroad from 1763 to 1765 by buying books for the musicologist and sending him accounts of concerts and recitals. When Burney himself went abroad from 1770 to 1772 he was given much practical help, such as letters of introduction to important friends and acquaintances of Garrick. (*National Portrait Gallery*)

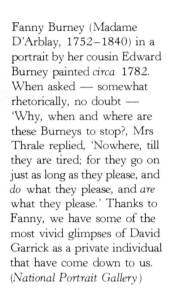

Fanny Burney (Madame D'Arblay, 1752–1840) in a portrait by her cousin Edward Burney painted *circa* 1782. When asked — somewhat rhetorically, no doubt — 'Why, when and where are these Burneys to stop?', Mrs Thrale replied, 'Nowhere, till they are tired; for they go on just as long as they please, and *do* what they please, and *are* what they please.' Thanks to Fanny, we have some of the most vivid glimpses of David Garrick as a private individual that have come down to us. (*National Portrait Gallery*)

and Germany, the Netherlands, and United Provinces, in 1773. They were received with enthusiasm, and Johnson told Burney that it was his 'elegant and entertaining travels' that he had in mind when he wrote his *Journey to the Western Islands of Scotland*.

Burney was now established as a man of letters, and was henceforth 'constantly invited and regarded as a member' by the intellectual society of London, and in particular by the blue stockings Mrs Vesey and Mrs Montagu. As his daughter Fanny wrote in her *Memoirs of Dr Burney* (1832): 'From this period the profession of Dr Burney, however highly he was raised in it, seemed but of secondary consideration for him in the world; where, now, the higher rank was assigned him of a man of letters, from the general admiration accorded to his Tours.' That admiration was almost universally regarded as merited, and even more so by those who knew him intimately. On the other hand, Fanny did a considerable amount of editing when preparing her father's memoirs for publication, and destroyed a large amount of fascinating material which did not entirely accord with the image she was determined to present of him. [15]

London society was still small enough for almost everyone of distinction to know one another, but even so, there were smaller, frequently overlapping circles within that society, with certain members belonging to several circles. Nor was society static. Friendships waxed and waned, reputations were made and lost. People who at first acquaintance accepted the general view about such and such a person, might well find that he or she was quite a different character when properly known.

That summer of Dr Burney's departure (1770) the Garricks had once more paid visits in the country. In the first week of August, for example, they were with the Earl of Exeter at Burghley House, where other members of the company included Richard Owen Cambridge, a gentleman of letters and leisure; William Patoun, the painter and connoisseur; Benjamin West, the American-born history-painter, and Capability Brown, who had landscaped the grounds at Burghley. [16] From there Garrick probably went on to Thurlow, the home of Francis Hare-Naylor in Suffolk, since there is a letter sent from there dated 10 August, and probably for this year. [17]

Despite the summer break, Garrick was forced by ill health to go to Bath again, where he spent October and part of November. He came back to London on 20 November to find a letter from William Hunt of Stratford about money — £80 — he had lost on the Jubilee. [18] Garrick's reaction was that he had had to pay out some £2,000 or more out of his own pocket, whilst conveniently ignoring the success of the Drury Lane venture afterwards: of course, the proceeds of that went into the general coffers of the theatre. Doubtless his health did not help, and what also irritated Garrick was the fact that Hunt had written two letters to George Garrick which had gone unanswered. Garrick had known nothing of them, and he disliked being put in that situation. It was an unfortunate and delayed aftermath of that event, and in the New Year Garrick took his brother to task in a strongly worded letter of 25 January 1771: 'Dear Brother, I sit down at this time to do a most disagreeable thing to me, which is to tax you with neglect, unkindness, and I will not add injustice to me. I have suffered much of late, I have hid my uneasiness as well as I could, I have had moments of good spirits, but my mind [h]as still returned to you, and your behaviour to me.'[19] He then went on to say that he had noticed that George was seemingly always in a hurry to get away from him, as if to avoid having to discuss matters. Garrick pointed out how George had access to all Garrick's private thoughts, permission to open his letters, and access to all his business affairs. However, George, it seemed, had for some time been keeping up a country house, horses and a coach, without giving Garrick the least hint of their existence. David had intended paying the Jubilee deficit out of the Peter Fermignac estate (a first cousin who had died on 26 March 1770), but had not pressed George because he assumed that he was in financial difficulties — or certainly not at ease. Instead he now discovered that George was really quite well off. He thereupon wanted the estate settled. Garrick still had received no account by June 1771, and in fact the estate had not been fully administered as late as 1806.

Garrick's state of mind was not improved by a bad attack of gout which afflicted him during the first half of February (1771). Such was the national interest that the *London Chronicle* carried regular reports on his progress. This attack lasted for almost two months, and more and more

An engraving entitled *The Procession*, showing Johnson and Boswell followed by Johnson's Negro servant, Francis Barber. Once Boswell had made Johnson's acquaintance, it was not long before he became friendly with the Doctor's circle, which automatically brought David Garrick into ken, and the two men were often in each other's company and exchanged letters. (*Mansell Collection*)

Garrick began to feel that it was time for him to contemplate retirement. As he wrote to Boswell on 18 April: 'Nothing till lately could subdue my spirits, but I begin to discover that I am growing old, and though I have no Apollo at my elbow, yet sickness *vellit et admonuit* [plucked my ear and warned me] that it is time for me to get into port and drop my anchor.'[20]

He was contemplating another peregrination for the summer, but before he could leave he had to deal with more repercussions of the Jubilee debts, and word of a pirated version of his play being mounted in Dublin. Despite the noises he made, in reply to a letter from the actor John Moody, there was very little that he could do about it. The letter, dated 6 June 1771, was of more use for the practical advice it gave Moody about the piles with which he was afflicted: 'I am very sorry that you have been plagued with that cursed distemper the piles. Live abstemiously for a little while, and take every night a large teaspoonful of flower of brimstone (night and morning) mixed up with honey or treacle, and you will be the better for it. You should make up a gallipot of it and take it by way of sweetmeat. Thank your stars for the piles. If you had not them, you would have gout, or stone, or both, and the Devil and all. While I had the piles I had nothing else. Now I am quit of them I have every other disorder.'[21]

The summer was a very social one. On 8 July the Garricks saw Lord and Lady Camden at Egham, and then visited General Conway and his wife, Lady Ailesbury, at Park Place, Berkshire. They went on to stay with Lord Edgcumbe at Mount Edgcumbe in Devonshire — which Garrick described as 'this enchanting place' to Dr Burney — and, on the way back, with Lord Lyttelton at Hagley in Worcestershire. Garrick also had invitations to visit the Earl of Hardwicke, and the Burkes at Gregories. To the former, however, he proposed the following year, when he would be happy to visit the Hardwickes at either Wimpole Hall in Cambridgeshire or Wrest Park in Bedfordshire, and to the latter he expressed the hope that he would be able to call on his way back from Hagley. After the summer holiday, it was back to the theatre and the prospect of a change of London home.

In 1768 the brothers Adam leased a property known as Durham Yard, between the Thames and the Strand, which belonged to the Duke of St Albans, and planned to build a terrace of houses overlooking the river. The plans were by Robert Adam, but the business itself was chiefly in the hands of his brothers. To symbolize their brotherly involvement, they decided to call it the Adelphi. Unfortunately, their grand design was a financial failure, and in the end had to be disposed of by lottery. In 1773 Parliament authorized the Adam brothers to conduct the lottery, tickets for which went on sale in December that year, and the lots were drawn on 1 March 1774.

It was known, however, as early as December 1771 that the Garricks were proposing to move to the Adelphi, into number 5 Royal Terrace, though the project was still not complete when they moved in during March 1772. In a letter to the Greek scholar and friend of Dr Johnson, Bennet Langton, dated 14 March 1772, Garrick said that his wife was 'almost killed with the fatigue of removing to the Adelphi, where we shall be fixed in the next week. Mr Beauclerk is to be our neighbour.'[22] This was Topham Beauclerk, a relative of the Duke of St Albans, who was to live at number 3, whilst Robert Adam himself lived next door to the Garricks.

The front of the terrace faced south across the Thames, and was only demolished immediately prior to World War II. The plate from the third volume of *The Works in Architecture of Robert and James Adam Esquires* shows us what the effect of the terrace was in the eighteenth century, and a photograph taken in the years leading up to its demolition gives some idea of the finished appearance. Cleaning of the stonework, which would certainly have been carried out today, would give a less heavy impression.

Of the interiors, only fragments survive. The medallions painted by Antonio Zucchi for the drawing-room ceiling at number 4 — Adam's own house — were saved and subsequently passed though the antique trade. The whole ceiling from Garrick's own drawing-room was saved and presented by the National Art Collections Fund to the Victoria and Albert Museum, where it has been restored and may be compared with the drawing for it now in Sir John Soane's Museum. Also in the possession of the Victoria and Albert Museum is a painted pine and marble fireplace from the ground-floor front room at number five, and a painted pine doorway from number ten.

A glance through the list of work carried out by the Adam brothers at this time gives the names of patrons, many of whom were either close friends or acquaintances of the Garricks. There was the rebuilding of 20 St James's Square for Sir Watkin Williams-Wynn, and work for Richard Rigby, who had plans to turn Mistley into a spa. Only an attractive fountain in the village, incorporating a swan, remains to testify to what might have been, though the two towers of Robert Adam's church still

(*right*)
The ceiling from Garrick's house, saved when the Royal Terrace was demolished in 1936, and re-erected in the Victoria and Albert Museum. (*Victoria and Albert Museum*)

(*far right*)
The fireplace from the ground-floor front room of Garrick's house, of painted pine and marble, designed by Adam. (*Victoria and Albert Museum*)

A doorway of painted pine from number ten, Royal Terrace, Adelphi, *circa* 1770. The elegance of proportion and application of Classical detail to domestic accommodation made the terrace one of the architectural glories of London, and its loss a tragedy. As Sacheverell Sitwell wrote, 'The Adelphi, wilfully, and of cupidity was pulled down. Willing hands did more damage to London than a German landmine.' (*Victoria and Albert Museum*)

survive. Unfortunately, the hall was demolished in the nineteenth century when the railway advanced to Harwich, and the body of the church went in 1870. The designs, however, published in volume two of the *Works*, show plans for lodges, gates, an inn, bathing pavilion, fountains and pools and a bathing-centre.

Mrs Montagu also appears amongst the patrons of the Adam brothers, and in the Soane Museum are complementary designs for a carpet and ceiling for her house in Hill Street. She was to move to Portman Square by this time, however — at any rate by the mid-1770s — and presumably the carpet went with her. Unfortunately, the second house was burnt down in 1941.

One of the unifying features of this circle of friends was their convergence of views on what was innovation in architecture and interior decoration. With Mrs Montagu, perhaps, it was simply the pursuit of fashion — or what Samuel Foote had labelled 'Taste'. As she wrote in a letter of 20 July 1779 to the Duchess of Portland, it was 'according to the present fashion' that she was having her ceilings painted 'in various colours'. But if one looks above the transient, one sees a trio of such men as Robert Adam, Joshua Reynolds and David Garrick as representing — in the words of one of Robert Adam's biographers — 'a high quality of endeavour' in their respective fields of architecture, painting and theatre, and indeed setting 'new standards of taste and perfection'. [23] There would always be Dr Johnson round the corner to condemn the work as consuming 'labour disproportionate to its utility', and indeed when, as at Kedleston, this ran to Adam's gilding the sash-bars of the windows on the outside of the house, then one can have some sympathy with such a view. Then there were times when even those who were usually more appreciative of Adam than not, such as Horace Walpole, might well have their reservations about some of his work. Walpole was never complimentary about the Adelphi, and of the entrance gateway and screen to Syon House he wrote: 'It is all lace and embroidery, and as *croquant* as his frames for tables; consequently most improper to be exposed in the high road to Brentford.' [24]

Garrick was no slavish follower of fashion, for although he admired this 'new' taste, in company with one section of his friends, there were plenty on the other hand who were not carried away by Adam. Moreover, these were aristocratic friends to whose judgement Garrick might have been expected to defer if he was simply currying favour or hoping to climb socially. We see the same taste reflected in the furniture from his villa at Hampton, now in the possession of the Victoria and Albert Museum. He bought what he did because it pleased both himself and his wife, and he did not need to make any apologies for their taste.

At about the time that the Adelphi plans were becoming reality — i.e. the beginning of June 1770 — we have the first extant letters from Garrick to Mrs Montagu. They were now great friends, though when Garrick first mentioned her in the correspondence, as we saw, in a letter to Colman of November 1764, she was 'Madame la précieuse', and he rather gloated over the fact that all she had obtained from Lord Bath's will had been a pair of ear-rings and a ring.[25] Perhaps at that point Garrick's friendship with Colman was more important to him, for he had in fact known Mrs Montagu since at least 1752, when they had dined together. In the interval his friendship with Colman had waned, however, and Garrick's affection for Mrs Montagu had blossomed, so that by 2 May 1772, when he wrote to her from Hampton, he encouraged her to breathe the fresh air with 'Adam and Eve' in what was, by implication, a Garden of Eden only a few miles from town. 'I could wish that your supreme spirit on the full gallop would but just recollect that it has a body (alas for us not the stoutest) to drag after it. You can never die, but you will hurry off your flesh by degrees, upon earth, and then your spirit, having shaken off encumbrances, will mount to its proper element and habitation, and repose itself to all eternity. I shall miss you some fine morning, and upon enquiring after you, some of my astronomical friends will tell me that you passed over St Paul's about a quarter after eleven.'[26]

Some two or three weeks later he had another friend to worry about, though this worry was of a very different nature. As mentioned on page 109, Isaac Bickerstaffe, publicly accused of homosexuality, which was then a capital crime, had fled to France earlier in the month, and a saddened Garrick wrote to Robert Jephson on 19 May referring to: 'The late accident which, I fear, will embitter the life of miserable B[ickerstaffe]! The affair is reported here just as you seem to have heard it. He is gone, and has written to Mr Griffin the bookseller a letter which shocked me beyond imagination. All his friends hang their heads and grieve sincerely at his misfortune. My wife and I have long thought him to be out of his mind. He has hurried away in the midst of conversation, without any apparent reason for it. The story they tell, if true, is a most unaccountable one; but the watch, seal and ring are in the soldier's hands, and B would not claim

Adam's designs for the church at Mistley in Essex (1776) extended to the pulpit, which in this drawing embraces elements of both Classical and Gothic forms, with even a hint of Chinoiserie. In 1763 Adam had collaborated with 'Capability' Brown on the church at Croome D'Abitot in Worcestershire, providing the interior fittings for the church Brown himself had designed, and an interest in Gothic style can be found even earlier in Adam's career. (*Sir John Soane's Museum*)

A drawing for a carpet for Mrs Montagu, *circa* 1766, now in Sir John Soane's Museum. Adam's design subtly echoed the ceiling of the room in Mrs Montagu's house in Hill Street for which the carpet was designed, though the roundels of the ceiling corners became ovals in the carpet. On the other hand, the Chinoiserie in the ovals reappears in the ceiling in a set of eight Chinoiserie motifs around the central circle, which is rare in Adam's work. (*Sir John Soane's Museum*)

them, but absconded. This business has hurt me greatly, as well as my wife. The stage has a great loss.'[27] On 24 June, Bickerstaffe wrote a pitiful letter in French to Garrick, who endorsed it: 'from that poor wretch Bickerstaffe — I could not answer it'.

That was not to be the end of the matter, however, as far as Garrick was concerned. He was always being bombarded with plays, either from the authors themselves or some patron or friend who, seemingly incapable of distinguishing good from bad, or blinded by affection, expected Garrick to welcome the piece with joy and gratitude. There certainly had been occasions when he accepted work sent to him in this way, and there were times, it must be said, when he had tried to help a friend by putting on an indifferent play, and then lived to regret it. Bickerstaffe's hurried departure unfortunately coincided with a contretemps over yet another unsolicited play which Garrick had refused. The affair is recorded in a sequence of four letters to Doctor William Kenrick, who maintained that he had submitted his play *The Duellist* to Garrick, who returned it without having read a single line.[28] This turned into an ill-tempered wrangle, and Kenrick maintained that his publisher had told him that Garrick, Griffin and Becket had planned to waylay him and beat him. There was a letter dated 20 June, now lost, but summarized in a Puttick and Simpson catalogue of 1862, which Garrick wrote to Thompson from the Adelphi, in which he said that he had been going to beat Kenrick 'for his infamy'. Kenrick's eventual retaliation was to publish in July 1772 a lampoon called *Love in the Suds, Being the Lamentation of Roscius for the Loss of his Nyky*. 'Nyky' was, of course, none other than Bickerstaffe, and in this way Kenrick tried to associate Garrick's name with the scandal.

On 7 July, Garrick instituted a suit for libel against Kenrick. On 7 October, however, the *Morning Chronicle* told its readers that Garrick had dropped his prosecution, though this was not true. Eventually, on 23 November, Kenrick made an apology to Garrick in the *Public Advertiser* and promised to withdraw *Love in the Suds* and stop its sale. It had been an unpleasant episode, to say the least.

Increasingly now Garrick talked of retirement, and in a letter of 17 June 1773 to Richard Penn (1735–1811), grandson of William Penn, who had placed a bet on the actor's age and then written to him to verify it, Garrick replied: 'Your Excellency knows that persons upon the stage, like ladies upon the town, must endeavour by dress, paint and candlelight to set themselves off for what they are not, and that a publication of registers would ruin the practice of half the Antonys and Cleopatras in London. My age (thanks to Your Excellency's proclamation of it) has been published with a proper certificate in all the papers, so that I have been obliged to resign all the love-making ravishing heroes and gentlemen in the dramatis personae... Your opinion, though erroneous, is a kind of warning to me, which my vanity has prevented me from taking before; and as you have so kindly pulled off my mask, it is time for me to make my exit.'[29] There is a rather bitter-sweet tone to the letter, and despite the generally light, tongue-in-cheek air, not far below the surface is the sadness of mortality. Time was running out, and for someone like Garrick, who had always reacted to any sort of reflection touching himself, it was a hard path to tread.

As an example of how Garrick was ever sensitive to what other people said, Joseph Cradock, in his old age, wrote that: 'Garrick rendered his life miserable by believing and encouraging tale-bearers and feeling hurt in the extreme at every little squib that appeared in the daily prints and novels of the day. Tom King, the actor, and Becket the bookseller were the persons who brought Garrick every disagreeable paragraph and tittle-tattle of the day. Becket was a sort of runner for Garrick. I have called on Garrick in the morning and no person could be in higher spirits, and when I have repeated my visit about an hour or two after, I have found him quite the reverse; depressed by the daily tales etc of the above gentlemen.'[30] There is no doubt that reputation was of immense importance to Garrick, and indeed, as a Shakespearian, he could well say with Cassio, that if he had lost his reputation, then he had indeed 'lost the immortal part of myself, and what remains is bestial'. Such deep concern may well have amounted to vanity, in the eyes of some who had dealings with Garrick, and whenever he has been given a bad press, vanity has been one of the charges most often levelled against him.

If he was indeed vain, then one slight that he bore patiently for almost nine years was the fact that he was not admitted to The Club which had been founded in 1764 by Johnson and some of their closest friends. Membership was to be restricted to eight, then twelve, and The Club met at the Turk's Head in Gerrard Street, Soho, once a week at seven p.m. Garrick thought that it sounded a most admirable institution, and is reputed to have said to Reynolds: 'I think I shall be of you!' When this was reported to Johnson, however, the Doctor was by no means of the same opinion: 'He'll be of us! How does he know we will *permit* him? The first duke in England has no right to hold such language.'

Another member of The Club for a time (he later withdrew) was a rich attorney, now retired and a magistrate, John Hawkins, who lived on Twickenham Common, not far from Garrick's villa at Hampton. According to Hawkins' daughter, Letitia Matilda, Garrick often asked her father whether he had been at The Club, and what they had talked of. He ventured to suggest that he was excluded because he was neither a poet nor a writer — but there were others in The Club who were in risk of similar disqualification. What Hawkins had not the heart to tell Garrick, apparently, was the fact that when he had approached the Doctor on Garrick's behalf, the answer was unequivocal: 'He will disturb us, sir, by his buffoonery.' There was an ungracious side to Johnson that was often no less than boorish. Even so, Boswell denied that he had gone so far as to threaten to blackball Garrick if he was proposed for The Club, which is what Mrs Thrale maintained. When Garrick was finally elected in 1773 — the same year as Boswell — he behaved with discretion and did not disturb The Club. In fact, Johnson was moved to remark that Garrick 'was the first man in the world for sprightly conversation', and after his death he moved that Garrick's place should not be filled for a year by way of tribute. Moreover, after his death it became known as The Literary Club.

The snows of the winter of 1773/4 gave way to floods, and Kitty Clive wrote from her cottage at Twickenham: 'I might date this letter from the Ark. We are so surrounded by water that it is impossible for any carriage to come to me, or for me to stir out — so that at present my heavenly place is a little devilish.' Hardly a promising start to a year that was to mark the twenty-fifth anniversary of the Garricks' marriage, and one which found Garrick himself complaining of gout and a bad cold. There was to be a further source of trouble, and none of his own doing, caused by the demise of his partner James Lacy on 25 January 1774.

Lacy's only son, Willoughby (1749–1831), inherited his father's position and wealth, but not his wisdom. He lived far too extravagantly, and was heavily in debt. He eventually sold his part of the Drury Lane patent to Sheridan, which was to be a source of considerable trouble for Garrick. Before this, however, Lacy had aspirations to a partnership with Garrick throughout the whole domain of the theatre, which had never actually been the case with his father, despite what Garrick had felt on occasions, and been driven to have clarified.

On 25 February, Willoughby Lacy wrote to Garrick that he had taken legal advice and that he had, in his opinion, 'an equal right' with Garrick in 'every branch of the business relative to the theatre'.[31] This had anticipated matters somewhat, for Lacy had told Garrick that he would, by the following day at 3 o'clock, answer Garrick, instead of which he sent a note — the one referred to above — announcing that he had consulted a lawyer. In a rather frosty note, therefore, of 26 February, Garrick let Lacy know that if he had taken legal advice, then Garrick would do the same: 'After waiting till three o'clock (according to your appointment) to receive your answer on my several proposals for referring our differences, I was surprised to find (by your note, which I received late last night) that you have consulted Counsel in a less amicable way than I proposed. You do me justice in supposing that I have no wish to deprive you of any right you are entitled to. I commend your prudence, and before I give you a final answer I shall follow your example and be properly advised.'[32] Lacy's reply to this, dated 28 February, was endorsed by Garrick: 'From Lacy Junior to sell his part of the patent.' It was to be some time, however, before it actually came to that.

On 6 March a new member of The Club, George Steevens, wrote to Garrick: 'Many thanks both for your suffrage and your congratulations, for they are equally honourable to me. I shall not fail to join The Club on

Engraved portrait by Heath of Hannah More (1745–1833), published on 1 May 1798. Garrick gave her the nickname of 'Nine', as the embodiment of the Nine Muses, and developed a deep friendship with her, almost as if she were his own child. Not all Garrick's circle appreciated Hannah More, however, and an exasperated Kitty Clive once wrote: 'Pray what is the meaning of a hundred Miss Moors [sic] coming purring about you with their poems and plays and romances? Send them to Bristol with a flea in their ears.' (*Mansell Collection*)

Friday evening. Dr Johnson desires I will call on him, and he will introduce me. Pray, what is the usual time of meeting?'[33] From Garrick's reply, dated 8 March, it seems that at the same time as Steevens had been elected, Goldsmith had proposed Edward Gibbon (1734–94), but he had been blackballed on that occasion.

On 18 May 1774, Garrick handed over to the Theatrical Fund — which he had set up by donations and benefit performances in May 1766 — 'possessions and securities' amounting to £2,918. 11s. 9d., as the records of the Fund tell us. It was a cause very dear to his heart, and secured for the acting profession what Handel and others had also done for the musical profession in an age when retirement might well spell destitution.

That same month brought Garrick an introduction to a person who was to figure largely in his last years. Hannah More (1745–1833) came to London from Bristol for the first time in May 1774, with two of her sisters. She knew Sir Joshua Reynolds and his sister, by whom the girls were introduced into London society. Hannah More also knew Mr James Stonhouse (1716–95), to whom she wrote a long letter, including details about Garrick's acting. When Stonhouse knew how much it would mean to Hannah to meet Garrick, he wrote to the actor on 21 May and enclosed a copy of her letter to himself. By 25 May, Garrick had met Hannah and was sending his coach for her and her sisters. In a reference, no doubt, to her letter, he wrote: 'What can Mr Garrick say for the most flattering compliment which he *ever* received? He must be silent.'[34]

For some reason a deep chord was struck almost at once, and Garrick never seems to have had anything but admiration for this woman young enough to be his daughter. Indeed, that may well have been the role she fulfilled for him. Hannah More certainly had some talent as a poet and playwright, but whether she really deserved her nickname, bestowed on her by Garrick, of Nine — implying that she was the embodiment of all the nine muses — is another matter. Even so, Garrick felt able to relax with her, in a way that he found possible with relatively few persons. After his death she rather tended to press her company on Mrs Garrick, though it would have taken more than Hannah More to control totally a person of her character. In the end there was no dramatic break in their friendship. Hannah More simply took to religion, and found the world of the theatre no longer to her taste. She was even unable to bring herself to go and see Mrs Siddons in a revival of her play *Percy* — with which Garrick had given her a good deal of help — and so she and Mrs Garrick drifted apart.

CHAPTER NINE

RETIREMENT

An engraving by Ridley of Reynolds' portrait of Richard Sheridan, published on 30 June 1799. Sheridan was Garrick's successor at Drury Lane, and he received from Garrick both a theatre and an acting company that were in excellent condition. It was perhaps inevitable, therefore, that Sheridan should — in Garrick's opinion — have presided over a decline in the theatre's fortunes. (*Mansell Collection*)

(*see previous page*)
Detail of view of Garrick's house at Hampton (see pages 70 and 71). (*Mansell Collection*)

IN August 1774, Garrick decided to hold an entertainment at Hampton, which was duly reported in the *London Chronicle*: 'Last night Mr Garrick gave a splendid entertainment or Fête Champêtre at his gardens at Hampton. Signior Torre conducted a most brilliant fire-work; an elegant concert of music was performed; and the company, which consisted of a great number of Nobility and Gentry, expressed the utmost satisfaction on the occasion. The temple of Shakespeare, and gardens, were illuminated with 6000 lamps, and the forge of Vulcan made a splendid appearance.'[1]

The entertainment became a means of reviving relations with Mrs Clive, who reproached Garrick for neglecting her. Since 1769, in fact, she had had a house on Horace Walpole's property at nearby Twickenham, and there was no apparent reason why Garrick should not have been a regular visitor, apart from his busy existence, perhaps. Garrick's reply to her, which he himself endorsed: 'My letter to Clive about the renewal of our friendship', breathes the spirit of deep affection and mutual understanding that could only come from such a long-standing friendship that had had its ups and downs. He began with the name he had used for her since at least 1768, 'Pivy', and then promised to take tea with her later that day, possibly 26 August: 'If your heart (somewhat combustible like my own) has played off all the squibs and rockets which lately occasioned a little cracking and bouncing about me, and can receive again the more gentle and pleasing firework of love and friendship, I will be with you at six this evening to revive by the help of those spirits in your tea-kettle lamp that flame which was almost blown out by the flouncing of your petticoat when my name was mentioned. *Tea is a Sov'reign balm for wounded love.* Will you permit me to try the poet's recipe this evening? Can my Pivy know so little of me to think that I prefer the clack of lords and ladies to the enjoyment of humour and genius? I reverence most sincerely your friend and neighbour [Horace Walpole], not because he is the son of one of the first, of first ministers, but because he is himself one of the first ministers of literature. In short, your misconception about that fatal champetre (the Devil take the word) has made me so cross about everything that belongs to it that I curse all squibs, crackers, rockets, air-balloons, mines, serpents and Catherine wheels, and can think of nothing and wish for nothing but laugh, jig, humour, fun, pun, conundrum, carriwitchet and Catherine Clive! I am ever my Pivy's most constant and loving. . . . My wife sends her love and will attend the ceremony this evening.'[2] It does not require a great deal of reading

between the lines to realize what Kitty Clive had taxed Garrick with —
his preference for 'the clack of lords and ladies', for example, and his
coolness towards Horace Walpole — but neither of them was getting any
younger, and it was preferable to spend what time was left to them in
amity.

At a time when Garrick was becoming increasingly aware of his
mortality, those around him seemed to be fading, too, and new faces were
appearing. George Garrick was quite ill this year (1774),and had to spend
time in Bath to recover, which meant more work for Garrick himself.
Then, on 17 January 1775, Sheridan made his début on the London
stage as a writer with *The Rivals* at Covent Garden. Also in 1775 Garrick
tried to get Sheridan's wife, Elizabeth Linley, to appear for him, but her
husband would not agree to it. George was still not well at the beginning
of March that year, when Garrick wrote to Boswell in answer to a letter of
his of 4 February.[3] The letter itself is chiefly interesting for the image of
Dr Johnson quarrelling with James Macpherson over the authenticity of
the Ossianic poems. Johnson's *A Journey to the Western Islands of Scotland*,
in which he further belaboured Macpherson, appeared that same year
(1775), but Boswell's *Journal of a Tour to the Hebrides, with Samuel
Johnson*, did not appear until 1785.

By 1 April, Garrick himself was in Bath, from where he wrote a
sequence of letters to George Colman.[4] Relations had now improved
between the two men. It was in Bath that year, on 18 April, that Hannah
More's first play, *The Inflexible Captive*, was acted at the Theatre Royal. It
had already had a single performance in Bath, however, in February
1774. Garrick did not say in his letters to Colman that he had actually
seen it, but that it had been played with success. From Bath, Garrick
seems to have gone over to Bristol to spend the day with Hannah More,
for he wrote to her on 4 May from Bath referring to such a visit. It was
soon going to be time for him to return to London: 'We begin to think of
leaving this land of Circe where I do this, and do that, and do nothing,
and I go here and go there and go nowhere. Such is the life of Bath and
such the effects of this place upon me. I forget my cares, and my large
family in London, and everything.'[5] Certainly he was back in London by
15 May 1775, and on 27 May the theatre season ended.

That was by no means the end of Garrick's worries, however, for
there were contracts to renew for the following season — with Jane Pope,
for example — and with George still ill, no help from that quarter. He
then had to deal with the troubled amours of his niece Arabella, who had

Mrs Richard Sheridan (née
Elizabeth Linley) as Saint
Cecilia, a portrait by Reynolds
engraved by Thomas Watson.
The assimilation of Elizabeth
Linley to Saint Cecilia was by
no means inappropriate, since
she was a singer of some
accomplishment, and earned
herself the name of 'The Maid
of Bath'. Sheridan married her
in 1773, having taken her
away from Bath to escape her
persecutor, a Major Mathews,
with whom Sheridan fought
two duels. (*Mansell Collection*)

come from Paris to London with Madame Descombes, with whom she lodged, together with her sister Catherine. An officer of dragoons, by name of Molière, who lodged in the same house, had made approaches to Arabella, and although Madame Descombes had put a stop to the affair as soon as she became aware of what was going on, she felt that it would be best to accompany the girls to England.

On 24 June, Madame Descombes went alone to the Adelphi to see the Garricks, who were soon to leave for Mistley, for a few days only, and it was from there on 26 June that Garrick wrote to Arabella, in reply to her letter, written on the day that Madame Descombes was giving her account of the matter. In the circumstances, Garrick was fairly adept at handling things, though at the same time issuing a dire and possibly over-dramatic warning for the future: 'Your letter is so properly written, with such a feeling of your situation, a true compunction for the cause of it, and a resolution to take warning for the future, that I will forgive you, never upbraid you again with the distress you have brought upon us, and yourself, provided that you will show your gratitude by telling every circumstance of this unhappy affair, that I may be the better able to deliver you from the villain, and that hereafter you will let your good sense and delicacy combat with your passions, and not involve yourself and family in the greatest affliction by another unwarrantable, indecent and ruinous connection. Indeed, my dear girl, I cannot account for your rash and almost incredible behaviour. You seemed to have lost the greatest ornaments and safeguards of your sex — *delicacy and apprehension*. When that great barrier that nature has cautiously fixed between passion and prudence is so easily overleaped, even by *our* sex, we see the daily ill consequences, but when *your* sex is possessed with such a madness, the horror that attends it is best described by the number of the most miserable wretches that have fallen a sacrifice to their imprudence.'[6] The descent into circumstantial detail in the postscript is pure comedy: 'Pray send me a full state of this matter, that I may be better able to cope with him and his friends. He says you are violently in love with him, that you will be unhappy without him. Is this true? Is not he near fifty and very plain? [He was, according to Arabella, about thirty-five.] *Good God!* . . . was not he the person you told me in one of your letters was a painter, who knew me, and was with you upon some water party? Pray let me know.'

One must bear in mind, however, that the Garricks never had any children of their own, and seem to have been very fond of their nieces and nephews, as well as the children of their friends. We see the two girls through the eyes of Fanny Burney, for example, in company with their aunt and uncle in 1771; and for Garrick's behaviour with someone who was not related, one may take Letitia Hawkins' description: 'If he saw my brothers at a distance on the lawn, shooting off like an arrow out of a bow, in a spirited chase of them round the garden.'[7] What is also interesting from this same account is the fact that Letitia Hawkins was more afraid of Garrick than of Johnson, giving as her chief reason the fact that neither she nor Johnson himself thought the Doctor to be 'an extraordinary man'. As far as she could recollect — and she was writing some forty years or more after Garrick's death — 'Garrick had a frown, and spoke impetuously; Johnson was slow and kind in his way with children.' But her own description of Garrick's behaviour with her brothers somewhat contradicts this, and from Fanny Burney's accounts of Garrick's light-hearted behaviour in their house, he seems to have been a great favourite with children.

As far as his nieces were concerned, David thought well enough of them to settle £6,000 on each of them, and Arabella eventually married an English soldier, a Captain Shaw, whereas Catherine married only after her uncle's death. Probably he had done the right thing by acting so swiftly and positively when he first became aware of the affair with Molière in late June 1775. All was not quite over, however, for on 26 July, Molière wrote to Arabella to try and reopen the dialogue, but her experiences seem to have been sufficient to stifle any feelings she still may have had for him.

An almost inconsequential letter to the writer Henry Bate of 31 July 1775 introduces into Garrick's world a person who was to become one of the English theatre's greatest stars, Sarah Siddons: 'If you pass by Cheltenham in your way to Worcester, I wish you would see an actress there, a *Mrs Siddons*. She has a desire, I hear, to try her fortune with us. If she seems in your eyes worthy of being transplanted, pray desire to know upon what conditions she would make the trial, and I will write to her the post after I receive your letter.'[8] Sarah Siddons (1755–1831), the daughter of Roger Kemble, had married a young actor, William Siddons, in 1773. Eventually Garrick engaged her — on the advice of both Bate

Sarah Siddons (1755–1831), as depicted by John Downman in a portrait engraved by P. W. Tomkins, a pupil of Bartolozzi. Garrick brought Sarah Siddons to act in London somewhat before she was ready for the experience, as a result of which her début was not a success. Ultimately, however, her talent triumphed, and she went on to become the greatest tragedy actress England has ever produced. (*Mansell Collection*)

Mrs SIDDONS.

and King — for the following season, i.e. 1775–6.

There are two letters from Garrick to William Siddons dating from October 1775, full of goodwill towards the couple. Mrs Siddons was at that date seven months pregnant, and although Garrick was eager to know exactly when he might expect her in London, he was fully prepared to make allowances for her. He had in any case been ill himself, and had to apologize for the fact that his hand 'shakes with weakness, but I hope you will understand this scrawl.' It was, he said, one of the first letters he had written since his recovery. As he went on: 'I wish much to know how Mrs Siddons is, and about what time I may have the pleasure of seeing you in London. I beg that she will not make herself uneasy about coming, till she will run no risk by the journey. All I desire is that I may have the earliest information that can be had with any certainty, for I shall settle some business by that direction, which may be of immediate service to Mrs Siddons and the manager. If in the meantime you find it convenient to have any pecuniary assistance from me, I shall give it you with great pleasure. Let me once more intreat that Mrs Siddons may have no cares about me to disturb her, and that she may not be hurried to the least prejudice of her health.'[9] Evidently the offer of an advance was welcome to the couple, for twelve days later Garrick wrote again to confirm that he would make a draft of fifteen pounds available at any time.[10] There is record of at least a further twenty pounds later in the year, and indeed it had been suggested by Henry Bate in a letter of 19 August to Garrick that he should support the Siddons pair until she was ready to come to London. The baby may have been born early, for in a letter to Garrick of 9 November, Siddons told him how his wife had been taken ill on stage during a performance, and then early next morning produced their daughter, Sarah Martha Siddons, who was to predecease her mother and die in 1803. In response to this news, Garrick expressed the opinion that it might be better if Mrs Siddons were not to come to London to appear that season, but to wait until the next one. However, the couple arrived in December, and on the 29th of that month, Mrs Siddons made her début. Garrick had been right in his instinct. Despite his offer to choose one of the parts that she herself would feel most at ease in, her début was not a success. Because of illness, and a certain amount of stage fright due to her immaturity, she did not live up to expectation, and was not engaged again until 1782, when she began her long and successful career.

In the summer of 1775 the Adam brothers refurbished the Drury Lane theatre, and it was possibly Garrick's intention that he would hand over the theatre to his successor, when the time came, in perfect condition. The Bridges Street façade was graced with pilasters, a pediment with the royal arms, a balcony and a colonnade, and an ornamental trophy sat on top of all. The interior was entirely remodelled and decorated, with all the delicate Adam charm.

There is in Sir John Soane's Museum, a design by Robert Adam, dated 8 May 1775, for the proscenium of Drury Lane inscribed: 'Method

Samuel de Wilde's portrayal (engraved by Leney) of Mrs Siddons as Euphrasia in *The Grecian Daughter*, published in *Bell's British Theatre* on 19 May 1792, which therefore fixes it relatively early in De Wilde's career. Although some of his commissioned work dates from 1790, his first theatrical subjects at the Royal Academy date from 1792. (*Mansell Collection*)

proposed for finishing the front of the stage which covers the first curtain and is never changed, the apotheosis of Shakespear [*sic*] by the tragic and comic muses.'[11] There is also a design for the ceiling, dated 19 July 1775, in the same museum. For a general view of the interior, looking from the stage into the auditorium, and for the Bridges Street façade, one may consult *The Works in Architecture*.[12]

Bridges Street façade of Drury Lane remodelled by Robert Adam for Garrick in 1775. (*Mansell Collection*)

(*below*)
Adam's design for the ceiling at the Theatre Royal, Drury Lane, which is dated 19 July 1775, from the Adelphi. It was Garrick's intention to hand over the theatre to his successors in the best possible state, so to this end he engaged Adam to refurbish it. So successful was Adam's work that it was almost twenty years before Sheridan decided on any major changes. (*Sir John Soane's Museum*)

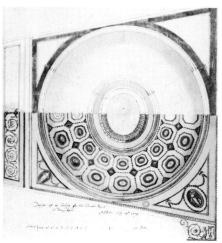

It is noteworthy, however, that although Adam raised the height of the ceiling by some twelve feet, he did not increase the actual size of the building, and so his work was essentially one of remodelling. Another of the ways in which he added to the sense of space, however, was by replacing the previous heavy pilasters with much more slender supports. The box fronts were redesigned, and the boxes themselves lined with

Adam's design for the proscenium of Drury Lane, dated 8 May 1775, depicting the Apotheosis of Shakespeare, whose bust is held up by the Tragic and Comic Muses. Garrick always regarded the theatre as being dedicated to Shakespeare. (*Sir John Soane's Museum*)

A drawing by Capon, engraved by Howlett, of the interior of Drury Lane 'as it appeared in 1792', prior to Sheridan's rebuilding of 1794, though the perspective is somewhat fanciful. (*Mansell Collection*)

crimson spotted paper. The pillars were 'inlaid with plate glass on a crimson and green ground'. The effect of all this was described as '*leste and brilliant*'. [13]

On 15 September, Garrick was at Lichfield, from where he wrote to Henry Bate, full of praise for Georgiana Spencer, daughter of the first earl, who had married the fifth Duke of Devonshire the year before (1774): 'The Grace of Devonshire is a most enchanting, exquisite, beautiful young creature. Were I five-and-twenty I could go mad about her; as I am past five-and-fifty I would only suffer martyrdom for her. She is no gamester, my friend, nor was there ever any gaming at Chatsworth.' [14] In this last, Garrick was very ill-informed. It was a family vice, and indeed for all

Georgiana, Duchess of Devonshire, in a painting by John Downman engraved by Bartolozzi. One of the more notorious members of the English aristocracy in her day, Georgiana was the daughter of one of the women Garrick most admired in the world after his wife — namely, Georgiana, Countess Spencer. For such a charming person as the Duchess of Devonshire, therefore, Garrick declared that he would 'suffer martyrdom'. (*Mansell Collection*)

Georgiana's mother's intelligence, it afflicted her, too. There is extant an interesting letter from Lady Spencer, in which she attempted to analyse why she gambled. She was writing to Mrs John Howe, née Caroline Hoare (1722–1814): 'I could without *much* difficulty avoid ever touching a card, but I cannot without a very great exertion check the tide of spirits and, while rashness supported by a careless indifference about money is dashing away, call in prudence and avarice to my assistance; yet this is a weakness excusable only in very young people, and what is ever to cure me of this intemperance, if I may so call it, I know not, since age really does not seem to take its natural and proper effect upon me. I agree with you that the real foundation of high play is avarice, but you have not the imprudence and consequently cannot know the feel I mean, which is throwing away the money when I win, as if it was what it always appears to me at such times, only counters; when I win I care not at the moment what comes of each stake.'[15]

There is an amusing vignette of Georgiana herself from Fanny Burney, who saw her in the park one Sunday morning in April 1776: 'We saw the young and handsome Duchess of Devonshire, walking in such an undressed and slaternly [sic] manner. Two of her curls came quite unpinned, and fell lank on one of her shoulders; one shoe was down at heel, the trimming of her jacket and coat was in some places unsown; her cap was awry; and her cloak, which was rusty and powdered, was flung half on and half off. Had she not had a servant in a superb livery behind her, she would certainly have been affronted. Every creature turned back to stare at her. Indeed I think her very handsome, and she has a look of innocence and artlessness that made me quite sorry she should be so foolishly negligent of her person. She had hold of the Duke's arm, who is the very reverse of herself, for he is ugly, tidy, and grave. He looks like a very mean shopkeeper's journeyman.'[16] Fanny Burney was to meet the Duchess properly, however, in 1791, when she was able to form a much more precise idea of her character, and although she did not capitulate, by any means, she was prepared to make allowances for Georgiana's situation.

Sheridan's *The Duenna* came on at Covent Garden on 21 November, and was so successful that the King and Queen went to see it a week later. It was to play no less than seventy-five times during the season of 1775–6, and in an effort to present some opposition, Garrick played nine times, in six of his chief parts, between 25 November and 23 December

171

1775. He went to see *The Duenna* for himself, and told Colman that he liked it much, 'with some few objections. It will do their business.'[17]

Garrick wrote to Colman again towards the end of the year — on 29 December — and it was now fixed that he would retire the following year and sell this 'theatrical property'.[18] We also know that Sheridan told his father-in-law, Thomas Linley, in a letter dated 31 December, that he and Garrick had met on 28 December — i.e. the day before Garrick's letter to Colman — and that Garrick was 'really serious'.[19] However, Garrick informed Sheridan that he wanted to give Colman the first refusal, whilst telling him in the same breath that he did not think that he would take up the offer. So when Garrick wrote to Colman the next day, it was in the knowledge that if he declined, then he had Sheridan's offer up his sleeve: 'I saw a gentleman yesterday of great property, and who has no objection to the price, viz: 35,000 pounds for my part. I must desire you to speak out, whether you have any thoughts of succeeding me in Drury Lane, for I must see the party again on Saturday evening to talk over the matter, and determine on my part.' Colman replied the following day that if Garrick was only offering him his share of the patent, then his answer was an unequivocal 'no'. If, on the other hand, Garrick was in a position to treat for the whole of the patent, or was reserving his own half, then Colman was prepared to talk further.[20]

Garrick's reaction was to arrange a meeting with Lacy in the presence of a solicitor and the treasurer of the theatre, and tell him that he was on the point of settling, and that if Lacy was willing, then he might have the same amount for his share. If, however, Lacy did not want to sell, then this would not prevent Garrick from doing so, and at once. When Colman was told of this, and that Lacy's answer had been that he was not prepared to sell, then Colman had no further interest in the matter.

There is an interesting letter written by Garrick to Dr John Hoadly at Southampton, dated 3 January 1776, in which he informed him that Dr James Ford, a wealthy obstetrician, was to be one of the parties involved in the new management, but rather of more interest are Garrick's views on the then London stage: 'The present race of theatrical heroines with all their airs, indispositions, tricks and importances . . . have reduced the stage to be dependant upon the wills of our insolent, vain and, let me add, insignificant female trumpery. There must be a revolution, or my successors will suffer much. I had a resource in my own acting that counteracted all the evil designs of those gentry.'[21]

Garrick then started telling all his friends of his decision to sell his part of the patent and retire from the stage completely. On 7 January he informed Richard Rigby, and on 18 January, James Clutterbuck, to whom he wrote: 'You shall be the first person to whom I shall make known that I have at last slipped my theatrical shell and shall be as fine and free a gentleman as you would wish to see upon the South or North Parade at Bath . . . I grow somewhat older, though I never played better in my life, and am resolved not to remain upon the stage to be pitied instead of applauded. The deed is done and the bell is ringing, so I can say no more.'[22] The contract was signed that very day, and also involved in the purchase was Simon Ewart, a relative of the Sheridans who was a London brandy merchant, though he in fact withdrew later from the enterprise.[23] When Kitty Clive heard of this mixture of talents she wrote to Garrick on 23 January: 'What a strange jumble of people. I thought I should have died with laughing when I saw a man midwife amongst them [Dr Ford]: I suppose they have taken him in to prevent *miscarriages*!'[24]

If the letters to Hoadly and Clutterbuck are a true indication of what Garrick felt — that the new generation was causing the theatre to decay and that he would prefer to go whilst he was still at the peak of his form rather than enter into a decline — then it was indeed very wise of him to go when he did. As time was to tell, he would have had nothing but worry with the young Lacy as a partner at Drury Lane, and Garrick no doubt felt instinctively that with Sheridan a bright new star had appeared in the firmament; much as he, in his day, had blazed his way into the limelight. A discreet eclipse now was the better part of valour. Then, despite what he said to Clutterbuck about never having played better in all his life, his health was not very good, and there were his two homes, his lovingly assembled library, and the company of his devoted wife — all of which he wanted to enjoy whilst there was still time to do so.

Garrick's concern as he prepared to bow out was not only for himself, however. He wanted an Act of Parliament to secure the Theatrical Fund, and in order to achieve this, he enlisted the aid of Sir Grey Cooper in a letter of 29 January.[25] A petition for a bill was duly brought into the House of Commons on 7 February, when it was referred to a committee headed by Cooper and Edmund Burke. From then on its passage was swift. Cooper presented his report on 13 February, a bill was drawn up, and the Royal Assent was given on 25 March. It had cost £116. 9s. 10d., which Garrick paid on 11 April.

Madame Necker came over to London to see Garrick act for the last time in 1776, and Hannah More somewhat enthusiastically recorded a dinner given by the Garricks on 24 April for their distinguished visitor and her party: 'We had beaux esprits, femmes sçavantes, academicians, etc., and no English persons except Mr Gibbon, the Garricks, and myself; we had not one English sentence the whole day.' (From F. Hedgcock: *A Cosmopolitan Actor, David Garrick and his French Friends*)

He also had to deal with members of his company, such as Jane Pope, whom he wished to see settled at the theatre before he left, and Mrs Abington who was, as ever, being difficult. She wrote to him on 4 March to tell him that she had a 'fixed determination to quit the stage'.[26] He endorsed her letter, referring to her as 'that worst of bad women', and in his reply advised her against giving up too hastily, but at the same time he agreed to play in her benefit on 7 May. In the event, she did not retire, but continued to play at Drury Lane until 1782, and then went over to Covent Garden.

As time went by, and 24 June approached, Garrick wrote to his brother Peter on 21 March that he began to feel as he used to when a schoolboy, and it was time to break up for the holidays. In a rather boastful way to his brother he told him how he had been 'enrolled a member among the first and greatest people in this kingdom', referring to General Joseph Smith's Savoir Vivre Club. On the opening night its members had been informed that they would have credit up to £40,000 at the gaming tables. The Savoir Vivre did not, however, last for long. In May, Smith was sent to prison for bribery, and the club was closed.[27]

Garrick now played some of his most famous parts for the last time. On 11 April, to a crowded house, it was Abel Drugger: 'I thought the audience were mad,' he wrote to brother George the following day, 'and they almost turned my brain.'[28] He could almost be forgiven for having his brain turned. Suzanne Necker, wife of Louis XVI's finance minister and mother of Madame de Staël, had come over to England at the end of March with her husband to see Garrick act before he retired. On 9 May he played Benedick for the last time. He was indeed the man of the moment. Invitations arrived, such as the one from Sir James Caldwell in Ireland, to which Garrick replied on 14 May. Rather touchingly, one of the things that militated against acceptance was the fact that Mrs Garrick was 'so sick and distressed by the sea' that he had not 'the resolution to follow [his] inclinations on account of her fears'. They had been married almost twenty-eight years, he said, and he had not left Mrs Garrick one day since they were married. He could not leave her now.[29] Even so, Caldwell repeated his invitation by letters of 16 May and 8 June.

Inevitably, the demand for tickets for the final performances was phenomenal. As Hannah More wrote: 'The eagerness of people to see him is beyond anything you can have an idea of. You will see half a dozen duchesses and countesses of a night, in the upper boxes. For the fear of not seeing him at all has humbled those who used to go, not for the purpose of seeing, but of being seen, and they now courtesy to the ground for the worst places in the house.'[30] As for Garrick himself, when it was all over, he was to keep his box as part of the sale contract. As the *London Chronicle* announced in January, the 'new proprietors, as an act of their own, have stipulated that Mr Garrick shall continue to keep that box which has of late years been set apart for the accommodation of his family'.

At this point Lady Spencer, too, announced her desire to see Garrick play. On 23 May he wrote to her: 'I have spoken to Mrs Garrick of Your Ladyship's request to take a peep at the farewell bow of your most sincere humble servant. She will think herself honoured that Your Ladyship will be a witness of her husband's behaviour in his last theatrical moments.'[31]

Inevitably, this sudden frantic rush towards the end caused all sorts of problems, and Sir Grey Cooper, who had helped Garrick get his Theatrical Fund bill through Parliament, complained that, whereas he had requested a box, he had been given a row of seats instead. This he might possibly have borne, had he not heard that the Dean of Derry and Monsieur Necker had boxes every night that Garrick played. The Dean of Derry was Thomas Barnard, a member of The Club, though in his reply of 26 May, Garrick denied that the Dean had had even a single place through himself. Madame Necker, he conceded, was different, but then she had come over from France expressly.[32]

On 27 May, Garrick played Richard III for the first time in four years. He said that he felt that he would be able to play it, but he dreaded the fight and the fall: 'I am afterwards in agonies.' Nevertheless, he played it again on 3 June, and for the last time for a command performance on 5 June. According to the *London Chronicle*, the house was so crowded that the start of the play was delayed for some two hours.

Garrick's actual farewell performance — as Don Felix in Mrs Centlivre's *The Wonder* — took place on 10 June. Perhaps one of the most touching accounts comes from Mrs Garrick herself, writing to Hannah Moore: 'I never shall forget his pale but charming looks when he took his leave; how the whole house felt them you will better describe in your imagination than I can, had I even more time than I have at present, being within a minute of eleven, and have only time to tell you that I have saved his buckles for you, which he wore in that last moment, and which [were] the only thing[s] that they could not take from him.'[33] In writing to

Madame Necker on 18 June, Garrick himself said of the occasion: 'When I came to take the last farewell, I not only lost almost the use of my voice, but of my limbs, too. It was indeed, as I said, *a most awful moment*. You would not have thought an English audience void of feeling if you had then seen and heard them. After I had left the stage, and was dead to them, they would not suffer the *petite piece* to go on; nor would the actors perform, they were so affected. In short, the public was very generous and I am most grateful.'[34] What he had actually said on stage was: 'This is to me a very awful moment: it is no less than parting for ever with those from whom I have received the greatest kindness, and upon the spot where that kindness and your favours were enjoyed.'[35] The same source — Murphy — goes on: 'Every face in the theatre was clouded with grief. Tears gushed in various parts of the house, and all concurred in one general demonstration of sorrow. The word, farewell, resounded from every quarter, amidst the loudest bursts of applause.'[36]

To Thomas King, on 25 June, Garrick sent a theatrical sword as a memento, with the Ghost's words from *Hamlet*: 'Farewell, remember me!'[37]

CHAPTER TEN

MAN OF LEISURE

Despite having refused to consider selling his share at the beginning of the year when Garrick first put it to him, Lacy was now, in late June 1776, of a different frame of mind, and had spoken to Garrick about it. In a letter to Lacy of 27 June, Garrick gave his considered opinion.[1] It was all very well offering to sell to a friend of Garrick's, and thereby keep a balance of power in the theatre, but why, asked Garrick, did Lacy think that it would be necessary to have a balance? That seemed to imply that he had suspicions, which was hardly a good start, one would have thought, to his working relationship with people who, as far as Garrick was concerned, had shown themselves hitherto to be men of their word. As Garrick pointed out, Lacy may well have flattered Garrick and sought his advice and the benefit of his experience, but 'I cannot say that you hitherto have much profited by it'. In the event, Lacy was obliged to sell out to Sheridan.

By 11 July, Garrick was at Mistley, and was then due to go to Wiltshire, but since the trip was put off for some days, he invited Lady Spencer and party to come down to Hampton on a visit. After this, Garrick went to stay with Lord Pembroke at Wilton, where he was on 9 August, and from where he possibly paid a visit to Stourhead, since Henry Hoare was a neighbour at the Adelphi, and was also at that time with Garrick at Wilton.[2] He seems to have been back again at Hampton on 18 August, however, having disappointed Hannah More, who had hoped to see him at Bristol, for on that day he wrote to Frances, daughter of his friend and doctor, William Cadogan, inviting her to Hampton when he came back from three or four days at Brighton, then rapidly becoming a fashionable resort.[3] For one who was taking retirement, Garrick was leading a remarkably active life. There was then an invitation to Chatsworth, which would furnish the opportunity to visit Lichfield at the same time, as he told brother Peter in a letter of 19 August.[4]

After Chatsworth in September, it was the turn of Althorp and Ampthill, the country houses of, respectively, Earl and Countess Spencer and the Earl and Countess of Upper Ossory. Lady Spencer wanted to make the journey down from London as comfortable as possible for the Garricks, and so suggested that they spend the night at her house in St Albans, Holywell House: 'The beds and rooms are well aired,' she wrote on 6 October, 'and more comfortable than at an inn.'[5] There would be no one to cook for them, however, though meals could be sent in from a nearby inn. A coach would then meet them at Newport Pagnell. Lady

An unfinished portrait by Reynolds of Lady Spencer with her daughter Georgiana, the future Duchess of Devonshire, now at Chatsworth. It was bought by the fifth Duke of Devonshire at the sale of Reynolds' effects after his death in 1793. This is a study for the finished version now in the collection of Lord Spencer at Althorp, though painted in the reverse direction. The study probably dates from 1759 and the finished version from 1761. (*Courtauld Institute, London*)

Spencer was very much to the point. Her servants had instructions that they were to receive no gratuities from guests. This was no doubt a welcome piece of information, even taking into account the Garricks' wealth, since it has been estimated that if one dined out at a great house at that time it could cost anything from ten shillings to two guineas in tips or 'vails' for the servants, who would be lined up inside the front door as guests left. Garrick appreciated Lady Spencer's frankness and endorsed her letter: 'Lady Spencer's letter from Althorp. Nature for ever!'

Apparently Garrick had, at some point, upset or offended Lady

Spencer, and the friendship that had so flourished during and after their Grand Tour had been interrupted. According to a letter of 9 October 1776 from Garrick to Lady Spencer, he dated his restoration 'to grace and favour' from the previous year, 1775. Certainly there was no hint of coldness now. On 16 October, Lady Spencer noted in the Chace Book at Althorp: 'Lady Spencer and Mr Garrick were out in the cabriolet and viewed the fox several times over Holdenby Grounds.' (Garrick was given a pony, which he later told Lady Spencer he was riding at Hampton when he was back in November.) Two days later, on 18 October, Garrick wrote to John Taylor that he would leave Althorp 'with the utmost regret', and go to Ampthill, which turned out to be nothing compared to Althorp as far as kindness was concerned.[6] What undoubtedly made life all the more enjoyable this autumn was the fact that he had no new theatre season to work for or go back to. He would have been happy to stay at Althorp much longer, especially when he actually sampled life at Ampthill and found it a very different atmosphere. He communicated this to Lady Spencer, who wrote to him on 30 October saying: 'Your reception at [Ampthill] is just what I should have supposed. There never was anybody who had the talent of making other people feel ill at ease so supremely as that person.'[7] She referred to the Countess of Upper Ossory, Anne Fitzpatrick, who had been married to the Duke of Grafton, but after the dissolution of the marriage had eloped with John, second Earl of Upper Ossory. Garrick endorsed this letter: 'Heavenly Lady Spencer to me.'

'Heavenly Lady Spencer' was to bring Garrick to earth somewhat over the next subject of their correspondence, namely a flattering letter of 5 October from Madame Necker to Garrick, which he sent on to Lady Spencer. The letter from Madame Necker was indeed enough to turn Garrick's head. In it she had told him that, as soon as he had left the stage, Voltaire and others had tried to dethrone Shakespeare, but she said that whenever anyone tried to denigrate Shakespeare to her, she replied: 'You have only seen his corpse, but I myself have seen him when his soul still animated his body. They reply: "You are mistaken. It was nothing more than a majestic phantom, that Mister Garrick, that powerful magician, had conjured up from the tomb. The spell is broken, and Shakespeare has to return into the night." '[8]

In writing to thank Madame Necker, on 10 November 1776, Garrick was fulsome: 'I take up my pen with fear and trembling to thank you from my heart of hearts (as Shakespeare calls it) for the most flattering, charming, bewitching letter that ever came to my hand. I shall keep it as the most precious monument of your unbounded partiality to me and of my own vanity. It shall be left by my will to be kept in the famous mulberry-box with Shakespeare's own handwriting, to be read by my children's children for ever and ever.'[9] He then went on to tell her how Edward Gibbon happened to be with him at the time he received the letter, and Garrick confessed that he was unable to prevent himself from showing it to him: 'He read, stared at me, was silent, then gave it me, with these emphatical words emphatically spoken: *"This is the very best letter that ever was written."* ' Garrick managed to remember to congratulate Monsieur Necker on having been appointed joint Controller General of the Finance on 22 October that year. His endorsement of the letter, however, leaves no room for doubt as to its effect on him: 'A charming letter from Mrs Necker and my answer.'

It was this letter, then, that Garrick sent to Lady Spencer on 15 November. Her reply, dated 27 November, is delightfully frank: 'I have no great partiality for studied letters, nor do I much admire those you have sent, except one expression which I like in Madame Necker's: "You have only seen his corpse, but I myself have seen him when his soul still animated his body".'[10] Garrick endorsed the letter: 'Lady Spencer, always natural!'

Lady Spencer was never put off, however, by this or any other example of Garrick's egocentricity, and was keen that he and his wife should spend Christmas at Althorp. Garrick found himself in something of a quandary, since he had learned subsequently that Lady Spencer had had a miscarriage after his last visit. Two things, on reflection, gave him cause for alarm. He had done his mad Lear turn during his last visit, and after it Lady Spencer had said: 'Indeed, you should not do that any more!' Then he had taken Lady Spencer out riding. Perhaps he had gone too fast? She did not regard him as being in any way responsible, but it was a shock to him, even so.

As Garrick grew older and basked in his retirement, he had no scruples about turning down an invitation from the Earl of Sandwich in December 1776, and then, on finding that he was free after all, asking to be re-invited: 'It is not (I know) *selon les règles du bon ton* [done in polite society], but when I consider that I am near sixty, and that many such holidays will not fall to my share, may I be permitted to hope for a remission of my sins and an admission to your table tomorrow.'[11] With true aristocratic indulgence, the Earl replied that he was exceedingly happy to hear that Garrick was to join them after all.

It was not until early December, in fact, that Garrick finally 'signed and sealed the last great parchment of all' in connection with the sale of his share of the Drury Lane patent, as he told Hannah More in a letter of 17 December 1776.[12] Two days later Lady Spencer wrote to him again, and in her letter referred to the words 'a nation's taste depends on you' in application to Garrick. The ever-sensitive Garrick interpreted this as a criticism of himself, and replied with much further explanation. His need to justify himself had again taken over, when much of Lady Spencer's letter was charming. She inquired after Mrs Garrick's health, and went on to remark on their married bliss and fidelity: 'Pray let me hear, without loss of time, how Mrs Garrick does; she must not ail anything. You, I am sure, can neither see, hear, nor understand without her. After all, it is comfortable to find that a few people can live a good many years together without wishing one another at the d——. It will tomorrow be one-and-twenty years since Lord Spencer married me, and I verily believe we have neither of us repented our lot from that time to this.'[13] Garrick endorsed the letter: 'Lady Spencer, delightful and natural', and yet took what he regarded as the critical parts as the only ones to be responded to, in his reply of 21 December.[14] Luckily Lady Spencer remained 'delightful and natural' — or at least natural — in her reply of 22 December: 'Never send me such a Jeremaid again, as long as you live. I dote upon all your nonsense, but I shall never dare make any more saucy observations upon it if you take what I say in such sober sadness.' With the new year Garrick set things off on a new footing with the Countess: 'To the goddess of my idolatry, I present the first fruits of the year 1777, with my prayers, which will do her no good, and with my warmest wishes, which will do her no harm.'[15]

Towards his brother George his feelings were much less amicable at this time. George had written on 27 December: 'I can assure you that the pangs I have felt from your withdrawing your love and affection from me for a long time . . . [have] been the cause of my many and very long as well as very expensive illnesses.'[16] In the event, Garrick did not send the reply he had prepared, but it shows what his first reaction was: 'If mine was an affectionate letter I am sure yours is the reverse.'[17] He was furious at the charge about the expensive illnesses, and it seems as if George's mismanagement of the Fermignac estate was still rankling with Garrick.

Late in 1776 Garrick renewed acquaintance with a lady who had first

(see opposite page)
The Thrales' house at Streatham where, at one time, Dr Johnson was a constant visitor. Drawn by C. Stanfield, it was engraved by E. Finden for the ninth volume of Boswell's Life of Johnson. By 1821, Mrs Piozzi declared to Fanny Burney: 'The village of Streatham is full of rich inhabitants, the common much the worse for being so spotted about with houses, and the possibility of avoiding constant intercourse with their inhabitants (as in Mr Thrale's time) wholly lost.' (Mansell Collection)

known him when she was a child, Hester Lynch (1741–1821), who had married the wealthy brewer Henry Thrale in 1763. Mrs Thrale was the one who sought to renew the friendship, though it was almost inevitable that they should have met again, since Dr Burney gave lessons to the Thrale daughter, and Dr Johnson was also a friend of the family and had been since 1765. Henry Thrale, who is reputed to have died of over-eating in 1781, gave splendid dinners at his Southwark brewery and at his home, Streatham Park, then south of London. Such was his reputation for being a bon viveur that reports appeared in the papers in April 1777 that he was dead. It turned out to have been something of a macabre April Fool in the end.

Garrick himself now became aware of his own mortality from time to time, as he wrote to Lady Spencer on 10 April 1777: 'My head is much clearer than it has been for some time past, but a certain tumult in my heart at times has whispered me very kindly that I am mortal. I never was conscious till lately that my tenement was frail, and a tolerable blast would overset me.'[18] Garrick was not well at all, and for the next two

An engraving by Ridley from a miniature portrait by Barber of Hester Lynch Thrale, later Piozzi, dated 30 June 1798. After the death of her first husband, Mrs Thrale remained a widow for some time and then greatly upset Dr Johnson — and several other friends — by marrying Gabriel Piozzi, an Italian Roman Catholic musician. After a brief exchange of letters with Fanny Burney at this point, their friendship ceased for many years, though it was resumed later. Mrs Piozzi died in her eighty-second year, and yet (according to Fanny Burney) she 'owed not her death to age nor to natural decay, but to the effects of a fall in a journey from Penzance to Clifton'. (*Mansell Collection*)

weeks at least he had a very heavy cold and a sore throat, with attendant hoarseness. He and his wife were obliged to postpone a visit to Streatham to the Thrales, but it did not prevent Garrick from continuing to work for one of his charitable concerns, the Theatrical Fund, of which he was now 'Father, founder and protector'. [19] At this time he was working to ensure a good attendance for a benefit performance on 28 April. For their part, the Drury Lane company were grateful for his activities on their behalf, and on 25 March 1777 they had drawn up a decorated Testimony of Duty and Affection, and early in April the whole company waited on him at the Adelphi: 'The Company . . . assembled in the Green-Room executed the deed constituting D. Garrick, Esquire, master of the corporation. They proceeded in coaches to his house in the Adelphi. Mr Garrick affectionately received them at the top of the stairs and inducted them into the drawing-room. A book of laws was then presented to him . . . a blue ribbon from which hung a medal [by Reynolds] was put round his neck . . . T. King read the deed. He made a heartfelt oration and invited him to dinner.' [20]

Things were not always so glowing at the Theatrical Fund, however, for when a dinner was held at the Globe Tavern, Fleet Street, on 17 May that same year, Garrick was heard by Tom King to say that he was 'coolly, not to say indelicately treated', and that King himself had been 'the foremost in tokens of disrespect'. King took the initiative later in the year, and on 11 July wrote to Garrick to apologize for the conduct of some of the members, but also suggesting that Garrick may have been mistaken. He added, towards the end of his letter, however, that though he respected, loved and admired Garrick, he would not seek him. [21] This was turned into Garrick's opening gambit in his reply of 17 July, written from Mistley, but what followed indicates that he had really minded about the affair: 'I must confess that my reception at the Fund dinner was as surprising as it was disagreeable and unexpected. I seemed to be the person marked for displeasure, and was almost literally sent to Coventry, though I ventured among you after a very severe illness and had dressed myself out as fine as possible to do all the honour I could to the day and the committee. I never was more unhappy for a time. However, let it be forgotten, and when we meet let not a word be said of what is past.' Garrick could not prevent himself from making a deprecatory remark about the theatre, by way of a parting shot: 'Poor old Drury! It will be, I fear, very soon in the hands of the Philistines.' [22] The episode ought to have warned Garrick that, once he had given up, things would never, and could never, be quite the same again, and as sad as the truth might be, it was one that had to be faced up to. Whatever he felt about 'poor old Drury', it was experiencing one of its most brilliant moments in 1777.

(above)
The screen scene from Sheridan's *The School for Scandal*, 1778. This is one of the few contemporary engravings giving a clear idea of a play in performance. Garrick attended the first night in 1777, though he felt that in this scene the characters stood for too long, after the collapse of the screen, before speaking. (*British Library*)

In his letter to Lady Spencer of 10 April, Garrick had given news of a new play by Sheridan: 'A new comedy is preparing at Drury Lane called the *School for Scandal*, in which may be seen a variety of characters which will strike everybody with some resemblance of their friends. I am told there is a great deal of wit, and will prove a very seasonable antidote to the daily poison of the newspapers.'[23] *School for Scandal* came on at Drury Lane and had its first two nights on 8 and 9 May 1777. Garrick wrote to Sheridan on 12 May following, inquiring after Mrs Sheridan's health. He had attended the first night, and professed that he was 'mad' about the play. Nevertheless, he could not prevent himself from pointing out that, in the famous screen scene, the characters stood for too long before they spoke. An anonymous 'gentleman' with whom Garrick had discussed the matter, and who had been present on the second night, agreed with Garrick. His advice to Sheridan was that: 'though they should be astonished and a little petrified, yet it may be carried to too great a length'. He then softened the edge of the criticism by saying that: 'all praised at Lord Lucan's last night'.[24] In fairness to Garrick, however, when writing to Richard Cumberland later in May that year, he gave the dramatist his due: 'Mr Sheridan hath indeed shown a wonderful genius in his last play, which Mr Garrick thinks must be of the greatest consequence to the stage and the present management.'[25]

Retirement from the stage did not mean that Garrick was at the same time free from the chore of reading plays submitted to him by aspiring dramatists, or from extricating himself from those who endeavoured to enlist his aid — either on their own behalf or that of some playwright they supported — in trying to get works performed on the London stage. It was by now merely part of the daily round, but something that Garrick might well have hoped to cease to deal with. What was no doubt even more regrettable was that such relationships were made more difficult on occasion by the activities of brother George.

Mrs Hannah Cowley had had a considerable success with her play *The Runaway* during the previous season, but felt that she had somehow lost Garrick's affection. George, it appeared, had told her that it was because she and her husband had not called on the Garricks. As she told Garrick in her letter: 'Had I conceived that the continuance of our intercourse depended on me, I should have flown to the Adelphi with transport — but I imagined that your engagements in the great world allowed you no time for little folks.'[26] Moreover, she had had the distinct impression during her last visit that Garrick would gladly have been spared it. So Mrs Cowley had subsequently devised a plan for having some reason for calling on the Garricks, by resolving to present David with a specially bound copy of *The Runaway*. She knew that he was fond of that particular kind of binding, and she had written her own dedication to Garrick in it. The play would therefore serve as an 'apology, for Mr Cowley's intrusion, or mine, whenever we might be admitted'. Every time that Mr Cowley had subsequently gone to the Adelphi he had taken the book in his pocket, and on each occasion he had brought it back 'with concern'. Not only had there been 'repeated denials', but these had, moreover, been delivered by the Garricks' servants 'in the most insulting manner'.

In a somewhat urbane reply of 27 May, Garrick wrote that, far from neglecting the Cowleys, he himself felt neglected by them. Had he been informed that any servant had behaved impertinently, then that servant would have been dismissed instantly, but the only occasion that he knew of when Mr Cowley had called was during an illness when he was unable to see anyone, apart from the members of his own family. If the Cowleys had nothing else arranged for the following Sunday morning, and the weather were fine, then Mr and Mrs Garrick would be happy to see them at the Adelphi. [27]

Such was his patience with 'little folks', even when he was courted by 'the great world' at the same time. Lady Bathurst, for example, wanted to see the Garricks in Brighton that summer, but although, as Garrick put it in his letter to her: 'the sea and the situation of the town are most agreeable to us', he was kept back in London and Hampton on account of family business. [28]

Some of the family business may well have been the arrival in London of the niece of Mrs Garrick, Elisabeth Fürst (1766–1840), known as Liserl. She reached them in June 1777, and did not return to Vienna until after Garrick's death. Notwithstanding Liserl's arrival, there was the annual visit to Mistley that summer, in July, and also to Farnborough Place to see the Wilmots. Afterwards Garrick was to welcome Dr Cadogan and his daughter Frances to Hampton, along with Hannah More, and he also issued an invitation to Martha Hale (Haly Paly) to come and try some roast venison. Presumably it was the same 'most luxurious basket of venison' that had arrived from Althorp, and for which he wrote to thank Lady Spencer on 26 July. [29] Around 7 or 8 August he was expecting Rigby to pay him a visit at Hampton, which was to be an affair of state, whilst Garrick himself was to pay a visit to Chatsworth later in the month, according to a letter written to Lady Spencer on 22 August.

Lady Spencer was going to pay a visit to the Continent, first to Holland, and it was suggested that she go via Mistley, and then embark from there. Garrick seems to have kept from her his views on the Dutch that he expressed to Benjamin Van der Gucht in a letter of 29 July: 'Your accounts of the Dutch perfectly tally with my own ideas of them, and I have long laid it down as a maxim that minds so warped to traffic can never bend to the politer arts and, what is worse, their hearts are shut up to the finer dealings of friendship and affection. I shall wish much to peep among them, but to live with them, I could not be bribed with the whole produce of their famed city of Rotterdam.'[30] Well, Lady Spencer survived Holland, and then wrote to Garrick from Fontainebleau on 7 October.[31]

It was strange how, even in his retirement, and after knowing people for many years, Garrick could be put off by remarks made by third parties. There is a long letter to Lord Camden dated 16 September — what Lady Spencer would have called a Jeremaid — in which a message, brought by a Mr Palmer of Bath, had made Garrick 'half consider the matter as a kind of reproach', which in turn made him 'a little serious'.[32] He had hoped that the Camdens would pay an annual visit to Hampton, but this did not seem to be the case. Worse than that, there was no invitation to Chislehurst, either, this year. Garrick realized that he ran the danger of appearing silly, but he could not help himself. Unfortunately, Lord Camden's reply does not seem to have survived. One hopes that he was able to be as straightforward with Garrick as Lady Spencer had been.

However, Garrick was in any case ready to go off on a long journey himself, first to Sir Watkin Williams-Wynn in North Wales, and then to Peter Garrick in Lichfield. According to a letter written to Peter from Wynnstay, dated 26 September, Garrick had been an object of curiosity in Shrewsbury: 'The town was in alarm at my coming, and the Raven Inn besieged. I little expected so much honour from Salopian swains, and Welsh mountaineers.'[33] Since the Garricks had no time to stay at Lichfield on the way back, brother Peter had to go to Birmingham to meet them. At all events, Garrick was still at Wynnstay on 30 September, and when he wrote to Marie Jeanne Riccoboni from Hampton on 17 October, he said that he had returned only the night before. When he wrote to Lady Spencer on 22 October, she was still on the Continent, and he had learnt

Nathaniel Dance's portrait of Charles Pratt, first Lord Camden (1714–94), Lord Chancellor of England, and one of Garrick's most influential friends. Garrick sent his nieces Arabella and Catherine to Madam Decombes' *pension* in Paris, which was also attended by Lord Camden's daughters. Lord Camden was both an executor of Garrick's will and one of the pallbearers at his funeral. (*National Portrait Gallery*)

of Foote's death the day before. Contrary to what Garrick believed, however, Foote had not died on his arrival at Calais, but in Dover whilst waiting for his passage. Another milestone had been passed.

As the end of the year approached, arrangements had to be made. Garrick wrote to Lady Spencer on 30 November, though in his wife's name, and in a rather heavy-handed German-English. He wrote again on 11 December, by which time the Garricks were about to set out to spend Christmas at Althorp. They arrived there by 15 December, when Garrick wrote a letter to brother George full of almost telegraphic instructions. Lady Spencer prevailed upon them to stay longer than originally intended, and when Garrick wrote to Mrs Thomas Ráckett senior on 21 December, he apologized for the fact that Mrs Garrick's niece was still with her, where she had been sent during their absence. [34] Liserl's Christmas was going to be a rather unfamily affair. The Garricks thought that she ought to go back to the Adelphi, and they would send Mrs Garrick's maid from Althorp for her, as well as George Garrick's wife, to

A drawing of the west end of the baths designed for Mistley, Essex, by Adam, records a dream, inspired by the current fashion for watering-places, that Richard Rigby had, but which never came to fruition. At the same time it shows how Garrick and his circle patronized one of the greatest architects of their day, and that Adam did not refuse to put his talent to utilitarian ends. (*Sir John Soane's Museum*) relieve Mrs Rackett. From the list of guests, which included the Duke and Duchess of Devonshire and the Earl and Countess of Jersey, with the Duke and Duchess of Marlborough expected too, one can see at least part of the reason why Garrick was in no hurry to leave Althorp.

From a letter possibly written to the Earl of Upper Ossory at this time, it would seem that the Garricks had again been invited to Ampthill, but they had declined. In view of their reception previously, they were presumably very happy to be able to do so, though their host could have had no suspicion of their discomfort on their earlier visit.

No doubt it is understandable, but the tone of the letter Garrick wrote to his niece on Christmas Day 1777 is decidedly patronizing: 'Your aunt and I . . . are glad that my mirth the day we parted, and your yawning afterwards have not killed you . . . I was going to see some of the best, as well as the greatest, persons in the kingdom, and who do everything to make me happy . . . your situation must be comfortable and pleasurable if you please. I hope you were not uneasy that I took this jaunt. I must see my best friends, and cannot lose the privilege of pleasing myself.'[35] It was hardly Liserl's fault, one feels, that she became a nuisance so comparatively soon after her arrival. Garrick does not seem to have been especially fond of her, though he left her £1,000 in his will, and after his death she went back to Vienna and married on 2 July 1781.

Despite Lady Spencer's injunction to Garrick not to do his Lear act again, it seems that he performed it at Mrs Montagu's in January 1778, when the Spencers were present. It was, of course, one of his most famous party pieces, and was said to have been studied from life on an occasion when he had seen just such a mad old man. Even in retirement, then, there was a marked inability or reluctance to put the stage completely behind him. When one has such a talent, it is hard not to display it from time to time, or indeed to turn a deaf ear to requests from others to display it. Garrick was no exception. Indeed, for one who had been so totally a man of the theatre, it would have been possibly more strange had he never slipped back into that world from time to time. But as Mrs Montagu's guests watched him in January 1778, no one could have realized how short a time Garrick was destined to be with them. He had entered the last year of his existence.

CHAPTER ELEVEN

THE END

DESPITE Garrick's retirement, both from the stage and the theatre itself, there was a nagging problem that refused to go away, created by the finances of Drury Lane, in which Garrick was still involved, because James Lacy had eventually mortgaged his share in it to him. There had also been Lacy's share of the cost of the alterations to the theatre, and an abortive attempt at finding coal on his Oxfordshire estate.[1] James Lacy died, therefore, owing Garrick some £4,500, and it soon became apparent that his son Willoughby would not be able to keep up the interest payments. Garrick did not consult Lacy, however, but went ahead with a scheme of his own to try and assign the mortgage to the men who had bought his own share of the theatre patent. Lacy's counter move was to try and sell half his share, but the partners did not agree, and certainly did not greet the proposal with the enthusiasm he had envisaged. Lacy therefore agreed to a further loan from Garrick, with an additional security put up by his partners. To ensure that the interest was handed over, however, it was agreed that Garrick should appoint a deputy, who was to take the money from the house receipts, which amounted to £6 each acting day, according to the Drury Lane account books for 1776–7.

This expedient was no remedy for the basic malady, however, and Lacy's debt went on increasing, to the point where, at the end of the second season, that of 1777–8, Lacy was in a desperate situation. He proposed granting renters 'money arising on Mr Lacy ['s] moity to be applied in reducing Mr Garrick's mortgage, and exonerating Mr L.' in this way from his obligations. However, as with his previous proposal, he failed to gain the agreement of his partners. Garrick saw the dangers, and put the matter into the hands of his solicitors, and a business-like letter to Lacy, Ford, Sheridan and Linley, dated 16 March 1778, reminded them that four months had passed since Gregory Bateman, a lawyer, had announced that he had authority to pay Lacy's debts, and had asked for an account of what was owing to Garrick, but since then nothing further had been heard.[2] Initially, then, Garrick served notice on all the partners, and indeed since they had to be consenting parties to whatever solution might eventually be found, they were closely involved in the matter. However, the negotiations had to have their fundamental agreement between Garrick and Willoughby Lacy, and there was a somewhat peppery exchange of letters between them towards the end of March 1778.

(see previous page)
Zoffany's unfinished portrait of Garrick *circa* 1770, now in the possession of the Garrick Club. Garrick helped Zoffany considerably in the early part of the artist's career, and Garrick's commissioning of a painting of himself in *The Farmer's Return* in 1762 established the artist's reputation. The unfinished state of the portrait only serves to accentuate the lasting impression Garrick made on those who saw him act. (*Garrick Club*)

Garrick was not at all an unreasonable man in such matters, and indeed, at the very time that he was thus engaged in dealings with Lacy, he was most generous towards Richard Berenger, who was so deep in debt that he dared not set foot outside his house for fear of writs and arrest. Friends and relations came to his aid, however, and raised the £2,600 required to pay off his creditors. Garrick not only cancelled his own claim on Berenger to the extent of £280. 10s. 0d., but is said to have donated a further £300.[3] With Lacy junior, therefore, he was equally prepared to be generous — though the sums involved were astronomical by comparison.

Nevertheless, it was surprising to Garrick, to say the least, to receive a letter from the partners of the theatre, sent on their behalf by Benjamin Victor on 6 May, which announced: 'I am directed by the proprietors to inform you that it will not be in their power for the future to pay the interest of Mr Lacy's mortgage until the debts and expenses of the theatre are discharged.'[4] As Garrick pointed out in reply the following day, his mortgage was 'as just a debt as any upon the theatre', and it was therefore 'as reasonable for me to expect my interest should be paid as punctually as any other expense of the theatre'.[5] For good measure he wrote to Lacy as

Reynolds' portrait of Garrick reading to his wife, 1773. Although painted before Garrick's retirement, there is a somewhat autumnal quality to the picture which makes it easy to imagine what that retirement was like. At the same time, of course, the painting reflects both the devotion of the pair to each other throughout their married life, and Garrick's love of books and book collecting. (*National Portrait Gallery*)

well, presenting his compliments, and expressing regret that 'the proprietors have so ill managed their affairs as to make it necessary for them to send him such a letter as he received yesterday.'[6] And indeed, all his careful husbandry, and concern to hand over the theatre in good standing, seems to have been squandered overnight.

Lacy's answer, on 15 May, maintained that the letter from the proprietors had been sent without his knowledge or consent, and that as far as he was concerned, the amount of interest owed for the season was complete. Moreover, as long as he had any part of the property, he would never agree to any defalcation.[7] Fine words, but Lacy was at the same time treating with Sheridan for the purchase of his share, which Garrick naturally heard about in due course. What particularly aroused his anger was the price — £45,000 — when he had sold his own share of the patent to Sheridan and the others for £35,000 only two years previously.

Garrick therefore put an end to his dealings with the proprietors of the theatre — at least officially — with a short letter in mid-August 1778: 'The rudeness of your letters — which is always the sign of a bad cause — I shall pass over with the utmost contempt, but as you have proposed . . . an arbitration, I cannot, as an honest man, refuse to meet you upon any ground. I therefore desire that your attorney will, without delay . . . settle and prepare this matter, and that all other correspondence may cease between you and your humble servant.'[8] Nevertheless, he managed to reply to Willoughby Lacy that month in a kindly manner, despite the fact that Lacy had written to him in July from Cork, where he had gone to perform, asking for money. In the event, the debt to Garrick left by Lacy senior increased from £4,500 to £22,500.

What must have been further irritation to Garrick as far as the proprietors' supposed difficulties were concerned, was the fact that on 24 June, Sheridan and Thomas Harris had become proprietors of the Opera House in the Haymarket. In a letter to Hannah More from Mistley dated 9 July, Garrick expressed his misgivings about the whole venture: 'The Haymarket goes on but heavily.' The hot weather did not help, and even though the King had been two or three times, the boxes were not full. Garrick then admitted that, as far as Sheridan and Harris were concerned, 'I am a little thoughtful at my situation with them, but not uneasy. My security is tolerably good.'[9] His instinct about the Opera House was right. The theatre did not prosper under the management of Sheridan and Harris, and by October 1780 the £300 shares were selling for £250; and

Blowing up the PIC NIC's; _or _ Harlequin Quixotte attacking the Puppets. Vide Tottenham Street Road

James Gillray's *Blowing up the Pic-Nics*, 1802, shows how Garrick's personality continued to make itself felt long after his death. The Pic-Nic Society had been formed by a few well-known actors and actresses of the time to perform exclusive entertainments for their own benefit. Sheridan (who, it is said, once played Harlequin, as Garrick did) led the protest in the press — hence 'Harlequin Quixotte attacking the Puppets' — for he felt that the scheme could have led to reduced patronage for minor players and entertainments. (*Mansell Collection*)

finally in 1781 William Taylor bought them out. Garrick did not live to witness such an end to the venture.

The letter to Hannah More is mostly in a buoyant mood, and Garrick was able to laugh at the rumour then circulating in London that he and his wife had parted. It was worthy of Mr Sheridan's *School for Scandal*. As far as the theatre in general, and writing in particular, were concerned, however, Garrick freely admitted that: 'My theatrical curiosity diminishes daily, and my vanity as an author is quite extinct.' It must have been particularly saddening for him that the theatre he had loved and run so successfully for so long should so soon be experiencing difficulties. By comparison, the cost to his own pocket was relatively insignificant.

George accompanied the Garricks to Mistley this summer, but he was ill, and his illness worried David. However, he himself was taken ill later that month, and on 21 July Mrs Garrick was so alarmed that she sent for Dr Cadogan. It seems, from a letter of 23 July to Frances Cadogan, that Garrick passed two or three gallstones. [10] He was still ill when he wrote to Lacy on 5 August, and then later in August he had a violent bilious attack which left him very weak. He still complained of it when he wrote to Joseph Cradock on 14 September, so decided to go to Broadlands, Lord Palmerston's house in Hampshire, to try and recuperate. [11] It seemed as if the shadows were lengthening around him, however. Thomas Linley had drowned on 5 August, and Lady Spencer had had another miscarriage. Before he left for Broadlands, Garrick wrote to her from Hampton on 14 September: 'Since my pain has left me I have been diverting myself with *Tom Jones* . . . for as tragedies and comedies are now too much for the old gentleman, he must be gently and gradually set down at rest with novels, tales, fables and lighter food of the mind.'[12] Luckily at Broadlands the Garricks found: 'a good host, a sweet place, and warm welcome'. [13]

At this time Garrick made his last will, for it is dated 24 September 1778, and was witnessed by Lord Palmerston and Mr and Mrs Ricketts. He was still at Broadlands on 28 September, when he wrote to Lord Sandwich, and sounded much more like his old self.

The next day, Garrick saw the King review the troops at Winchester. From Broadlands he had gone to stay with Hans Stanley at Paultons, where he had a bad attack of bile and, in his own words, 'underwent the torment of martyrs'. [14] In fact, he had thought himself very near to death. He had hoped to go also to visit Richard Cox, who was staying at Quarley Manor, the house near Winchester that he had inherited from his father, but Garrick was evidently in no fit state to travel, despite what he wrote to Cox on 28 October. On the same day, Mrs Garrick wrote to Cox, too, asking him to put them off, because she feared for her husband's health. [15] The clouds were inexorably thickening.

Nevertheless, as Christmas approached, the Garricks were once more invited to spend it with the Spencers at Althorp. On 13 November Lady

Spencer wrote to Garrick, telling him of the silk that was to be made up into 'uniform' for the ladies at Althorp during the holiday season.[16] A month later, however, Mrs Garrick wrote to Lady Spencer and told her that her husband had had a new attack of gout and they would be obliged to put off their visit until after Christmas — much as they would regret not having the yellow room again.

Garrick's condition seems to have improved slightly, for on 28 December, Lady Spencer wrote to him: 'We shall be happy to see you on Thursday [31 December] either well or ill dressed, but do not put us off any longer.'[17] It was perhaps a foolhardy thing to do at that time of year, but the Garricks duly set off on the morning of 30 December, according to a letter to Joseph Warton, and seem to have been expected at Althorp on 3 January (1779).[18] However, though Garrick seems to have recovered somewhat when he arrived, he was again attacked by gout, and now had the added complication of shingles, so decided to return to London, for in such a situation, home would be best. On 14 January he wrote to Lady Spencer, en route, from Dunstable, and again the following day when he arrived back at the Adelphi. This is the penultimate letter of Garrick's to have survived. On 18 January he sank into a coma, and died on the morning of 20 January. Traditionally his last words were: 'Oh dear!'

The funeral was a splendid affair with the procession stretching from the Adelphi to Westminster Abbey. Richard Sheridan was chief mourner,

W. Darling's engraving of the invitation to David Garrick's funeral in Westminster Abby [sic]. The opening paragraph of the order for the funeral, devised by Sheridan, runs: 'Four men in mourning with staffs covered with black silk and scarfs [sic] on horseback as porters. Six ditto with mourning cloaks, etc. A man in mourning to bear the pennon, scarf, etc. Two supporters. Six men in cloaks as before. Surcoat of arms. Helmet, with crest, wreath and mantlet. State lid of black ostrich feathers, surrounded by escutcheons. Hearse full dressed with THE BODY.' (British Museum)

197

and may well have been responsible for the organization of the ceremonial, which was considerable. There were representatives from the theatres of Drury Lane and Covent Garden, as well as what was soon to be known as The Literary Club, and the pallbearers were the Duke of Devonshire, Lord Camden, Earl Spencer, the Earl of Ossory, Viscount Palmerston, Sir Watkin Williams-Wynn, Richard Rigby, Hans Stanley, John Paterson and Albany Wallis. In Westminster Abbey, Burke was heard to sob as the coffin was lowered into the floor, and Dr Johnson, too, openly wept.

The Spencers had returned to London shortly after the Garricks, and Mrs Garrick noted in her journal that Lady Spencer visited every day during her husband's final illness. His death must have affected Lady Spencer deeply, and although it was not the custom for women to attend funerals, she wanted to be present right to the end. There is a letter at Althorp from Richard Rigby, offering Lady Spencer a window of a warm room in the Pay Office from which she would be able to watch the procession: 'Mr Rigby presents his respects to Lady Spencer, and is ashamed that he did not explain sufficiently the nature of the offer, which he took the liberty to make, of a room for her ladyship to see the last of poor Garrick's remains. It is a small room belonging to his office, to which there is not the smallest imagination of suffering any other person to have access to Lady Spencer. Lady Spencer will please to come through Mr Rigby's house to the office where she will neither be seen by, or [sic] see, a creature. Without troubling Lady Spencer any further upon this melancholy business, or desiring any reply, if Lady Spencer chooses to come a little before twelve on Monday [1 February] she will find herself put to no sort of inconvenience.'[19] There had been a meeting of minds between David Garrick and Lady Spencer, which in no way diminished their affection for their respective spouses. Now it was over, but Lady Spencer did not forget Mrs Garrick, and there is at Althorp a touching letter from the latter, dated 20 January 1800, thanking Lady Spencer for the gift of a turkey: 'My spirits were today very low! It is the anniversary of the one-and-twentiest year of my dear husband's decease! And he is as fresh in my memory as ever.' She was not quite half-way through her widowhood at that point.

After her husband's death, Mrs Garrick seems to have realized from the start that henceforth she was destined to have a long and lonely life. Hannah More, who had rushed to London as soon as she heard the news of Garrick's death, recorded how she went first to the Adelphi, only to find that Mrs Garrick was going to stay with the Angelo family until the funeral was over. When they met, according to Hannah: 'She ran into my arms, and we both remained silent for some minutes; at last she whispered, "I have this moment embraced his coffin, and you come next".'[20] Hannah More remained for some time, comforting Mrs Garrick, with something of a proprietory interest, to the irritation of old friends such as Kitty Clive, who found it almost impossible to get through to the widow. But as Hannah More found out for herself, Mrs Garrick was not the person to crumble into helplessness. When Hannah remarked on her ability to cope with the situation with such apparent ease in the days and weeks after the funeral, Mrs Garrick replied: 'Groans and complaints are very well for those who are to mourn but a little while; but a sorrow which is to last for life will not be violent and romantic.' She was wise, since she was to live for a further forty-three years.

After two years she began to move in society once more, and one of the very first dinner-parties she graced included the Spencers, their son and new daughter-in-law, Joshua Reynolds, Bennet Langton, Edward Gibbon, Dr Johnson and the inevitable James Boswell. Hannah More, who reported the occasion, was alarmed to find that James Boswell, when he came to the tea-table after dinner, was in his cups, 'and addressed me in a manner which drew from me a sharp rebuke, for which I fancy he will not easily forgive me'.

After this renewal of contact, Dr Johnson went to visit Mrs Garrick the next morning. She told him that she always felt more at her ease when she was with people who had suffered the same loss as herself. Considering the disaster that Johnson's own marriage had been, this was somewhat romantic of Mrs Garrick, and to have accepted it without comment would have made Johnson — by his own standards — something of a hypocrite. However, he rose to the occasion, and rather than administer one of his crushing replies, gently told her that 'that was a comfort she could seldom have, considering the superiority of his [Garrick's] merit and the cordiality of their union'.

That union had certainly been a long and happy one, and seems truly to have been built on the love that survives passion. Garrick had realized early on that what he needed was the matrimonial stability created by the partners' dedication to each other. The affair with Woffington had taught him that, if nothing else. Nor, on the other hand, could one ever imagine

A caricature of Mrs Garrick done by Robert Cruikshank in September 1820, when she was in her ninety-seventh year. When she eventually died, on 16 October 1822, she had been a widow for forty-three years and had faithfully obeyed the instructions in Garrick's will to keep up their two houses. Although she worried increasingly about her income as the years went by, Garrick had left an estate valued in the region of £100,000. (*British Museum*)

Garrick having anything to do with the marriage of convenience which Miss Betsy Sterling so praises to her sister in *The Clandestine Marriage*: 'Love and a cottage! Eh Fanny! Ah, give me indifference and a coach of six.'[21] We have ample testimony from those who knew them that the marriage was a genuine partnership, and that Garrick relied on his wife's opinion and advice to a much greater extent than was perhaps realized by those who only encountered his decisive business character. Of course, in basic matters of the theatre Garrick had his own sure instinct, but there were often areas where he was less sure. Certainly on matters of taste he often seems to have deferred to his wife, and in the various references to her, that word 'taste' is the one most frequently encountered. Some people found her rather too discreet and tasteful, but doubtless they would have been the first to make adverse comments had Mrs Garrick been assertive. Indeed, in an age when scandal was the breath of life to many people, it is amazing that so little was ever put about concerning Mr and Mrs Garrick. *Love in the Suds* was never taken seriously for one moment by anyone who had the slightest acquaintance with Garrick; the story of the Garricks' supposed parting was one of the very few occasions for gossip about them, and it only made them laugh.

It was always assumed that the fact that they had no children was a matter of sadness for them, but one wonders how much room for children there would have been in such a close relationship, or how any children might have fared. Intense devotion on the part of the couple to each other does not necessarily make for emotionally healthy children when it comes to forming their own relationships in life. And there would have been the problem of being the children of such a father. It seems fitting, therefore, that there was no Garrick dynasty, that there was only the one brilliant star in the firmament, that blazed out and then disappeared.

In some respects Garrick's gift to posterity, though not mortal, was none the less a kind of begetting. Indeed, what he produced was more lasting and influential than any child of his could have been. He set the theatre in this country on a new path, but in order to do so, he first had to change public taste. As Johnson expressed it for him in the prologue he wrote for the opening of Drury Lane in 1747:

> The stage but echoes back the public voice;
> The drama's laws, the drama's patrons give,
> For we that live to please, must please, to live.
> Then prompt no more the follies you decry. . . .

It was up to the audience, in the last analysis, to dictate how the theatre should evolve. If he could not carry them with him, then Garrick could do nothing. They had to be persuaded into wanting, and then expecting, and even demanding, something better.

There were, of course, occasions when baser instincts prevailed, but even then there were no controversies about the nature or quality of the plays or the acting. The *Chinese Festival* riots and the half-price admission uproar had nothing at all to do with the nature of what Garrick was doing or had done to reform the theatre, except, possibly, insofar as the charging of proper admission would facilitate better financial returns, and by extension better productions on stage.

What is so remarkable from one point of view is that there was, and has been, relatively little criticism of what he achieved in the theatre. The purists may deplore his doctored versions of Shakespeare's plays and other works, but set in the context of his own day, his must surely have been a benign influence in that regard. He brought back to the stage the nation's greatest dramatist at a time when his reputation was at a low ebb. Even allowing for the hyperbole of the age, Johnson's prologue quoted above indicates how Garrick saw the problem that confronted him when he took over:

> The wits of Charles found easier ways to fame,
> Nor wish'd for Jonson's art, or Shakespeare's flame,
> Themselves they studied — as they felt they writ;
> Intrigue was plot, obscenity was wit.
> Vice always found a sympathetic friend;
> They pleas'd their age, and did not aim to mend.

When seen from this standpoint, the theatre was certainly in need of some kind of reform.

As to the man himself, it is more difficult to be so categorical. Even Dr Johnson is in print as taking two completely opposing views of Garrick. He was accused of being mean, and yet we know that he was often extremely generous, and although he often had to be firm with actors and actresses, he would never let them be treated unfairly, and made sure that all the Drury Lane staff were provided for. Then Garrick was said to be snobbish and vain. Most of us could, to a greater or lesser degree, be accused of being both snobbish and vain. The danger lies in allowing our judgment to be distorted as a result; but there again, which of us would freely admit to that affliction?

The Apotheosis of Garrick, by
George Carter (1737–94),
painted in 1782. On the right,
seventeen actors and actresses
in their favourite
Shakespearian roles take their
leave of Garrick, who is being
carried up to Parnassus where
Shakespeare and the Muses of
Tragedy and Comedy are
waiting to welcome him.
Horace Walpole thought it
'ridiculous and bad', and it is
hard to disagree with him.
(*The Governors of the Royal
Shakespeare Theatre,
Stratford-upon-Avon*)

It is interesting to read again in this light, Oliver Goldsmith's *Retaliation*, written after Garrick had produced the following epitaph for Goldsmith at a coffee-house one evening:

> Here lies Nolly Goldsmith, for shortness call'd Noll
> Who wrote like an angel, but talk'd like poor Poll!

Goldsmith's answer runs to thirty-two lines, and though it begins and ends with praise, there is a somewhat sour filling to the sandwich. Garrick was, according to Goldsmith, 'an abridgment of all that was pleasant in man'. He was an actor without rival, a great wit, and had an excellent heart. However, whereas on the stage he was natural, off it he acted constantly. He was changeable, and by implication somewhat devious:

> Though secure of our hearts, yet confoundedly sick
> If they were not his own by finessing and trick.

Moreover, according to Goldsmith:

> He cast off his friends as a huntsman his pack,
> For he knew when he pleased he could whistle them back.

There is little evidence to support Goldsmith's claim, and in any case it does not say a great deal for the friends if they were so easily handled.

The last charge is the most extensive — some ten lines out of the whole piece. In it Goldsmith accused Garrick of being a glutton for praise, swallowing all that came his way, and mistaking 'the puff of a dunce' for fame. It reached such a point, Goldsmith maintained, that Garrick's palate became insensitive almost to the point of disease, so that whoever peppered the praise most highly was the one most sure to please.

Goldsmith had never really forgiven Garrick for failing to accept his play *The Good Natur'd Man*, though because they moved in the same circles, and were members of The Club, they managed to get on with each other, at least outwardly. But that it was simply outwardly is revealed by the two references to Hugh Kelly in Goldsmith's verse. It was Kelly's *False Delicacy* that Garrick had brought on at Drury Lane when Colman accepted Goldsmith's play — rejected by Garrick — for Covent Garden. Apart from Kelly, only Kenrick and Woodfall were mentioned by name in the *Retaliation*, with the implication that all of them had, as 'dunces', applauded Garrick and then been paid in kind. In the event, Garrick had little reason to hold anything but contempt for any of the trio, had

Goldsmith but known it. Even so, he made his mark, and Garrick was duly chastised.

We may, perhaps, agree with Goldsmith on Garrick that 'the man had his failings' — but is that a crime? After all, he was running a theatre, not a cathedral. And on the other side of the coin, many eminent and intelligent people were happy to enjoy his friendship, and his name became a household word. Possibly he was no great man, except in the history of the theatre, but he was certainly a phenomenon, and one may surely concur with Dr Johnson: 'I am disappointed by that stroke of death, which has eclipsed the gaiety of nations, and impoverished the public stock of harmless pleasure.'

NOTES

All places of publication London, unless otherwise stated

CHAPTER ONE: EARLY DAYS [pp. 11–28]

1 Charles Dibdin, *The Professional Life of Mr Dibdin, Written by Himself*, 4 vols, 1803

2 Forster Collection, Victoria and Albert Museum, London (hereafter FC); Joseph Knight, *David Garrick*, 1894, pp. 5–7 (hereafter Knight); *The Letters of David Garrick*, ed. D. M. Little and G. M. Kahrl, 1963, I, pp. 1–2 (hereafter *Letters*)

3 Thomas Davies, *Memoirs of the Life of David Garrick*, ed. Stephen Jones, 1808, I, p. 6f. (hereafter Davies); Percy Fitzgerald, *Life of David Garrick*, 1899, p. 7f. (hereafter Fitzgerald)

4 FC; D. M. Little (ed.), *Pineapples of Finest Flavour; or, a selection of sundry unpublished letters of the English Roscius, David Garrick*, Cambridge, Massachussetts, 1930, pp. 6–8 (hereafter Little); *Letters*, 5, pp. 9–10

5 FC; Little, pp. 18–20; *Letters*, 9, pp. 16–17

6 FC; Little, pp. 20–25; *Letters*, 10, pp. 18–21

7 Percival Stockdale, *Memoirs*, 1809, II, p. 137f

8 *Private Correspondence of David Garrick*, ed. James Boaden, 1831–2, I, p. 3 (hereafter Boaden)

9 John Genest, *Some Account of the English Stage, from the Restoration in 1660 to 1830*, Bath, 1832, III, p. 609 and IV, p. 18 (hereafter Genest)

10 FC; *Letters*, 12, pp. 23–4

11 *Some Unpublished Correspondence of David Garrick*, ed. G. P. Baker, Boston, 1907, p. 4f. (hereafter Baker)

12 Folger Shakespeare Library, Washington, D.C. (hereafter FSL); *Letters*, 14, pp. 26–7

13 FC; Carola Oman, *David Garrick*, 1958, pp. 34–5 (hereafter Oman); *Letters*, 15, pp. 27–8

14 FC; Oman, pp. 36–7; *Letters*, 17, pp. 30–31

15 Frances Burney (Madame D'Arblay), *Diary and Letters*, 1842, I, p. 289

16 FC; Little, p. 25f.; *Letters*, 18, pp. 31–2

17 FC; Little, p. 27f.; *Letters*, 19, pp. 32–3

18 FC; Little, p. 28f.; *Letters*, 20, pp. 33–4

19 FSL; *Letters*, 21, pp. 35–6

20 Fitzgerald, p. 61 (and letter in the Garrick Club); Little, p. 31f.; *Letters*, 24, p. 40

21 FSL; *Letters*, 25, pp. 40–41

22 *see* 20, above

23 *London Morning Post*, 29 August 1786; *Letters*, pp. 64–5
24 Thomas Otway, *The Orphan*, IV, i, l. 68
25 Harvard Theatre Collection, Harvard College Library (hereafter HTC); William Cooke, *Memoirs of Charles Macklin*, 1804, p. 120

CHAPTER TWO: 'UNCOMMON APPROBATION' [pp. 29–48]

 1 FC; Little, p. 28f.; *Letters*, 20, pp. 33–4
 2 FC
 3 Arthur A. Houghton, Jr; *Letters*, 22, pp. 37–8
 4 FSL; *Letters*, 21, pp. 35–6
 5 FC; Little, p. 30f.; *Letters*. 23, pp. 38–9
 6 Davies, I, p. 44
 7 Joseph Cradock, *Literary and Miscellaneous Memoirs*, 1828, I, p. 198 and IV, p. 251 (hereafter Cradock)
 8 *see* 5, above
 9 Boaden, II, p. 337f.; *Letters*, 267, pp. 337–8
10 John Hill, *The Actor*, 1755, p. 73, though based on Sainte Albine's *Le Comédien*
11 Theophilus Cibber, *Two Dissertations on the Theatres*, 1756, p. 56
12 David Williams, *A Letter to David Garrick, Esq.*, 1772, pp. 30–1
13 George Alexander Stevens, *The Adventures of a Speculist*, 1788, II, p. 131
14 FC (copy); Boaden, I, p. 177f.; *Letters*, 345, pp. 435–6
15 Frances Burney, *Early Diary*, ed. A. R. Ellis, 1907, I, p. 120
16 Frances Burney, *Evelina*, I, letter 10
17 Richard Cumberland, *Memoirs*, 1807, I, pp. 80–82
18 Arthur Murphy, *The Life of David Garrick*, 1801, I, p. 105 (hereafter Murphy)
19 *A Dialogue in the Shades, between the Celebrated Mrs Cibber, and the No-less Celebrated Mrs Woffington*, 1766, pp. 15–16
20 *A Dissertation on Comedy*, 1750, p. 15
21 *London Morning Post*, 24 August 1786; *Letters*, 28, pp. 43–4
22 Davies, I, p. 119f.
23 Draft in Yale University Library; *Letters*, 36, pp. 58–63
24 *London Morning Post*, 15 September 1786; *Letters*, 34, pp. 55–6
25 *London Morning Post*, 2 September 1786; *Letters*, 40, pp. 68–70
26 *London Morning Post*, 7 September 1786; *Letters*, 42, pp. 73–4

CHAPTER THREE: ACTOR AND MANAGER [pp. 49–72]

 1 HTC
 2 *The Athenaeum*, 10 April 1880, p. 481f.; *Letters*, 47, pp. 81–4
 3 Genest, IV, p. 213

4 *The Autobiography and Correspondence of Mary Granville, Mrs Delany*, ed. Lady Llanover, 1st series, 1861, II, p. 453 (hereafter Delany)

5 Boaden, I, p. 53f.; *Letters*, 51, pp. 88–90

6 *Roscius Anglicanus*, 1789, Appendix, p. 22f.; *Letters*, 54, pp. 92–3

7 *Clarissa*, 1748, VII, p. 428

8 *Correspondence of Samuel Richardson*, ed. Anna L. Barbauld, 1804, I, p. 123

9 Horace Walpole, *Correspondence with George Montagu, 1736–70*, 1819, I, p. 28

10 Horace Walpole, *Anecdotes of Painting*, 1786, p. 486

11 *The Letters of Horace Walpole*, ed. Mrs Paget Toynbee, Oxford, 1903–5, II, pp. 197f., 346, 382, 392

12 FSL; *Letters*, 57, pp. 95–6

13 FSL; *Letters*, 58, pp. 97–8

14 FSL

15 FSL; *Letters*, 69, pp. 119–121

16 Davies, I, p. 144

17 *London Morning Post*, 28 September 1786; *Letters*, 87, pp. 143–4

18 Devonshire Letters, Chatsworth, 1st Series, 354.10; *Letters*, 90, pp. 147–9

19 Devonshire Letters, Chatsworth, 1st Series, 354.2; *Letters*, 91, pp. 149–50

20 *Public Advertiser*, 31 August 1786; *Letters*, 93, pp. 152–3

21 FSL; *Letters*, 95, pp. 155–6

22 FSL; *Letters*, 96, pp. 156–7

23 *London Morning Post*, 7 October 1786; *Letters*, 103, p. 166

24 *The Diary of David Garrick . . . 1751*, ed. R.C. Alexander, New York, 1928, *passim*

25 Bibliothèque de l'Arsenal, Paris, Archives de la Bastille, MS 11743, 357–83

26 Charles Collé, *Journal*, Paris, 1868, I, p. 324f.

27 FSL; Baker, pp. 41–4; *Letters*, 105, pp. 167–8

28 *London Morning Post*, 25 September 1786; *Letters*, 108, p. 172

29 Devonshire Letters, Chatsworth, 1st Series, 354.24; *Letters*, 152, pp. 225–7

CHAPTER FOUR: THE CHINESE FESTIVAL [pp. 73–92]

1 Frank A. Hedgcock (hereafter Hedgcock), *A Cosmopolitan Actor, David Garrick and his French Friends*, [1912], p. 102f., based on: *Supplément au roman comique; ou, mémoires pour servir à la vie de Jean Monnet*, London (Paris), 1772; Arthur Heulhard, *Jean Monnet, vie et aventures d'un entrepreneur de spectacles au XVIIe siècle*, Paris, 1884; Henri d'Alméras, *Mémoires de Jean Monnet, directeur du théâtre de la Foire*. There is also relevant correspondence in the Bibliothèque de l'Arsenal (Portefeuille de Bachaumont) and the Forster Collection

2 FSL; *Letters*, 81, pp. 135–6

3 FC, vol. XXII add.

4 Hedgcock, p. 128, n.1

5 FC, vol. XXII and Boaden, II, p. 386

6 FC, vol. XXII, p. 30

7 FC; Hedgcock, pp. 139–43; *Letters*, 200, pp. 274–6

8 Boaden, I, p. 252

9 FC; *Letters*, 173, pp. 251–2

10 FC

11 Massachusetts Historical Society; Robert Anderson, *The Life of Tobias Smollett*, Edinburgh, 1806, p. 186; *Letters*, 185, pp. 261–2

12 *The Letters of Horace Walpole*, ed. Paget Toynbee, VIII, p. 42

13 FSL; Walpole, ed. Toynbee, supplement, I, p. 87f.; *Letters*, 201, pp. 277–8

14 Devonshire Letters, Chatsworth, 1st Series, 354.26; *Letters*, 155, pp. 231–2

15 Devonshire Letters, Chatsworth, 1st Series, 354.31; *Letters*, 210, pp. 286–7

16 Hyde Collection, draft in FC; *The R. B. Adam Library*, Buffalo, 1929, I, pp. 2–3; *Letters*, 203 and 204, pp. 279–81

17 Quoted in J. Nichols and G. Steevens, *The Genuine Works of William Hogarth*, 1808, I, p. 212

18 Morgan Library, draft in FC; Boaden, I, p. 59f.; *Letters*, 299, pp. 369–70

19 Waterson Collection (draft); Boaden, I, p. 658; *Letters*, 859, pp. 954–5

20 Berg Collection; George Colman, *Posthumous Letters*, ed. George Colman, the Younger, 1820, pp. 309–11 (hereafter Colman); *Letters*, 903, pp. 1001–2

21 FC (copy); Boaden, II, p. 347; *Letters*, 292, p. 363

22 Genest, V, p. 14f.

23 *London Chronicle*, 1757–1823, XIII, 25–7 January 1763

24 *European Magazine*, XII, July 1787, p. 15; *Letters*, 611, pp. 715–7

25 *London Chronicle*, 28 February 1763, p. 205f.

CHAPTER FIVE: THE GRAND TOUR [pp. 93–112]

1 William Salt Library; *Letters*, 307 and 308, pp. 376–8

2 FC (draft); Boaden, I, p. 201f.; *Letters*, 315, p. 385

3 Berg Collection; Colman, pp. 258–60; *Letters*, 332, pp. 416–7

4 Morgan Library; Little, pp. 43–5; *Letters*, 319, pp. 390–92

5 *London Chronicle*, XIV, 15–17 and 17–20 September 1763, p. 270f.

6 Berg Collection; Colman, pp. 245–53; *Letters*, 321, pp. 395–8

7 Burney, *Early Dairy*, I, p. 150

8 *see* 3, above

9 FC; Hedgcock, pp. 182–5; *Letters*, 337, pp. 422–4

10 FSL; Lady Charnwood, *An Autograph Collection*, New York, 1930, p. 182f.; *Letters*, 339, pp. 426–7

11 FC (last of three drafts); Boaden, II, p. 362; *Letters*, 340, p. 428

12 Voltaire, *Oeuvres complètes*, Paris, 1881, XLIV, p. 131f.

13 Abbé Jean Bernard Le Blanc, *Lettres d'un Français à Londres*, Paris, 1745, II, p. 73f.

14 Berg Collection; Colman, pp. 261–5; *Letters*, 341, pp. 429–31

15 FC (copy); Boaden, I, p. 177f.; *Letters*, 345, pp. 435–6

16 FSL; FC (copy); *Letters*, 383, p. 487

17 Berg Collection; Colman, pp. 268–72; *Letters*, 347, pp. 439–40

18 Colman, p. 271, n.

19 Berg Collection; Colman, pp. 272–4; *Letters*, 350, pp. 443–4. [*The Fribbleriad* (1761) was an anonymous satire by Garrick on Thaddeus Fitzpatrick in retaliation for a pamphlet entitled 'An Enquiry into the Real Merit of a Certain Popular Performer' published in 1760.]

20 Berg Collection; Colman, pp. 277–81; *Letters*, 353, pp. 449–51

21 Boaden, I, p. 186; *Letters*, 360, p. 460

22 *Life of David Garrick by Arthur Murphy and Garrick's private correspondence edited by James Boaden*, extra-illustrated volumes bound together, X/clippings 225, HTC

23 Baker, p. 119 (extract); *Letters*, 374, p. 477

24 Hedgcock, p. 364, n.1

25 Berg Collection; Colman, pp. 293–6f.; *Letters*, 413 and 414, pp. 520–22

26 FC; *New Monthly Magazine*, XII, December 1819, p. 532; *Letters*, 415, pp. 523–4

CHAPTER SIX: FAMILY AND FRIENDS [pp. 113–128]

1 Morgan Library; *The Gentleman's Magazine*, xlix, June, 1779, p. 318; *Letters*, 423, pp. 533–4

2 FSL; *Letters*, 445, pp. 556–7

3 BM; *Letters*, 449, pp. 560–61

4 FC; Boaden, I, p. 252f.; *Letters*, 450, pp. 562–3

5 Boaden, I, p. 245f.; *Letters*, 455, pp. 568–9

6 FC; Boaden, I, p. 255f.; *Letters*, 456, pp. 569–70

7 HTC; *Letters*, 458, pp. 571–2

8 Boaden, I, p. 256; *Letters*, 459, pp. 572–3

9 Duke of Portland; Little, p. 54f.; *Letters*, 476, pp. 586–7

10 Boswell MSS, Yale; *Letters*, 479, pp. 588–9

11 FC (draft); Boaden, I, p. 279; *Letters*, 480, p. 590

12 FSL; Boaden, II, p. 364; *Letters*, 485, pp. 593–4

13 FC (copy); Percy Fitzgerald, *Life of Mrs Catherine Clive*, 1888, p. 71; *Letters* 487, pp. 595–6

14 FC (copy); Fitzgerald, *Clive*, p. 73f.; *Letters*, 488, pp. 596–7

15 Morgan Library; Little, pp. 55–7; *Letters*, 498, pp. 604–6

16 BM; *Letters*, 481, p. 591

17 William Kenrick, *A Letter to David Garrick, Esq.*, 1772, p. 22; *Letters*, 500, p. 607 (hereafter Kenrick)

18 FSL; Baker, pp. 94–6; *Letters*, 512, pp. 618–9
19 FC (draft); Boaden, I, p. 311; *Letters*, 515, pp. 622–3
20 FC (copy); Boaden, I, p. 304; *Letters*, 507, pp. 612–3
21 Wentworth Woodhouse Muniments, Burke 1/80, Sheffield City Libraries Archives Division; Dixon Wecter, 'David Garrick and the Burkes', in *Philological Quarterly*, XVIII, October, 1939, p. 369f.; *Letters*, 385, p. 490
22 Wentworth Woodhouse Muniments, Burke 1/211, Sheffield City Libraries Archives Division; *Correspondence of Edmund Burke*, 1744–97, ed. Charles William, Earl Fitzwilliam, and Sir Richard Bourke, 1844, I, pp. 155–7; *Letters*, 511, pp. 616–7
23 Delany, 2nd series, 1862, I, p. 155f.
24 Sir John Hawkins, *The Life of Samuel Johnson*, 1787, p. 427f.
25 FC (copy); *Monthly Mirror*, VIII, August 1799, p.102f.; *Letters*, 528, pp. 634–6
26 FSL; *Letters*, 532, p. 640
27 HTC: *Letters*, 510, pp. 615–6

CHAPTER SEVEN: THE SHAKESPEARE JUBILEE [pp. 129–142]

1 FSL; *Letters*, 535, pp. 642–3
2 Shakespeare Birthplace Trust Records Office (hereafter SBT) ER 38/1, f.1
3 SBT DR 413; *London Chronicle*, XXV, 13 May 1769, p. 458; *Letters*, 537, p. 644
4 *London Chronicle*, XXV, 23–5 May 1769, p. 495
5 Royal Shakespeare Theatre Picture Gallery, Stratford-upon-Avon; *Letters*, 540, pp. 647–8
6 William Cooke, *Memoirs of Samuel Foote*, 1805, II, p. 86
7 SBT ER 1/38, f.17
8 SBT ER 1/38, f.13; *Letters*, 545, pp. 651–2
9 BM; *Letters*, 546, pp. 652–4
10 *The Gentleman's Magazine*, xxxix, July 1769, p. 364f.
11 SBT ER 1/38, f.36
12 *Public Advertiser*, 16 September 1769
13 George G. Fortescue; *The Manuscripts of J. B. Fortescue, Esq.*, Historical Manuscripts Commission, Report 13, pt.3, 1892–1927, I, p. 160
14 *The Tempest*, IV, i, 152–6; *A Midsummer Night's Dream*, V, i, 12–17
15 SBT ER 1/38, f.22; *Letters*, 553, p. 660
16 SBT ER 1/83, ff. 20v–21v; *Letters*, 554, pp. 661–2
17 Robert B. Wheler, *History and Antiquities of Stratford-upon-Avon*, Stratford-upon-Avon, [1806], p. 167 f.
18 *See* Johanne Stochholm, *Garrick's Folly*, 1964
19 *The Gentleman's Magazine*, September 1769, xxxix, p. 422
20 Cradock, 1, p. 217

21 *The Town and Country Magazine*, September 1769, I, p. 477

22 *London Magazine*, October 1769

23 Herbert Randolph, *Life of General Sir Robert Wilson*, 1862, I, p. 27

24 FSL; Cradock, I, p. 219; *Letters*, 560, pp. 665–6

25 SBT ER 1/38, f. 38; *Letters*, 561, pp. 666–7

26 *The Jubilee*, MS in Huntington Library; *Three Plays by David Garrick*, ed. Elizabeth P. Stein, New York, 1926, p. 109

27 Sir Sidney Lee, *A Life of William Shakespeare*, 1925, p. 601

CHAPTER EIGHT: ADELPHI TERRACE [pp. 143–160]

1 FC (copy); Boaden, I, p.366; *Letters*, 557, pp. 663–4

2 SBT ER 38/1, f. 34

3 FSL; Charles Nisard, *Mémoires et correspondences historiques et littéraires, 1726–1816*, ed. Jean-B.-A. Suard, Paris, 1858, p. 160; *Letters*, 562, p. 668

4 FC; Boaden, II, p. 365; *Letters*, 564, p. 669

5 Voltaire, *Oeuvres complètes*, Paris, 1883, I, p. 391

6 FC (draft); Boaden, II, pp. 343–6; *Letters*, 565, pp. 670–74

7 Cardiff Public Libraries and FSL; Cecil Price, 'David Garrick and Evan Lloyd', in *Review of English Studies*, NS, January 1952, p. 32f.; *Letters*, 567–8, pp. 675–7

8 FSL; *Letters*, 573, p. 682

9 FSL; *Letters*, 574, pp. 682–3

10 Quoted in *King Lear*, Arden edition, p. xl

11 Charles Lamb, Works, ed. W. Macdonald, 1903, II, p. 33

12 Gabriel Wells and FSL (Letter to Suard in Nisard, op. cit.); *Letters*, 587–8, pp. 693–4

13 Charles Burney, *Music, Men and Manners in France and Italy*, 1770, BM add MS 35122, ed. H. E. Poole, 1969, p. 15

14 ibid., p. xx

15 Frances Burney (Madame D'Arblay), *Memoirs of Dr Burney*, 1832

16 FSL (draft); *The Works of Richard Owen Cambridge*, ed. George O. Cambridge, 1803, pp. lxi–ii; *Letters*, 600, pp. 704–5

17 FC (draft); *Letters*, 601, pp. 705–6

18 SBT ER 1/38, f.54; *Letters*, 617, pp. 721–2

19 FSL; Boaden, I, p. 411f.; *Letters*, 621, pp. 724–5

20 Boswell MSS, Yale: *Letters*, 628, p. 733. The Virgil quotation is from *Eclogues*, VI, 1.4

21 FSL; *Letters*, 635, pp. 743–4

22 Boswell MSS, Yale; *Letters*, 680, pp. 791–2

23 Doreen Yarwood, *Robert Adam*, 1970, p. 98

24 Letter to William Manson, 29 July 1773

25 Berg Collection; Colman, pp. 261–5; *Letters*, 341, pp. 429–31

26 Huntington Library; R. Blunt, *Mrs Montagu*, 1923, I p. 356f.; *Letters*, 687, pp. 779–80
27 Francis Edwards, Ltd; Baker, p. 91f; *Letters*, 688, pp. 800–1
28 The first and fourth letters are in FSL (draft); Boaden, II, p. 341; the second and third letters are in Kenrick, pp. 29–30; all are in *Letters*, 691–4, pp. 804–7
29 FC (copy); Boaden, I, p. 542f.; *Letters*, 773, pp. 874–5
30 Alan Downer, 'The Diary of Benjamin Webster', in *Theatre Annual*, 1945, p. 64
31 FC; Boaden, I, p. 612
32 FC (copy); Boaden, I, p. 612; *Letters*, 822, pp. 922–3
33 Murdock Collection
34 FSL; *Letters*, 839, pp. 936–7

CHAPTER NINE: RETIREMENT [pp.161–176]

1 *London Chronicle*, 18–20 August, 1774, p. 175
2 FC (copy); Boaden, II, p. 296; *Letters*, 855, pp. 950–51
3 Boswell MSS, Yale; *Letters*, 895, pp. 993–4
4 Berg Collection; Colman, pp. 306–11; *Letters*, 902–4, pp. 1000–3
5 Society of Antiquaries; *Letters*, 907, pp. 1005–6
6 FC (draft); Hedgcock, p. 387f. (in part); *Letters*, 919, pp. 1014–15
7 Burney, *Early Diary*, I, p. 117
8 FSL; *Morning Post*, 27 August 1823; *Letters*, 926, p. 1021
9 HTC; Little, p. 72f.; *Letters*, 944, p. 1038
10 FSL; *Letters*, 947, p. 1040
11 Vol. XXVII, no. 85; vol. XIV, no. 17
12 *The Works in Architecture*, vol. II, set v, p11. vi & vii
13 Walter H. Godfrey, 'The apron stage of the eighteenth century as illustrated at Drury Lane', in *Architectural Record*, XXXVII, 1915, pp. 31–35
14 SBT ER 90/2; *Letters*, 940, p. 1035
15 Earl Spencer
16 Burney, *Early Diary*, II, pp. 138–9
17 Berg Collection; Colman, p. 314f.; *Letters*, 963, p. 1053
18 FC (draft); Boaden, II, p. 118; *Letters*, 971, p. 1060
19 Thomas Moore, *Memoirs of Richard Brinsley Sheridan*, 1825, I, p. 181f. (hereafter Moore)
20 FC; Boaden, II, p. 118
21 FSL; *Letters*, 976, pp. 1063–4
22 E. Percival Merritt; John P. Collier, *An Old Man's Diary*, 1871, pt.I, p. 12; *Letters*, 978, pp. 1066–7
23 Moore, loc. cit.
24 Boaden, II, p. 128

25 FSL; *Letters*, 979, pp. 1067–8
26 FC; Boaden, II, p. 141
27 FC; Little, p. 79f.: *Letters*, 995, pp. 1084–5
28 FSL; FC (copy); *Letters*, 1005, pp. 1092–3
29 FC (copy); Boaden, II, p. 150; *Letters*, 1014, pp. 1099–1100
30 William Roberts, *Memoirs of the Life and Correspondence of Mrs Hannah More*, New York, 1835, I, p. 59f.
31 Earl Spencer
32 FC; Boaden, II, p. 152f.
33 Bristol Public Libraries
34 Boaden, II, p. 161f.; *Letters*, 1026, pp. 1110–1
35 Murphy, II, p. 135f.
36 ibid., p. 139
37 FSL (draft); Boaden, II, p. 162; *Letters*, 1028, p. 1112

CHAPTER TEN: MAN OF LEISURE [pp.177–190]

1 FC (copy); Little, p. 79f.; *Letters*, 1029, pp. 1113–4
2 FC (copy); *Letters*, 1031, pp. 1115–6
3 Baker, p. 68; *Letters* 1040, pp. 1123–4
4 FSL; *Letters*, 1041, pp. 1124–5
5 Boaden, II, p. 179
6 Morgan Library; Little, pp. 81f.; *Letters*, 1052, pp. 1133–4
7 Boaden, II, p. 185
8 Boaden, II, p. 624
9 FSL; Boaden, II, p. 189f., and also 625f.; *Letters*, 1061, pp. 1139–41
10 Boaden, II. p. 192
11 FC; Boaden, II, p. 162; *Letters*, 1071, p. 1147
12 FSL; Roberts, *Hannah More*, I, p. 75f. (extract); *Letters*, 1072, pp. 1148–9
13 Boaden, II, p. 195f.
14 Boaden, II, p. 196f.
15 Earl Spencer
16 Boaden, II, p. 198f.
17 FC; *Letters*, 1075, p. 1150
18 Earl Spencer
19 James Winston, 'Theatrical Records', FSL. The medal is now in FSL too.
20 HTC
21 Boaden, II, p. 235f.
22 FSL; Boaden, II, p. 237; *Letters*, 1108, p. 1171
23 Earl Spencer
24 HTC; Moore, I, p. 245; *Letters*, 1097, p. 1163
25 FSL; *Letters*, 1100, pp. 1164–5
26 Boaden, II, p. 223

27 FC; Boaden, II, p. 224; *Letters*, 1101, p. 1165
28 Fitzwilliam Museum, Cambridge; FC (copy); *Letters*, 1103, pp. 1166–7
29 FC (copy); Boaden, II, p. 186; *Letters*, 1114, pp. 1176–7
30 Garrick Club; T. F. Dillon Croker, 'Garrick in Retirement', *The Era Almanack and Annual*, 1877, p. 58; *Letters*, 1116, pp. 1178–9
31 Boaden, II, p. 275.
32 FC (copy); Boaden, II, p. 272f.; *Letters*, 1132, pp. 1190–92
33 FC; *Letters*, 1133, pp. 1192–3
34 FSL; *Letters*, 1149, pp. 1206–7
35 FSL; *Letters*, 1151, pp. 1208–9

CHAPTER ELEVEN: THE END [pp. 191–204]

1 HTC; FSL; BM, Winston MSS
2 FC (copy); Boaden, II, p. 291; *Letters*, 1162, p. 1216
3 Boaden, II, p. 297f.
4 FC; Boaden, II, p. 303
5 FC (copy); Boaden, II, p. 303; *Letters*, 1174, p. 1224
6 FC; Boaden, II, p. 303; *Letters*, 1175, p. 1224
7 FC; Boaden, II, p. 304
8 FC; Boaden, II, p. 310; *Letters*, 1191, p. 1240
9 FSL; Roberts, *Hannah More*, I, p. 74f.; *Letters*, 1184, pp. 1232–4
10 Baker, p. 65f.; *Letters*, 1188, p. 1238
11 FSL; Joseph Cradock, *The Czar*, 1824, p.viii; *Letters*, 1196, p. 1243
12 Earl Spencer
13 FSL; Baker, p. 72f.; *Letters*, 1198, pp. 1244–5
14 Boaden, II, p. 315
15 HTC; *Letters*, 1203, pp. 1250–51
16 Boaden, II, p. 317
17 Boaden, II, p. 326
18 John Wooll, *Biographical Memoirs of the late Reverend Joseph Warton*, 1806, p. 388f; *Letters*, 1217, p. 1260
19 Earl Spencer
20 Roberts, *Hannah More*, I, pp. 147–9, pp. 156–9
21 *The Clandestine Marriage*, I, ii

SELECT BIBLIOGRAPHY

Place of publication London, unless otherwise stated

ANDERSON, R., *The Life of Tobias Smollett*, Edinburgh, 1806

APPLETON, W. W., *Charles Macklin, an Actor's Life*, Cambridge, Mass., 1961

BARTON, M., *Garrick*, 1948

BLUNT, R., *Mrs Montagu*, 1923

BURKE, E., *Correspondence*, ed., Charles William, Earl Fitzwilliam and
    Sir R. Bourke, 1844

BURNEY, C., *Music, Men and Manners in France and Italy, 1770*, ed. H. E. Poole,
    1969

BURNEY, F. (Madame D'Arblay), *Diary and Letters*, 1842
    Early Diary, ed. A. R. Ellis, 1907

BURNIM, K. A., *David Garrick, Director*, Carbondale, Ill., 1961

CAMBRIDGE, R. O., *Works*, ed. G. O. Cambridge, 1803

CIBBER, T., *Two Dissertations on the Theatres*, 1756

COLLE, C., *Journal*, Paris, 1868

COLLIER, J. P., *An Old Man's Diary*, 1871

COLMAN, G., *Posthumous Letters*, ed. G. Colman the Younger, 1820

COOKE, W., *Memoirs of Charles Macklin*, 1804
    Memoirs of Samuel Foote, 1805

CRADOCK, J., *The Czar*, 1824
    Literary and Miscellaneous Memoirs, 1828

CUMBERLAND, R., *Memoirs*, 1807

DAVIES, T., *Memoirs of the Life of David Garrick*, ed. S. Jones, 1808

DELANY, MRS, *The Autobiography and Correspondence of Mary Granville, Mrs
    Delany*, ed. Lady Llanover, 1861

DIBDIN, C., *The Professional Life of Mr Dibdin, Written by Himself*, 1803

FINLAYSON, I., *The Moth and the Candle, a Life of James Boswell*, 1984

FITZGERALD, P., *Life of David Garrick*, 1899
    Life of Mrs Catherine Clive, 1888

GARRICK, D., *The Diary . . . 1751*, ed. R. C. Alexander, New York, 1928
    The Journal . . . 1763, ed. G. W. Stone, New York, 1939 (repr. 1966)
    The Letters, ed. D. M. Little and G. M. Kahrl, 1963
    Letters of, and Georgiana, Countess Spencer, 1759–79, ed. Earl Spencer and C.
        Dobson, Cambridge, 1960
    *Pineapples of Finest Flavour; or, a selection of sundry unpublished letters of the
        English Roscius, David Garrick*, ed. D. M. Little, Cambridge, Mass., 1930
    The Private Correspondence, ed. J. Boaden, 1831–2
    Some Unpublished Correspondence, ed. G. P. Baker, Boston, 1907
    Three Plays, ed. E. P. Stein, New York, 1926

GENEST, J., *Some Account of the English Stage, from the Restoration in 1660 to 1830*, Bath, 1832

HAWKINS, SIR J., *The Life of Samuel Johnson*, 1787

HEDGCOCK, F. A., *A Cosmopolitan Actor, David Garrick and his French Friends* n.d. [1912]

HILL, J., *The Actor*, 1755

KENRICK, W., *A Letter to David Garrick, Esq.*, 1772

KNIGHT, J., *David Garrick*, 1894

LAMB, C., *Works*, ed. W. MacDonald, 1903

LE BLANC, J. B., *Lettres d'un Français à Londres*, Paris, 1745

LEE, SIR S., *A Life of William Shakespeare*, 1925

MOORE, T., *Memoirs of Richard Brinsley Sheridan*, 1825

MURPHY, A., *The Life of David Garrick*, 1801

NICHOLS, J., and STEEVENS, G., *The Genuine Works of William Hogarth*, 1808

NICOLL, A., *The Garrick Stage*, Manchester, 1980

NISARD, C., *Mémoires*, ed. J. B. A. Suard, Paris, 1858

OMAN, C., *David Garrick*, 1958

PEDICORD, H. W., *The Theatrical Public in the Time of Garrick*, Carbondale, Ill., 1954

PRICE, C., *Theatre in the Age of Garrick*, Oxford, 1973

RANDOLPH, H., *Life of General Sir Robert Wilson*, 1862

RICHARDSON, S., *Correspondence*, ed. A. L. Barbauld, 1804

ROBERTS, W., *Memoirs of the Life and Correspondence of Mrs Hannah More*, New York, 1835

SMITH, H. R., *David Garrick, 1717–79*, 1979

STEIN, E. P., *David Garrick, Dramatist*, New York, 1938 (repr. 1966)

STEVENS, G. A., *The Adventures of a Speculist*, 1788

STOCKDALE, P., *Memoirs*, 1809

STONE, G. W., and KAHRL, G. M., *David Garrick, a Critical Biography*, Carbondale, Ill., 1979

WALPOLE, H., *Anecdotes of Painting*, 1786

Correspondence with George Montagu, 1736–70, 1819

The Letters, ed. Mrs Paget Toynbee, Oxford, 1903–5

WHELER, R. B., *History and Antiquities of Stratford-upon-Avon*, Stratford-upon-Avon, n.d. [1806]

WILLIAMS, D., *A Letter to David Garrick, Esq.*, 1772

WOOLL, J., *Biographical Memoirs of the late Reverend Joseph Warton*, 1806

YARWOOD, D., *Robert Adam*, 1970

INDEX